MW00795200

Witchcraft
& the
Rise of Wicca
Vol.2

FIRST PRINTING

Billy Crone

Cover Design:
CHRIS TAYLOR

To my sister, Heather.

If ever there was two people,
who knew firsthand
the ravages of spiritual warfare,
It would be you and me.

Prior to salvation,
both of us,
at various times,
have danced with the devils,
played their games,
and sang their songs.

We ingested their poison,
believed their lies,
and even tried to end these lives,
multiple times.

But God did what only He can do.
He rescued us from the dominion of darkness,
He saved us from the clutches of the evil one.
He set us free through Jesus Christ.

Thank you for not only putting up with me,
and for being a wonderful sister here on earth,
but for now, being a fellow soldier of Christ,
fighting the good fight,
in this greatest battle of all,
The Satanic War on the Christian.

Don't ever give up Heather,
We know who wins.

I love you.

Contents

Preface..vii

1. The Definition, Types & Location of Witchcraft................Vol.1
2. The Protection from Witchcraft....................................Vol.1
3. The History of Witchcraft in Babylon............................Vol.1
4. The History of Witchcraft in Egypt...............................Vol.1
5. The History of Witchcraft in Greece............................Vol.1
6. The History of Witchcraft in Rome..............................Vol.1
7. The History of Witchcraft in Asia.....................................Vol.1
8. The History of Witchcraft in India & Islands...................Vol.1
9.The History of Witchcraft in Africa...............................Vol.1
10.The History of Witchcraft in Latin America......................Vol.1
11.The History of Witchcraft in Europe............................9
12.The History of Wicca Part 1......................................43
13.The History of Wicca Part 2......................................73
14.The History of Wicca Part 3......................................107
15. The History of Wicca Part 4.....................................143
16. The Beliefs of Wicca..179
17. The Symbols & Calendar of Wicca............................217
18. The Practices of Wicca Part 1...................................265
19. The Practices of Wicca Part 2...................................301
20. The Promotion of Wicca...337

How to Receive Jesus Christ............................373
Notes.. 375

Preface

Other than the unfortunate common media exposure to Witchcraft growing up, my first awareness of this dark practice occurred in High School. Some friends were at a house party doing what sadly many did at that time, drinking, drugs, and various immoral behaviors. However, unbeknownst to the rest of the group, a girl was upstairs in that two-story home, in the bathroom, drawing a pentagram on the floor doing occult rituals. After a while, her absence was noticed by the rest of the group and soon she was stumbled upon by another person at the party. Needless to say, that person obviously began to freak out over the occult behavior of the girl right there before their very eyes. Not only was the girl obviously possessed, but soon the rest of the people at the party found out the hard way that her dark arts ritual did what it was apparently designed to do. A demon literally manifested itself right there in the bathroom and it began to slowly make its way downstairs to the rest of the inhabitants. Not only could everyone see the actual form of the demonic entity, but it ever so slowly creeped its way to the lower level. This only added to the horror of the moment as everyone was frozen in place, in stark terror, while screaming in fright at the same time. Word of this event soon began to spread in the small town I was living in, and it became one of the first "spiritual encounters" that opened my eyes to the reality of evil firsthand. Unfortunately, rather than running away as far as I could from these occult behaviors and practices, I soon began to dabble in them myself, leading to a dark miserable multi-year journey before Jesus Christ saved me from this deadly occult snare. It is my hope that you will not only become well-informed in this book about the beliefs and practices of Witchcraft, but that it will encourage any and all to run away from it, not to it, like I did as a non-Christian. One last piece of advice; when you are through reading this book, will you please READ YOUR BIBLE? I mean that in the nicest possible way. Enjoy, and I'm looking forward to seeing you someday!

Billy Crone
Las Vegas, Nevada
2020

Chapter Eleven

The History of Witchcraft in Europe

So far, we've seen that modern-day "Wicca" just means "witchcraft." We also saw it permeates the planet. In the last eight chapters, we've been dealing with the progression of witchcraft's growth history as it has spread throughout the world, which shows us over and over that nothing has changed up to the present time. It is all part of old-fashioned occult practices that started at the Tower of Babel. That was when God confused the languages and witchcraft spread over the earth from Babylon to Egypt, Greece, Rome, Asia, India, the island countries southeast of India, Africa, and then when man hopped the pond, he brought it to Latin America.

Genesis 10 tells us, "The nations spread out over the earth after the flood."

The Bible was right again about how mankind was able to traverse the oceans early on. The first men reached the Americas long before 1492 when Christopher Columbus "sailed the ocean blue." Some of those earlier explorers and immigrants brought witchcraft with them. And Latin

America got deeply into it, taking the horrible murderous practices to a whole new level, with cultures like the Mayans, who worshiped blood-thirsty demon entities. Those devils got the Mayans to the point of being saturated in human sacrifices. Again, it is no wonder God used others to take that evil culture out. The blood taken and offered to their demon entities was not just from prisoners and slaves they held captive and killed on a massive scale, everyone got into bloodletting by cutting themselves. Yet, we have been taught that these Latin Americans, who invented sports, like soccer, were mathematical geniuses with their calendar and study of astronomy, as well as having a wonderful peace with nature. But the truth is that their ball games, calendar, and everything else in their culture revolved around human sacrifices. That Mayan calendar told them when to kill people. And again, if their math was so good, why didn't it predict their own demise? By the way, does today's occult also schedule sacrifices on specific calendar days? Yes, they do, which again shows what the Bible tells us: This is nothing new.

The Aztecs also had a calendar of witchcraft that took them to a new level of human sacrifice, and they even went as far as cannibalism. According to the Aztecs' own account, their debauchery was so bad that just one dedication ceremony over four days was an excuse to slaughter 80,400 people. They were a sick civilization, so it is no wonder God took them out. Again, I am not for rounding up occults and witches to kill them. I am not advocating that! But when we look back at those people's behavior, it seems to make sense why God dealt with them so harshly.

Then we saw that the Incas with their mountain structures at Machu Picchu and how they were also involved with witchcraft's human sacrifice. Unsurprisingly, in Disney's quest to scour the planet, highlighting and promoting different witchcraft practices, they even made a cartoon out of Inca's witchcraft. And witchcraft is still widely practiced in Latin America today. It goes by a newer name, "brujeria," which just means "witchcraft."

Now, all this history has taken us on a tour through much of the old world and then Latin America but next I want to back track, jumping back over the big pond to a culture I skipped on purpose: Europe. I am covering it in this chapter so that we do so right before North America. Much of European witchcraft needs to be dealt with as well, as much of it came to North America whether or not people want to believe it or acknowledge that it's true. Of course, witchcraft includes an amalgamation of occult practices that also came from other parts of the world because America is one big melting pot of immigrants. We also got people from places steeped in witchcraft like Asia and Africa. In fact, the latter has a history of exporting African voodoo witchcraft to places in the U.S. like Florida, where it began, because people moved from the island countries south and east of Florida, as well as those that came by way of the slave trade. So, we got witchcraft from multiple cultures around the world. A lot that we have to deal with in North America, certainly Wicca, has its roots in European witchcraft. So that's what we'll take a detailed look at in this chapter.

Before we do that, let's once again demonstrate that the warning against witchcraft is all over in the Scriptures. Just like Bible prophecy, if we want to learn the whole Bible, as we should, at some point we need to deal with these kinds of occult practices. And we cannot dismiss it as a uniquely Old Testament issue that we need not concern ourselves with. Instead, it is also all over the New Testament. Let me share another passage where God does not mince words in His warning against getting involved with witchcraft and some of its horrible consequences. Here is a list of those things inspired by the sinful nature, which are not what you and I want to emulate or live by. The total number of sins we can commit is such a huge amount that only God knows how many there are, but Paul takes this opportunity in **Galatians** to point out witchcraft and gives us some of the deadly consequences:

Galatians 5:13-21: *"You, my brothers and sisters, were called to be free. But do not use your freedom to indulge the flesh (sinful nature); rather, serve one another humbly in love. For the entire law is fulfilled in keeping this one command: 'Love your neighbor as yourself.' If you bite and devour each other, watch out or you will be destroyed by each other."*

So, how do we stay away from that sin nature? Even as a Christian, how do we keep from being an instrument of division and destroying the fellowship and brotherhood of the Church? Well, Paul goes on with how we do that:

"So, I say, live by the Spirit, and you will not gratify the desires of the flesh."

That is a guarantee from God! If we live by the spirit, we will not gratify the desires of our sinful nature. That is the key to escaping the sin trap. And here is the ongoing war that goes on every day that we get out of bed:

"For the flesh (sinful nature) desires what is contrary to the Spirit, and the Spirit what is contrary to the flesh. They are in conflict with each other, so that you are not to do whatever you want. But if you are led by the Spirit, you are not under the law."

Just so we are clear on some aspects of our sin nature, Paul breaks it down to specific and obvious examples that show us when we're not living in the Spirit, but instead being seduced into following our flesh:

"The acts of the flesh are obvious: sexual immorality, impurity and debauchery; idolatry and witchcraft; hatred, discord, jealousy, fits of rage, selfish ambition, dissensions, factions and envy; drunkenness, orgies, and the like."

Right smack dab in the middle there is occult witchcraft! In fact, we know that those who permit witches in their midst will get issues like hatred, discord, jealously, envy, etc. Witches like to quickly divide people up. And we certainly see witchcraft practices leading to drunkenness, drug use, and debauchery, with the first two being classic ways of getting witches, or anyone, into an altered state of consciousness that can easily lead to a connection with demons.

So, the Bible gave us telltale signs of those times when we are not living by the Spirit. But keep reading because this last verse is what I want to emphasize:

"I warn you, as I did before, that those who live like this following their sin nature, will not inherit the kingdom of God."

Whoa! Does that mean we born-again Christians lose our salvation when we sin? No, that is not what Paul is talking about. Notice his phrase: "those who live like this..." It's about a pattern in life. We all know people who share this mindset: "Yeah, okay, I'm a sinner but, so what?" That person has no conviction of their sins. They do not care. In fact, it used to be, that people were only unconvicted and unworried about sin, but since then, it has gone even further to people who deny there are sins, so anything that they want to do is perfectly fine.

Contrary to that, Paul explains that people with desires and actions for living like that is a good indicator that the Spirit of God is not in them. That is because those indwelled with the Holy Spirit of God will be convicted against their sin nature. We should be troubled by our sinful behavior. Notice I did not say someone living by the Spirit would be sinless. We are all going to sin, myself included. Jesus was the only person to walk the earth while living a sinless life. But when we are not convicted of our sin, because it's become our way of life, that sin regularly causes factions, discord, and dissension through disruptive sins like drunkenness, orgies, witchcraft, hatred, and discord. Yet, some of us may still call ourselves Christian while that sinful lifestyle is what we practice. If that is you, "the you", as the Bible says, you will not inherit the kingdom of God.

Now, again, we are not staring at the challenge of us meeting the perfection standard. Only Jesus was able to attain that. But, as I said, when someone claims to be committing no sins, has no problem with sin, or even justifies sin, that is not a good indicator. But notice what Paul mentions, of all the sins he could have listed as a way of life, that you need to stay away from, because you will be risking your inheritance of the Kingdom of Heaven. Paul pointed out witchcraft.

And that is not by chance. What do we have today? Here in our own country, even in the American Church, we have people who not only flirt with, play around with, and dabble in witchcraft, but, believe it or not, there's a new trend in the Church involving those who call themselves "Christian witches." How low can you go, right? Unfortunately, I'm not joking. "Christian witch" certainly fits the term, "oxymoron," which would also include the classic examples of peaceful war, icy hot, government intelligence and the best of all, yummy chicken. Hey, life just works that way, right? It's like people who call foul the healthy meat; not true! Are you kidding me? Whoever said that better get their insurance copay ready.

But "Christian witchcraft" has got to be the worst of the oxymorons. Some people who do not have a problem with their involvement in witchcraft and some who do not even think it is a sin, will still claim they are Christians. But according to **Galatians 5**, how should that person categorize him or herself? Paul informs us that it would rightly be as someone who will not inherit the kingdom of God. That is a habit of life that shows there is no Spirit of God in you.

That said, unfortunately, the trend of people calling themselves Christian witches is taking off right now. Witchcraft is not only exploding in our secular society, but now we are even getting this rise in so-called Christian witches. In fact, they are having their own conferences. Here is a short promotional video for a 2020 Christian witch gathering that includes this sales pitch and examples of vendors attending:

Many different attendees are shown in various styles of witch outfits.

"CHRISTIAN WITCHES CONVENTION 2020!"

Books and other Witchcraft paraphernalia are shown at the vendor's tables.

"JOIN THE ADVENTURE IN SALEM, EASTER WEEKEND"

Amulets and these vendor books that are shown: *40 Money Mantras, 40 Money Spells,* and *Christian Witch: How an Ex-Jehovah's Witness Lives Magical & How You Can Too!*

"WITCHY VENDORS"

"READERS STUDIO"

A vendor's witch potion is shown.

"SATURDAY NIGHT WITCHES BALL"

Candles are shown and then witches all dressed up like a New Orleans Mardi Gras party.

"JOIN US"

A cake is shown with this writing: *"Happy YouTube 10 Year Anniversary,"* to a so-called Christian witch named, *"How You Lovin'"*

"TIX ON SALE"

"CHRISTIAN WITCHES CONVENTION 2020"

That is nuts! Even saying Christian witch seems crazy but now there is also a movement that has conventions. Just like you and I might attend a Christian convention to study the Bible, they are saying, "Hey, let's get all the 'Christian' witches together to learn more witchcraft! Tickets are on sale now!" Just when you thought the spread of witchcraft could not get worse, they try sneaking into the Church. How bizarre is that.

Unfortunately, it is just the tip of the iceberg. I'll give you a bit more about this and then we'll move on to the history of witchcraft in Europe. There is a so-called Christian Witch website, and I want to give you some comments from people on that website that go to show there is a natural slide toward being a Christian witch if you've already been involved with the charismatic movement in the Church. These are the words of people claiming to be Christian witches:

"The first annual Christian witches convention is set to be hosted in Salem, Massachusetts, and will feature internationally recognized Prophet Calvin Witcher who agrees with the convention's host that Jesus was a 'sorcerer' and the Bible is really a 'book of magic.'"

So, he claims to be a prophet. What other organizational leaders call themselves prophets, supposedly having the ability through power and touch to perform miracles? It is the charismatics and he's going to admit it because he was raised in Pentecostalism. One lady calls herself the Reverend Valerie Love. Hey, who holds to the false teaching of female pastors as a way of feminine empowerment, so that women can exercise their power as pastors and prophets? Again, it is the charismatics. Coincidentally, witchcraft offers the same. Now, listen to how Valerie Love describes the audience she is recruiting and notice she is not trying to attract the secular community. She is fishing inside the Christian Church:

"The Rev. Valerie Love, the force behind the event who describes herself as a practicing Christian witch and an ordained minister of spiritual consciousness, recently launched the Covenant of Christian Witches Mystery School to help Christians tap into magic, which critics are condemning as 'dangerous.' She insists there is nothing wrong with the idea of Christians practicing magic, despite biblical warnings against it."

Yes, I'm sorry, but the Bible says, "You will not inherit the kingdom of God." That is the reality. Here's more:

"Love revealed previously that she was 'born a witch' but was forced to stifle her identity as a Jehovah's Witness from age 4 to 30 when she finally left the 'cult.'"

That is really sad, but actually also consistent in that Jehovah's Witnesses is not Christianity. So, it is no wonder she is not a Christian.

You can take a look at that organization, and how to witness those trapped in it, by getting our study, *Jehovah's Witnesses & The False Teachings of the Watchtower Society*. It's a works-based false gospel. This woman jumped out of the frying pan and into the fire, trading cult for cult and going from bad to worse. It's unfortunate.

And here is a claim from the other one in that article, Calvin Witcher:

"The miracles from Jesus' adult ministry are clear examples of sorcery."

He says he's working "his way up" through witchcraft rather than how he had been trying to do so through Pentecostal techniques:

"Witcher, who describes himself as a believer in Christ who still speaks with tongues from his background in the Pentecostal church, said the Scripture has 'haunted me' and agreed that they were both still working on getting up to Jesus' level."

And he is looking to get to Jesus' level because his focus is on himself and his power. Who else promotes that today? Again, it is the charismatic movement. In fact, here are his words quoted from the article, so you know I'm not making this up or somehow presenting an unfair comparison:

"My background in Pentecostalism really set me up on a good foundation."

It was certainly a foundation that helped you to slide right into witchcraft. He continues:

"In Pentecostalism we had tools. We did anointing oils, prayer shawls, and we talked on the gifts of the spirit. Going into magic was a very easy segue."

Calvin says magic was an easy segue from Pentecostalism and then talks about a ritual he and his community practice called, "money magic."

He calls it magic but that is just the same practice as those who profess to "manifest money" through their membership in the charismatic community and more specifically, the Word of Faith people, who "name it and claim it" or "blab it and grab it." Many of those leaders are getting rich. Then Witcher goes on to claim Christian Church leaders have nefarious motives for teaching against the practice of witchcraft:

"Church leaders teach against it, to keep people as 'slaves.'"

That is just another charismatic mindset where anyone who calls them out on their unbiblical practices are supposedly not reading the Bible correctly. They claim we are against the Spirit of God in these last days. We are said to be fundamentalists and those charismatics do not want to hear Biblical doctrine from us because they profess to only needing the Spirit of God that moves and empowers them. It is a parallel to witchcraft that includes the same kinds of baloney. In fact, he spells it out even more plainly:

"All Christians are mystic, especially Charismatics…"

And without going through the rest of our whole huge *Charismatic Chaos* study, this again is more of the similar charismatic teachings that this guy is now using to do his witchcraft:

"There is no difference between me and the Father. There is no difference between me and Jesus…"

Another false teaching of the charismatics is that we can all become our own "little gods." We are supposedly little messiahs walking around the planet. So, you can see why I say the charismatic movement is preparing people for an unfortunate slide into even worse belief systems. And these witches are admitting it with their occult practices that they claim to be Christians. It has gotten so bad that people like this even feel justified saying they're Christian witches who do good for other Christians by sucking them into their so-called oxymoron organization. And if you look at the website, you will have noticed that

Love and Witcher are signing people up for their "mystery school class" that they say will bring a powerhouse word. What does that sound like? Again, it is similar to some teachings of Bethel Church in Redding, California, that we talked about in chapter eight with their supposed showers of gold dust.

Also, like Bethel, the witch website lists another aspect to come to the conference for and that is the wonderful music. Hey, it's all about an experience with hot rock music, right? No. That said, there is nothing wrong with well performed Christian music, but it can also be the focus of false faith services that use music to seduce people to their beliefs. Now, even without looking at Christian witches, we may think overall witchcraft in our society is still inconsequential. But listen to this:

"A report in The Christian Post last fall highlighted the astronomical growth of self-identified witches in the U.S."

Again, that does not even include those now claiming to be Christian witches.

Now, I want to give you one more aspect of this subject and then we will move on. And this is not an anomaly because it too is growing. From their own words, I want to show you how some slide from the "Church," straight into witchcraft. A lot of it comes from the charismatic community. This is called "The Christian Witches Creed," and it is rather lengthy, so I'll only give you a few short pages, which demonstrate blasphemy to the core as an ultimate oxymoron:

"I am a Witch, and proud of it, free to be as God created me, Living my Soul's Destiny, Magickal, Mystical, Mysterious me. I am Love, exceedingly."

No. You are exceedingly being led astray. It goes on:

"I am not here to please anyone."

Well, as a supposed Christian, who professes to be created by God, you should be here to please Him.

"I need no one's permission to be who I am, nor do I seek approval or require validation."

Can you smell the rebelliousness? Where does rebellion come from? It is from satan, who was the initial rebel. In fact, the Bible says rebellion is the sin of witchcraft. It's rebellion against God. Those who take that creed will stand accountable before God. How could anyone with that rebellious mindset be a Christian? There is no humility and desire to follow Jesus Christ. That creed is about serving self and not Jesus, who is our Lord; we are His servants. Here's more:

"I'm only here for Love. I am a Christian Witch; I love my cross and my wand. I consult my Tarot deck and my Bible. I adore and I'm devoted to Christ & the Goddess. There is no conflict in what I do, what I say or who I am."

You say you're saved and there is no conflict between Christianity and your witchcraft. But you better read **Galatians 5** in your Bible because those who live like that will not inherit the kingdom of God.

Now, here is the question for us here in the United States: Where did all our witchcraft practices come from? Again, some arrived out of the slave trade from countries like Africa, while other aspects were picked up in the amalgamation of cultures coming here from all over the world. But the more major influx has been from Europe, which makes sense because those who started the United States of America were from Europe.

So, let's get into the history of witchcraft practices in Europe:

"Belief in and practice of witchcraft in Europe can be traced to classical antiquity..."

As we saw already that antiquity included Roman society's decline as power morphed into the rise of the Roman Catholic Church in the Middle and Dark Ages. Do you know why it is called the "Dark Ages?" That is specifically because Roman Catholicism took over. And I am being completely serious about that. But the trail of civilization goes back to the Roman people who were steeped in witchcraft as they spread into what we now call Europe.

"Belief in and practice of witchcraft in Europe can be traced to classical antiquity and has continuous history during the Middle Ages, culminating in the early modern witch hunts, as well as the concept of the 'modern witch' in Wicca and related movements of contemporary witchcraft. The topic is a complex amalgamation of the practices of folk healers, folk magic, ancient belief in sorcery in pagan Europe."

And, of course, they are still dealing with it today because like here in the U.S., much of the witchcraft in Europe has been downplayed, as well as turned into something light and kiddish. It has become something we dress up as on Halloween or just a cartoon character that isn't identified as representing the real demonic entities behind what is sold as just a "fun" figure. But those demons are real, and it is a serious issue. Real witchcraft from Europe still has a major effect on customs they still have today. Here is a video transcript that will introduce you to some of that:

"The witch, an iconic Halloween character, is usually dressed all in black with green skin, a tall pointy hat, and flying on a broomstick across a full moon. But witches are not just a Halloween cliché. They have got a long and tumultuous history that we bet you didn't know. Though many stereotypes come from Western culture, witchcraft has existed around the world and throughout history, including Asian, African and many Native American societies. In medieval Europe, anywhere between 100,000 and 200,000 people were arrested on suspicion of witchcraft. About half of them were executed. And did you know, the accused witches were not just women, but men, too?

Even after the witch hunts ended, Western culture remained fascinated with witches. The witch-filled fairy tales of the Brothers Grimm and Hans Christian Andersen inspired L. Frank Baum to create his modern fairy tale: The Wonderful Wizard of Oz, which featured the most famous witch in pop culture history, The Wicked Witch of the West. And did you know Baum didn't intentionally make the witch's skin green in his book? But that is how she appeared in the Technicolor film version in 1939; the image stuck.

What about that tall, black, pointy hat that witches wear? Members of Europe's upper classes wore similar hats during the 15th century. The style later spread to commoners; the same poor country folk who are typically accused of paganism and witchcraft.

The broom, a common household tool, was used by pagans during ancient crop fertility rites. It later became a common symbol of witches, who were said to use their brooms to hide their wands during the witch hunts. People also believed that witches would rub a special ointment into their brooms and use them to fly across the sky and perform their magic.

And did you know that witches still exist in modern times? The modern form of witchcraft, known as Wicca, was founded in England in the 1950's. Its members worship nature and a female deity known as the goddess. There are now more than 400,000 Wiccans in the United States, but you probably will not recognize them on the street. They don't wear pointy hats and not a single one of them has green skin."

That was from the History Channel and, as they laugh it up, witches are even infiltrating the Christian Church.

Now, I want to break down some of those aspects and practices of witches, like those pointy hats and the brooms. There is a lot more to those items than what was just said, and it is pretty wicked, too. As with witchcraft in pretty much all societies, European witches seek to commune with demons. Some come up with other names besides demon, but you'll see that it's the same old effort from witches, trying to achieve an altered state of consciousness to connect with spirit entities. So, first, let's talk about how European witches have been heavily into drugs:

"A number of modern researchers have recognized the importance of hallucinogenic plants in the practice of European witchcraft."

They would make ointments and other herbal concoctions to rub on themselves as a way to achieve what they characterized as a "witches flight." They used hallucinogenic plants such as henbane, belladonna, mandrake, datura and others from the Solanaceae family of plants.

"All of these plants contain hallucinogenic alkaloids of the tropane family, including hyoscyamine, atropine and scopolamine, the last of which is unique in that it can be absorbed through the skin. These concoctions are described in the literature variously as brews, salves, ointments, philtres, oils and unguents. Ointments were mainly applied by rubbing on the skin, especially in sensitive areas, underarms, the forehead, the mucous membranes of a person's private parts, or on areas rubbed raw ahead of time. They were often first applied to a 'vehicle' to be 'ridden' (an object such as a broom, pitchfork...)."

Now, why would they do that? Well, let's get into what was really going on with the witch's broom.

Again, over the years we've been led to believe that the witch on a broom is just some funny little cartoon character. But that keeps us from understanding the occult background of the broom that has been used in European witchcraft. So, let's take a look at the reason witches are depicted as riding brooms in the night sky:

The witchcraft broom had everything to do with pharmakeia, the use of hallucinogenic drugs, to contact and commune with the demons. It sounds crazy, but let me tear that down for you:

"During the Middle Ages, parts of these plants were used to make 'brews,' 'ointments,' or 'witches' salves' for witchcraft, sorcery, and other

nefarious activities. Hallucinogenic compounds could be absorbed through sweat glands in the armpit or via the mucus membranes of the rectum or the female private part."

And the reason they would do that, as opposed to eating the hallucinogenic plants, was that it took a little while for the effect to happen if the drugs had to go through the digestive system. But when you get the drug to these particular areas of the body, the effect is more instantaneous. So that is how the practice got started. And, as weird and gross as it sounds, for these areas like the armpits, forehead and private parts, they would put the ointments on something, often a broom, and then ride around on that so the concoction would work its way into that area, giving the witch the desired effect. And this is not just some strange parallel for a short period of time because that practice by witches was recorded long ago. Here is more from this secular article in Forbes Magazine about these broom-type practices of witches back in the fourteenth century:

"The earliest clue comes from a 1324 investigation of the case of Lady Alice Kyteler: 'In rifling the closet of the lady, they found a pipe of ointment, wherewith she greased a staff, upon which she ambled and galloped through thick and thin.' And from the fifteenth-century records of Jordanes de Bergamo: 'The witches confess, that on certain days or nights they anoint a staff and ride on it to the appointed place or anoint themselves under the arms and in other hairy places.'"

And typically, clothes would block the area where a witch would want to put hallucinogenic drugs to start her ride, so, that's why a lot of classic depictions of witches had them, not only riding on brooms, but also with no clothes. Obviously, the reality of the true witch picture has been cleaned up since.

"These particular alkaloid hallucinogens tended to cause sleep, but with dreams that involved flying, 'wild rides' and 'frenzied dancing.' A 1966 description of this alkaloid intoxication was offered by Gustav Schenk: 'My teeth were clenched, and a dizzied rage took possession of me. But I also knew that I was permeated by a peculiar sense of well-being

connected with the crazy sensation that my feet were growing lighter, expanding, and breaking loose from my own body. Each part of my body seemed to be going off on its own, and I was seized with the fear that I was falling apart. At the same time, I experienced an intoxicating sensation of flying. I soared where my hallucinations took me, the clouds, the lowering sky, herds of beasts, falling leaves, billowing streamers of steam and rivers of molten metal.'"

So that is a description of their "flying" and those might not just be drug-induced trips in their minds. In our New Age movement study, *New Age & The Last Days Deception*, we talked about how those who get into an altered state of consciousness can actually experience something called, "astral projection," or "astral travel," where a person leaves their body to spend time in the demonic realm. That's not good. So, why would they do this stuff? Was it just because they didn't have anything to do? There was no ability to stream shows and not even cable television. Can you believe that? What else could they do? I guess that's an excuse to take drugs. Hey, they had to deal with the plague back then so maybe they too had a lockdown like our Covid experience. Seriously though, why did they get involved with those crazy behaviors? Well, it was all about the occult practices. After they have their drugged broomstick, which is the vehicle to get the hallucinogenic drugs into the person so they can start flying, then what?

"All of these concoctions were made and used for the purpose of giving the witch special abilities to commune with spirits (demons,) transform into animals (lycanthropy), gain love, harm enemies, experience euphoria and sexual pleasure, and most importantly, to "fly to the witches' Sabbath."

What in the world was a witches' Sabbath? Well, let's trace that trail: The Witch's Sabbath was a gathering of witches, where they did their hallucinogenic drugs. And by the way, they have a horned critter in the middle of their ceremony that they are worshiping and dancing around in their hallucinogenic drug-induced state. The whole thing is most likely about inviting demons to possess them. So, that is what their Sabbath was and it's just flat-out occult practices. It reminds me a lot of the satanist stuff that we will get to in the next study after witchcraft. Another name for the Witches' Sabbath is "Black Sabbath," which you might remember as a rock group by the same name. Now you know where they got that name. In fact, that was Ozzy Osborne's first band before he went on his own in the 1960's.

"According to the band, the group derived their name from one of their early songs, 'Black Sabbath,' which documents a band member's experience with the occult and his fascination with horror films. Additionally, Black Sabbath is a name that refers to a meeting of those who practice witchcraft, or Witches' Sabbath, or other occult or superstitious rites."

So the basic method for these types of witches is to put the drugs on the broom, somehow get that inside his or her body, head to the Sabbath, where everybody else is doing it, and then jump into the demonic frenzy of people, who are performing occult rites and rituals. And once they were in this drug-induced state, where they were probably connecting with demons, that were everywhere around those people, as well as inside of them, what would they do in that satanic state? Or was it just some crazy dancing? No!

Typically, three things would go on at these Witches' Sabbaths, or Black Sabbaths: First, there would be a procession of spirits (demons) that would join the human beings. That is demon possession, which was attained by getting into an altered state of consciousness, inviting the demons in. Unfortunately, I have been there, done that, and wish I wouldn't have bought the t-shirt. Second, there would be a lone spectral (a demonic, accursed, or otherworldly figure) that would appear over the procession. Third, there would be a procession of the human dead, which usually consisted of those who had died prematurely, violently, or as one of the group's human sacrifice. So, this practice is not just taking a trip to worship nature. This is not about leaving nature lovers alone. This behavior was just as sick as all the other debauchery we have seen. And it still goes on today in Europe.

"The book 'Compendium Maleficarum' (1608) by Francesco Maria Guazzo illustrates a typical witch-phobic view of a gathering of witches as the attendants riding flying goats (getting into their drug-induced hallucinogenic state,) trampling the cross, and being re-baptized in the name of the Devil while giving their clothes to him, kissing his behind, and dancing back to back forming a round."

What does Wicca say about their practices today? They claim it is just nature worship because they are concerned about climate change. Some of the other diabolical elements of the Witches' Sabbath involve poisoning wells and eating babies. Hey, that last one cannot be true, right? Yes, it is. What did we see in the last several chapters? Witches are into sacrificial murders of adults, infants, and children and they do so in bloody, horrible ways. It is all so sick and demonstrates why God tells us not to let this stuff permeate our country.

Again, I'm not for witch hunts. This kind of thing should be handled through the courts. And don't let anyone tell you we Christians are somehow hypocrites, because people in the past were involved in the witch hunts. First of all, I wasn't there for those witch hunts. And second, that was not Christianity. Those witch hunters were with the Catholic Church, which is not Christianity. It's the same mistake people make who say we Christians carried out the Crusades. That too was the Catholic Church trying to grab land and money. And by the way, during those Catholic Crusades and Catholic witch hunts, who also got hunted down by the Catholic Church? It was Christians and Jews. So, we Christians do not need to defend any of those bad behaviors by non-Christians. And again, I am also not condoning any of that vigilante justice. But you can see why God told us not to let this kind of thing permeate our country. Now, let's look back quickly at drug use in witchcraft and then we'll move on.

"Magic ointments produced effects which the subjects themselves believed in, even stating that they had intercourse with evil spirits, had been at the Sabbat (Sabbath) and danced on the highest mountains with their lovers."

That is getting into stuff that we will discuss in our satanism study: the "incubus" and "succubus." It's all demonic activity that has been downplayed today, just like the cartoon character of an old lady with a pointy hat, who flies around on her broom. They neutralize the real evil involved. Today, just like photos of people can be turned into cartoons (cartoonized), that is what they have successfully been doing with the occult. But when we study the true history, the facts behind these practices show the rotten behavior it is.

"At the end of the Middle Ages, the recurring beliefs about European witches were, the ride by night, pact with the devil, formal repudiation of Christianity, secret nocturnal meeting, desecration of the Eucharist and crucifix, orgy, sacrificial infanticide, and cannibalism."

"They supposedly also harmed local communities with their powers to cause impotence, turn milk sour, strike people dead, cause diseases, raise storms, cause infants to be stillborn, prevent cows from giving milk, prevent hens from laying, and to blight crops."

Now, here's another aspect that I thought was interesting, though I don't know how true it is: Witches not only have pointy hats but also ride brooms at night. They also normally have something on their faces, right? Most are depicted with warts. Why in the world is that? Is it just an innocent and fun cartoon? Is it part of the caricature that is to make them look ugly and creepy? Well, we may have thought that but, apparently, there is a much creepier reason. The description actually comes straight from witches through secular research on European witchcraft. I'm not sure it could happen, but it involves the familiar-spirit demons we have already seen in other cultures. Remember, the demons would supposedly possess animals that would then walk around and instruct the witch in deeper witchcraft practices, as well as give them power and protection. We saw that each country had their own familiar spirit animals like Japan's foxes and snakes and Africa's baboons and hyenas. Well, European witches had dogs and black cats. People like a cute little cat, right? But that's not what those represent. The black cat depicts a familiar spirit or demonic possessed animal. So, even that black cat is with a witch for an evil aspect of her craft.

That gets us back to the facial warts and I will warn you, their supposed use is depraved activity. It was believed that the warts were what witches used to suckle and nourish their familiar spirits. As crazy as that sounds, folks, it was supposedly the same way a lady would breastfeed a baby. But for what it's worth, I'm not saying that's really what happened. I'm just saying, the witches' explanation of the warts is that those are points where the familiar spirits could get their nutrition from a witch. That is just sick, weird, and creepy all at the same time. Wow! But again, all we see is that it is depicted as, "all in good fun," and has a sinister truth behind it. The evil part has been downplayed and the whole thing cartoonized.

Now, this is also going to sound crazy and weird, but witches were not only known for flying on broomsticks. Supposedly, they also occasionally rode humans. And when a witch, also known as a hag, had ridden a human, that person was said to have been "hagridden." And that is where a saying about horses comes from. Sometimes horses were found sweating in their stalls in the morning, which meant someone had been riding them that night. The perspiring horse was said to have been hagridden. And the horse may have been another of their vehicles to deliver the ointment to the witch. Apparently, they would spread it on the sitting area of the horse. That is just more craziness that is bizarre to read about, but important to know so we can deal with the evils of witchcraft.

Again, that drug use demonstrates it is nothing new, they are the same as other witchcraft practices, like the European witch spells that would supposedly give them the ability to perform magical actions.

"A spell could consist of a set of words, a formula or verse, or a ritual action, or any combination of these. Spells traditionally were cast by many methods, such as by the inscription of runes or sigils Latin word meaning 'seal' on an object to give that object magical powers."

Each of their figures represents a demon's image that witches would affix to a poppet or moppet (similar to our modern-day puppet, or Muppet). Then they would supposedly engage that particular demon, that they wanted to affect the person that the witch made the poppet to represent. It is more of the voodoo thing but with a European-witch style. There are a huge number of those sigils, which remind me of how the Asian community would use sealed calligraphy to supposedly give protection, by keeping the demons at bay; or even as a way to invite them in. It is the same sort of practice in this European version that is just done with different symbols called, sigils. Now, I can't go through all of them because it would take a whole chapter but using a demon-specific sigil was supposed to conjure up that particular demon, so that it would do whatever dirty deed a witch desired.

And some demon sigils today are the same as those mentioned in the Old Testament. Why? Well, like satan, demons have been kicking around in man's experience for a long time; ever since satan and the angels rebelled. A couple of those demons that are still mentioned today are Baal and Balaam. And how does God feel about murmuring? He does not like it any more than He does the demon called, "Murmur." Have you heard that one before? In our coming satanist study, we'll see the story about how one of these satan followers confessed to attending a Baptist Church for two years. Day in and day out, he would go around murmuring to others in his effort to bring down and destroy that Church. His goal was to cause whatever division he could. In fact, the Bible's **Galatians 5** is not just about witchcraft. It also warns against division-causing hatred, dissension, and discord.

Other aspects of witchcraft in Europe are the effort to summon up Lucifer and also getting involved with necromancy, which is the practice of conjuring up the spirits of the dead for the purpose of prophecy.

At places like burial sites or what they called, "crossroads," the European witch would conjure up a demon in hopes that it would inhabit him or her. With the burial site they believed that the practice of necromancy would cause the person in that grave to come up as a demon.

Do we see that same behavior being condemned by God in the Old Testament? Yes, and it was with King Saul's message that he received from the Witch of Endor. With that example of necromancy, there is the debate about whether the entity that came up was the Prophet Samuel. And here is a look at what we all recognize as a crossroads:

This is still something in effect today that has to do with the goddess Hecate that we saw earlier in this book with Babylon, Egypt, Greece, and Rome. A crossroads is the occult term for a "hotspot." I remember my days in New Age where a hotspot like Mount Shasta was where we were told we could more easily tune into the spirits. Another was Sedona, Arizona. So, there are certain places on the planet, which New Agers and other occultists believe are more charged. And the idea of a crossroads is the same sort of belief about places that supposedly facilitate an easier connection between the spirit world and ours; places where the veil is much thinner, so you get better action. That is their mentality that says crossroads are places where a witch can perform their more serious supernatural and paranormal practices.

And these crossroads are something still used for voodoo today, with those witches believing they need to visit a hotspot crossroads in order to open up a particular portal. They do so for specific reasons, including the ability to gain skills from the demons like playing a musical instrument, throwing dice, or dancing. By visiting a crossroads at certain times, like midnight, or just before dawn, they believe they'll meet a black man, whom some would call the devil. That color probably comes from voodoo being prominent in some areas where there is more of a black culture like Africa and Haiti. But the witches would try cutting a deal with the man, who would give them powers they did not have before.

Hey, I'm sure no one in the music industry today has gone to a crossroads and made a deal with the devil to give them supernatural abilities with music or dancing, right? Wrong. Though our society does not want to deal with it, this is happening all over the place, and with prominent people. I will give you one example in this transcript of a video where a huge star admits it, out of her own mouth. Beyonce claims she gets power from demons. In fact, she has a name for her demon that she calls, Sasha.

Beyonce: *"When I performed 'Crazy in Love' at the BET Awards, it was almost like my coming out."*

Announcer at BET Awards: *"Ladies and gentlemen, give it up for my girl, Beyonce!"*

Beyonce: *"I was very nervous, of course. Sasha was in full effect. Sasha is my alter ego. And when people see me, sometimes I think that when they meet me and they speak with me, they are expecting Sasha. I'm really kind of shy and not really shy, but more reserved and nothing like Sasha. But I guess I wouldn't be very entertaining on stage, so Sasha comes out and she's fearless. You know, she can, she can do things that I cannot do when I'm in rehearsal. I mean, I can try but then it just doesn't happen. I can sing notes and sing strong and do all these things that, when I'm just by myself, I can't do. And I remember right before I performed, I raised my hands up and it was kind of the first time I felt something else come into me. And I knew that was gonna be my coming out night."*

Oprah Winfrey is interviewing Beyonce in 2008: *"Like when you're getting ready to go onstage and perform, does Sasha Fierce, when does she show up?"*

Beyonce: *"Usually when I hear the crowd, when I put on my stilettos; the moment right before the show, when you're nervous and that other thing kind of takes over for you. Then Sasha Fierce appears in my posture and the way I speak, and everything is different."*

Hey, at least she was honest. I certainly don't recommend what she's doing but, apparently, it shows how people are still making pacts with the devil and Beyonce says this one was in an actual crossroads scenario that gave her supernatural abilities.

Now, if you're thinking crossroads sounds familiar from another area of our entertainment industry, you'd be right. In 1986, there was a film made about this stuff that everyone thought was just a fun and cool movie with Ralph Macchio from *Karate Kid*. That movie, *Crossroads*, is all about blues music and witchcraft. The whole premise surrounds people who visited a certain crossroads in the south. In fact, crossroads are popular in the blues industry that spawned a lot of songs about it. The movie was about how Ralph Macchio had to go up against the devil's guitarist played by the famous musician, Steve Vai. If Macchio's character could beat the devil's guitarist, then Joe Seneca's character, Willie, who had previously sold his soul to the devil, for his abilities (apparently like Beyonce), could get his soul back. That is actually what that movie was about and, unfortunately, it's based on real witchcraft.

European witches these days claim the same as other modern witches, who say they are not all the bad types that allow demons to suck on their warts as they commit infanticide and cannibalism. They will say they are good witches. But again, it is all the same old witchcraft whether they want to call it black, white, green, or whatever color of magic.

Some modern European witches paint themselves with interchangeable terms like good witch and white witch; a lot like how *The Wizard of Oz* had a good and bad witch. But they are both just witches and both are bad.

As I mentioned earlier, European witches also got involved with familiar spirits that were often animals. But in the limited research I was able to do for that area of the world, it is interesting how the Europeans would often skip the whole animal thing and commune directly with demonic entities. Of course, they didn't call it demonic. At first, they called them "fairies."

Fairy was their term for a fallen or demoted angel, which is a demon. That is what the witches would communicate with. Also, there is the usual occult owl in the background of some pictures you might see. But again, European witches would sometimes skip the familiar spirit animal that would teach, guide, lead, and give them powers. Instead, they would go directly to the demons that appear in different forms, one of those being a fairy. Now, that may sound familiar because, shocker, it is a version of Disney's Tinker Bell.

Tinker Bell is actually a manifested European demon that witches relied upon to hopefully help but, of course, demons are liars that do bad things. To ward off these demon fairies, witches had protective charms.

And back in an earlier time of Europe's Church, they had a way to get rid of the demon fairies like Tinker Bell. They rang Church bells. See, you thought those were just to signal the start of Church services. But it was to get rid of the fairy demons. That was their belief, which I think was obviously superstitious.

Another practice designed to ward off demon fairies involved the structures of Catholic Churches, which are not Christian Churches. As you've probably seen, Catholic cathedrals will often have tall spires that come to a high point. As crazy as it is and much like spikes put on walls to keep the birds from landing there, Catholicism felt those spires would keep the demons away because they would have no place to sit. Other supposed ways to ward off fairy demons were four-leaf clovers and wearing clothing inside out. But again, European demons have since been cartoonized.

"Before the advent of modern medicine, fairies were often blamed for sickness, particularly tuberculosis and birth deformities."

European witchcraft involves other types of demonic fairy creatures like goblins, gnomes, and sprites. Those are just more old-fashioned European terms for demons. And another that has been cartoonized is the leprechaun.

A leprechaun actually comes from two words in the Latin, which are "lepre" for "small" and "corpus," which means "body." So, it is a European demon that manifested itself with a "small body." Leprechauns are depicted as little bearded men with a coat and hat. They are said to cause a lot of problems. Here is the earliest known account of a leprechaun and it is from medieval times:

"Fergus mac Leti, King of Ulster, falls asleep on the beach and awakes to find himself being dragged into the sea by three luchorpain, Irish for, Leprechaun."

Again, today we've been taught to think of leprechauns as fun, but illusive cartoon characters, who like to dance and hoard their gold. But that is a false picture of that demon. So, it is another case of European witchcraft skipping the familiar-spirit, animal-guide demon and just manifesting the actual demon. That is what we're talking about when referencing leprechauns. It is crazy how the whole topic has been twisted. And guess who is involved in making movies about leprechauns that, of course, give us a false impression of those demons? You guessed it— Disney.

Disney's *Darby O'Gill and the Little People* is about a tribe of leprechauns and their king. It was made by Disney back in 1959. Another figure downplayed today but still a manifested European demon, is the hobgoblin.

Hobgoblin comes from two words: "hob" meaning "elf," which you will recognize from the long ears, and a "goblin" that is a mischievous and ugly fairy. So again, it was just another type of demon that was manifested. The hobgoblin's relatives were called brownies, which were demons that typically visited human dwellings while the family was asleep.

Also, with fairies in European witchcraft, one demonic tactic to lead people astray was called the "Will O' Wisp," which was Latin for "giddy flame." It was an orb of light that was often hard to discern because folks didn't know if it was just someone with a lantern out in the forest or on the swamp (bog). People believed the fairies (demons) would show that light to get them to go in that direction, and in that way the will o' wisps would lead them astray and into harm's way. It was also called the ghost light, which is related to something we will get into more when we do a full-blown study on the background of Halloween practices. That is the "Jack O' Lantern." But that and these will o' wisps, ghost lights or orbs in the sky, are all a part of the occult around the world. And by the way, once again there is a will o' wisp in the Disney movie, *Brave*.

Mexico has a version of these orb lights called, "luces del dinero," or "tesoro," meaning "money lights," or "treasure lights." In Asia it's called the "Aleya," a "marsh ghost-light." These orbs are also talked about throughout Europe in Finland, Sweden, Estonia, Latvia, and Lithuania. It's also called a "pixie-light" in parts of England, as well as a "spunkie" in Scotland and even Australian Aborigines have their version of these orbs that lead people astray, which they call the "min min light." Again, Disney portrayed these occults will o' wisps in *Brave*, but what other Disney production incorporated them?

They used them a second time in *Mater and the Ghostlight*, which is a seven-minute short film; an offshoot from their *Cars* movies. It was aptly named with the will o' wisp-type title: "Ghostlight." But all these lights are actually about demonic entities like fairies that would grab people's attention to draw them into harm's way. As crazy as it sounds, that is what those really are, while Disney and others want to make them okay by turning more demons into cartoon characters. They are demonic fallen angels and even secular sources say the lights can be viewed as subjects of satan. Yet, if we make cartoons out of them, that somehow makes it all okay.

Originally in Europe, fairies like "nymphs" and "tree spirits" were also worshiped as minor deities. The latter is something we will see from Wicca's modern feminist witchcraft today. They claim to be worshiping nature, but it is just the same old demons, repackaged. And here is what all the European interaction with demons led to:

Again, I am not saying we should emulate what they, including organizations like the Roman Catholic Church, did with those witch trials.

But these trials happened because witchcraft was all over Europe. They started having witch hunts as far back as 1233 and 1329. A time that is always thrown in Christian's faces, but was actually Catholicism, when they had great power. It was the peak of the witchcraft trials from about 1580 to 1630. Then it began to decline because, just like India and Africa, Britain passed a law against calling out witches.

"The Witchcraft Act was a law passed by the Parliament of the Kingdom of Great Britain in 1735 which made it a crime for a person to claim that any human being had magical powers or was guilty of practicing witchcraft."

That breech of the law would get you a year in prison. As a result of that law passing, what do you think happened with the practice of witchcraft after that? It began to spread. However, I want to mention one public voice that was against the law being passed. That was James Erskine:

He was the only prominent figure to speak and say they better not do that. But they didn't listen to him, which led to an explosion of witchcraft. Why else did it explode? The huge increase happened, not only because it was protected, but because they had their own early version of Disney. That was from the Brothers Grimm with their books called, *Grimm's Fairy Tales*.

Since fairies are just glamorized demons, those should be called, *Grimm's Demon Tales*. Their writing was demon stories about occult witchcraft practices that were made into children's stories. Does that sound familiar? As we will see, Disney tapped the Brothers Grimm fairy tales for a lot of Disney's cartoons. By now, that should not be a shock. But it was these Grimm guys who helped popularize witchcraft and other occult behavior in the 1800's.

So, witchcraft was first protected and then popularizing by that early form of media. In 1812, the Grimm brother's first edition came out with 86 stories. By the time their seventh edition hit the shelves in 1857, they were up to 210 fairy (demon) stories.

Again, Disney got a lot of their stories from the Brothers Grimm, including *Rapunzel*, which they renamed *Tangled, Hansel and Gretel, Cinderella, Little Red Riding Hood, Bremen Town Musicians, The Princess and the Pea, Snow White, Rumpelstiltskin* and *The Golden Goose*. On and on it goes.

And bringing European witchcraft up to modern time, another watershed creation has been a huge breakthrough in Europe that spread across the world. It involves this witchcraft critter from the British author, J.K. Rowling, who has also had a bunch of successful spin-offs from it:

"As of February 2018, the 'Harry Potter' books have sold more than 500 million copies worldwide, making them the best-selling book series in history, and have been translated into eighty languages. The last four books consecutively set records as the fastest-selling books in history, with the final installment selling roughly eleven million copies in the United States within twenty-four hours of its release."

Those are all about witchcraft, which is a big reason it is spreading rapidly in our world! Between books and movies, the *Harry Potter* brand is worth $25 billion dollars.

So, when we put all this promotion of witchcraft together, it makes sense that we now have what secularists are saying is an explosion of witchcraft all around the planet, with a lot of it having originated in Europe. From a news report called, "Britain's Young Witches," here is the video transcript about that growing number of worldwide witches:

Some witches are shown, along with this caption: *"Meet the coven of cackling witches, who cast magic spells and perform rituals. At the top of the table is medium and head witch, Charlotte Clark."*

Witch, Charlotte Clark, (with a British accent): *"As a child, I remember very, very strongly: I've always been very frightened of the dark; because in the dark, that's when the faces come forward. I used to kind of think, when I was a child and at school, I was a bit like, you know, Bewitched, the U.S. TV series witch. I thought I could move my nose and make things happen. It was quite weird. I was a weird child, I suppose. And it wasn't until I was in my early teens that I actually realized I was shown how to control all the different spirit energies that come forward. There is also another side to this: negative things. And there was a time where I realized that things could happen, mind over matter. So, be careful what you wish for."*

Reporter interviewing a witch: *"So what do we need?"*

Witch demonstrating witchcraft to the reporter: *"So, the first thing is a pentagram."*

Narrator: *"In Wicca each point on the pentagram or pentacle represents the five elements: earth, wind, water, fire and spirit."*

Reporter holding up a pentagram: *"As soon as I saw this, I slightly panicked. I am not going to lie. I can't be the only one that found this unnerving."*

Witch demonstrating: *"Yes, of course. I think when people see pentagrams, they instantly think of Satan."*

Narrator: *"That's not all. This altar also includes her wand, herbs, chalice, bloodstone, tarot cards, rune stones, and last but not least…"*

Witch demonstrating: *"We have a cauldron, if you'd like to pick that up, as well."*

Reporter picks up a hand-size cauldron: *"Look at this."*

Narrator: *"You heard right, that is a cauldron."*

Male witch, Stephen Aidan, being interviewed in the forest: *"The same as people talk about yoga, people will be able to just talk about their witchcraft practice."*

Female witch, Thea Jade: *"I sit in my garden with my pendulum, asking questions."*

Second female witch, Rowan Jasmin: *"Yeah, I think it will just become something that's completely normal—hopefully."*

Video of those three witches in the forest laughing together with this caption: *"The Modern Witch."*

Aidan: *"Someone who's a witch is someone who just practices witchcraft and magic. They're doing things from spell work to anything like prosperity or healing or anything they want to do."*

Jasmin: *"It's someone that's in tune with the elements around them."*

Jade: *"Honestly, it's someone that just practices witchcraft. It's so open."*

Jasmin: *"And also, it's lots of stuff in tiny jars, which is great."*

The three witches are shown walking away with this caption: *"Meet the witches proving it is not just double, double, toil and trouble."*

Aidan: *"The most magical times are at home when it's just me in a room with a candle. You feel like time stops when you are practicing."*

Jasmin: *"I use all sorts of things."*

Jade: *"I tend to do spells in little satchels."*

Aidan: *"I like to do a lot of my spoken magic and scrying with crystal balls and things like that. It's something that gives me that faith and hope and that connection to that spirit in nature."*

Jasmin: *"I use tarot card readings. I use crystals a lot, as well as meditating."*

Jade: *"My pendulum is one of my favorites. If I'm having a hard day and then I go home and I practice, it does calm me down. It makes me have a much nicer outlook on the world."*

Aidan and Jasmin are sitting on a log in the forest and laughing with this caption: *"They are among thousands bringing witchcraft to social media."*

Aidan: *"It was very much hush hush; very much unseen. But now, with things like social media, it is massive. It's huge."*

Jasmin: *"Because there are so many people putting their practice out there now, especially on Instagram, people are more accepting of it; this generation, especially."*

Jade: *"It can be there for anybody."*

Aidan: *"People are really out and proud in terms of their witchiness."*

Ending caption: *"These witches hope witchcraft will be more mainstream in the future."*

It's no wonder the practice of witchcraft is exploding with young, old, male, and female alike. In large part, it is because people are turning away from Christianity and toward something that has been popularized and glamorized, cartoonized. And those witches might experience some power, but that power is not from God. If you are a Christian dabbling in witchcraft, there is danger to being okay with that as you attempt to combine witchcraft and Christianity without conviction of how wrong it is. The Bible says you will not inherit the kingdom of God. And we'll see more about that in the next chapter as we get more directly into modern Wicca.

All this promotion of witchcraft in our media has led to what secularists are calling a revival of the occult. There is an explosion of witchcraft, but it's not just in Europe. The witchcraft from Europe has once again hopped the pond, with more of it getting to us in America because of ubiquitous movies like the *Harry Potter* series that is one more we have been given by Disney. And we just heard the other area of our society that is really helping push witchcraft. That is social media here in America and around the world, which is part of what we will take a look at in the next chapter.

Chapter Twelve

The History of Wicca
Part 1

So far, in our study of witchcraft, we have seen its definition, the different types, and how it is all over the world. We also talked about having protection from witchcraft, which is only for Christians through Jesus. And speaking of that, as we are giving this original study through our weekly Wednesday night format at Sunrise Bible Church, it seems we have received a badge of honor. We have been told that this study is now appearing on blogs of witchcraft sites that are now praying curses and hexes against us. But they are going to find out what the Bible tells us Christians: "Greater is He that is in me than he that is in this world." They will learn that God is the One in control. It's not satan—hello! So, those practicing witchcraft need to turn to Jesus. For us Christians, we need to spiritually deal with that threat, and we do not need to be afraid of it because we only need to call on the name and authority of Jesus Christ. We have not been given a spirit of fear. God has given us a spirit of power, love, and a sound mind.

We also learned that today's modern witchcraft, which is the definition of "Wicca," is nothing new. They try to relabel themselves but it's just old-fashioned witchcraft that's been going on since the Tower of Babel, and we demonstrated that history, in the last nine chapters. Like me, you have probably been blown away by how much our planet is permeated with witchcraft, which has been in the background through much of earth's history. So, it is no wonder cultures around the planet have been all messed up, just as much of today's population still is. From its origins in Babylon, the sewer pipe of witchcraft and other occult practices went to Egypt, Greece, Rome, Asia, the India area, with its large island chain to the southeast, Africa, and Latin America.

In the last chapter we hopped back over the pond from Latin America and took a look at European witchcraft, which is what today's Wicca has risen from. They just relabeled it, and besides a hodgepodge of witchcraft practices coming from other countries as well, Europe is where we have gotten a lot of what we have here in North America. We saw that European witchcraft is just as bad as all the other cultures we have looked at throughout history. And like those others, European witches have been involved with drugs that are so important to the occult, as one of their ways to get into an altered state of consciousness and open themselves up to the spirit realm so they can connect with demons. As a way of getting the drugs into the body quicker, witches spread them on their brooms and then ride them. Once high off the drugs, they go "flying," not only through visions but possibly also astral projection (out of body experiences).

We talked about how European witchcraft has been cartoonized to the point that people don't realize it's a true evil threat to society. We also got to know what is involved with the "Witch's Sabbath," or "Black Sabbath." European witches have also been into witchcraft spells, speaking with the dead (necromancy), and visiting spiritual hotspots that they call "crossroads," where they make deals with the devil to acquire special abilities. We saw that is what Beyoncé apparently did through her "spirit," she calls, "Sasha." Beyoncé says it takes over when she gets on stage. Like witches in today's modern culture, European witches try to say there are good and bad witches, just like the depiction we see in *The Wizard of Oz* with one of those witches being portrayed as good Glinda, the so-called good witch of the North.

We also saw how European witches used the same familiar spirits (demons) as other witchcraft cultures, like Asia, with their snakes or foxes and Africa's baboon or hyenas. European witches use dogs and black cats. In that witchcraft practice, demons can either possess a non-Christian or an animal. Those are the only two options. We are familiar with the idea of witches having a familiar-spirit black cat, but their use of dogs has also been common in Europe. And it traces all the way back to Egypt and Greece with their goddess, Hecate.

With European witches, we saw how they did not wait for the demons to possess their animals. Instead, they go directly to demons that they call, fairies. Those demons just appear on the scene. Of course, Europeans haven't called them demons, but what we saw is that's really what was going on. A witchcraft fairy has always meant the same as a witchcraft demon. Besides fairies, those demons also appeared as leprechauns, hobgoblins and will o' wisps. That last one, also called a ghost light, is a demon that leads people astray, into danger.

Like witchcraft in India and Africa, European witches began to really grow in number after they were protected by laws denying people the ability to say someone is a witch so they were protected, while at the same time witchcraft began getting glamorized by the media of that day. Even before Disney came along, the tool that glamorized occult practices was *Grimm's Fairy Tales*, which more rightly should have been called *Grimm's Demon Tales*. Like Disney has done now for decades, they began cartoonizing witchcraft and other occult practices to make them palatable for kids, as well as adults. In fact, those Grimm-brother's books are where Disney got a lot of their stories. And coming along to really boost Disney's efforts has been an extremely popular phenomenon that has been advancing witchcraft all over the world, for a couple of decades now, including a massive influence here in the U.S. It's the *Harry Potter* series that came out of Europe. And that is what we ended with in the last chapter, which brings our study to the practices of witchcraft today.

What we're going to see is how today's witchcraft has simply been repackaged and renamed as "Wicca," even though it's just the same old occult practices that we've been seeing all over the world for thousands of years. They've given it a new name because those involved don't want to go around saying they are into witchcraft. Most people would freak out. Although, today, many witches are coming out of the "broom closet" and being proud to call themselves witches.

Now, before we get into the activities of today's Wicca, I want to look at the history of its rise and how it got to us in the United States of America. Besides our planet's increase, as prophesied by the Bible, of earthquakes, famines, pestilence, wars, and rumors of wars, why are witchcraft and other occult practices also growing rapidly? Is that just by chance? No! It is another huge sign that is given in the Bible to tell us when we are living in the last days. Most people do not get that. In fact, it is preparing the people of earth for the soon-arriving Seven Year Tribulation society. The Scriptures tell us that people at that time are going to be so incredibly hardened and wicked that, no matter how much wrath God pours out, they still will not turn from their sins. And it is because they're steeped in occult practices.

Again, I believe the rise we're seeing today is preparing them, and I'm not making that up, because it comes straight from the Bible in **Revelation 9**, which tells us the status of the people in the Seven Year Tribulation. It is not good! A lot of **Revelation's** chapters layout 3 major judgments that come on the earth: the seals, trumpets, and bowls. Then we see the return of Jesus Christ in **Revelation 19**. With chapter 9, starting at verse 13 and moving forward to 21, we will be looking at the time of the 6th trumpet. Again, the trumpet judgements come after the seals where we have already seen a quarter of the earth's people have been annihilated. If that were to happen today, it would be not be millions. Instead, that is nearly two billion wiped out. And this next wave of judgments, the trumpet judgments, is where another third of the earth gets annihilated.

Now, we'll see how that happens, but the big question is this. With all the people being slaughtered through wickedness, asteroids slamming into the land and oceans, earthquakes going off, global wars, giant tsunamis, a third of the earth getting burned up, and all the rest of God's judgement, don't you think the people of our planet would get the message that God is not happy with what they have been doing? Can you see them turning to God, getting right with Him? You would think He would get their attention. But the people talked about in this glimpse of the future from **Revelation**, (the worst time ever on the face of the earth), have hardened hearts. And we are going to see why. Let's take a look at **Revelation 9**, beginning with verse 13, which picks up after a fourth of mankind has already been annihilated:

"The sixth angel sounded his trumpet, and I heard a voice coming from the four horns of the golden altar that is before God. It said to the sixth angel who had the trumpet, 'Release the four angels who are bound at the great river Euphrates.' And the four angels who had been kept ready for this very hour and day and month and year were released to kill a third of mankind.

The number of the mounted troops was 200 million. I heard their number. The horses and riders I saw in my vision looked like this: Their breastplates were fiery red, dark blue, and yellow as sulfur. The heads of the horses resembled the heads of lions, and out of their mouths came fire, smoke, and sulfur. A third of mankind was killed by the three plagues of fire, smoke and sulfur that came out of their mouths. The power of the horses was in their mouths and in their tails; for their tails were like snakes, having heads with which they inflict injury."

So, they got people coming and going. Now, after all that, did the rest of mankind get right with God? Did they all confess that He got their attention, so they would now turn back to Him and live godly lives? No! And this explains what has given those people such a hardened heart:

"The rest of mankind who were not killed by these plagues still did not repent of the work of their hands; they did not stop worshiping demons, and idols of gold, silver, bronze, stone and wood, idols that cannot see or hear or walk."

What will they be worshiping? It will be about their demon worship! And what has always been the occult's main focus? It too is demons! How about the more specific practices of witches? It's about demons and all kinds of other aspects that God talks against right here in **Revelation**, including idol worship. Behind every idol is a demon. What entity is instilling all that occult behavior into people? Again, it is demons. These people, in occult witchcraft, are not just involved with demons, they're actually worshiping them. It's along the lines of what we'll see with Wicca. They claim to worship so-called gods and goddesses. But those are just demons. And how about the murders we have seen that go on as a part of the practice of witchcraft around the world? Here is more from **Revelation**:

"Nor did they repent of their murders, their magic arts, their sexual immorality or their thefts."

Of course, magic arts mean sorcery (witchcraft). Sexual immorality is a huge part of the occult. Basically, they believe anything goes, which leads to some really horrible behaviors.

So, the Bible's depiction of the coming Seven Year Tribulation is the picture of people whose hearts are so hard that, no matter what God does to get their attention, they still won't respond. They will not repent. The Greek word used in the Bible is "metanoia," which is "meta" meaning "after" and "nous," which is "mind." Here is a good explanation of that.

"The term suggests repudiation, change of mind, repentance, and atonement; but 'conversion' and 'reformation' may best approximate its connotation."

They will not turn away from it. They will not let it go. Why? It's because our planet will be majorly involved with the occult and witchcraft at the time of the Seven Year Tribulation. And the Bible speaks against pharmakeia, which is drug use that is fostered through the magical arts, as it is mentioned there in **Revelation**. Drug usage is huge in witchcraft. So, that is what it's talking about with the magic arts.

Today, do we see a rise of people involved in the occult; those preparing to create that unfortunate, non-repentant, and occultish society talked about in the Bible, with that soon-arriving Seven Year Tribulation? Yes! What have we been seeing throughout this book? Do you understand the prophetic significance of what we are dealing with in this study? Along with the earthquakes, wars, and rumors of wars that show us we're living in the last days, we are seeing this rise of witchcraft and its newly repackaged Wicca, including here in the United States and even with the youngest of children, as well as teenagers and adults. These days witches are even coming out in the open and being proud of their evil craft. In fact, they are even praying against our president and that news is actually reported in a positive light. So, that is another sign we are living in the last days because those are the people who have needed to rise on this planet to fulfill that **Revelation 9** passage. It's here now! And the practice is spreading rapidly, just in time for the Seven Year Tribulation.

That's what we're going to see with modern witchcraft (Wicca). Before we get to the history of Wicca, I want to talk about just how much it is exploding. In the last chapter we left off with Europe, and that is where we're going to see that Wicca started. It came from there to America. But let me give you the current statistics about how much witchcraft has permeated Europe. And think about this: Not that long ago, our Christian heritage came out of Europe where the Protestant Reformation started. But now it's gotten very dark and even an English reporter from CBS News admits it here:

"England is positively crawling with witches, warlocks, wizards, and water diviners. There is hardly a village in the Kingdom where you will fail to find someone gazing into a crystal ball, offering to tell your fortune, or getting involved in close encounters with aliens."

We'll get into the alien theme a bit later, which relates to the will o' wisps, or ghost lights from the last chapter. Again, those are orbs of light, sometimes in the sky that appear, and people feel the need to go toward them to see what they are. Could that be part of what's going on with some UFO behavior today? Yes! And we are going see that in this chapter. Here is more from the British reporter:

"Forget Salem, Massachusetts in the U.S. when it comes to the occult, we've cornered the market. Harry Potter is not just a bestseller and an international movie hit, it is real life for many of us. There are parts of England where one in 10 of the people believe they have the power to teleport their neighbors, pick them up and spirit them away, literally. The northern country of Yorkshire, for example, is packed with telepathists, time travelers, enchanters, mediums, and astrologers. Essex, to the east of London, contains the highest number of people subscribing to ancient pagan customs and rituals, and my own home country, Kent, just south of the capital, has three times the national average of psychic healers. This is not just mumbo jumbo. It is the result of detailed academic research."

Why would that happen? It's because two thousand years ago God let us know that would be going on around our planet during the Seven Year Tribulation; one more indication that we are living in the last days before Jesus' return. Here is more from the English reporter:

"Everywhere the paranormal is booming. Ancient spells are available on every sidewalk."

I also have to share this headline with you because you might think that's just England and this rise of Wicca is not really a serious movement in the United States:

"Witches Outnumber Presbyterians in the U.S.; Wicca, Paganism Growing 'Astronomically'"

Why is it growing astronomically? This has been seen during the years since the *Harry Potter* series hit the big screen in 2001. According to the studies, from that time forward the books and movies have influenced a massive number of people around the world; not just in Europe but around the world, including the United States. This is from the Pew Research Center:

"It makes sense that witchcraft and the occult would rise as society becomes increasingly postmodern. The rejection of Christianity has left a void that people, as inherently spiritual beings, will seek to fill."

And you wonder why we are putting out this study. Why would I take so much time in the pulpit, as well as getting this book out, when some say it's not what we as a Christian Church should be focusing on? But this warning against witchcraft comes from the Bible, which the Church has failed to preach about. The Church is not equipping their people to help fight this evil that is destroying so many lives and sending countless numbers to hell. And it is not just me whipping this study out of thin air. Even the secularists are saying that the rise of witchcraft is being facilitated because pastors aren't teaching this part of the Scriptures, which also includes other occult practices. These warnings are all over the Bible in the Old and New Testament. Yet, because the whole Bible isn't being taught, so many Christians today will sit there listening to their pastors their whole lives, and never hear anything about the dangers of the occult and how they and everyone they know, including their children, need to stay far away from that evil. Because no one has said to them, "Don't you even think about going down that road to witchcraft!" Even Christians are flirting with, getting involved in, somehow condoning, or at least ignoring, the quickly spreading wildfire of witchcraft that is bringing destruction all around our planet.

"Wicca has effectively repackaged witchcraft for millennial consumption. No longer is witchcraft and paganism looked at as satanic or demonic. It's a 'pre-Christian tradition' that promotes 'free thought' and 'understanding of earth and nature.'"

I like what this guy said:

"As mainline Protestantism continues its de-evolution, the U.S. witch population is rising astronomically."

They are leaving the Church and then going to the occult. They want a spiritual experience, but they cannot find it in the Church, which is sad. There is so much baloney going on today in the Church that they're going someplace where they can at least feel spiritual. Why do we Christians need to deal with witchcraft? I love how this guy puts it:

"The Church needs to wake up to the reality of this."

Since we started this study, there have been people commenting online with things like, "I don't want to hear this. I don't need to study this." But where is it that I am getting this teaching and equipping from? Is it just because I cannot find anything else to preach on? No! We are a Bible Church and Get A Life Media is a Bible ministry. All over the Scriptures, both the Old and New Testaments deal with witchcraft, the occult, sorcery, and pharmakeia. So, we must hit it at some point. And we do because we are faithful to the Bible. As that guy said, the Church needs to wake up to this evil in our midst. People need to be warned. They need to know all of Scripture, not just about our wonderful future in Heaven.

This aversion to preaching all of God's Word is part of the long-line of the apostasy going on in the Church, which is another sign we are living in the last days. It isn't just the lack of equipping Christians on Bible prophecy. The Church is also not talking about hell, sin, God's wrath, and certainly not the occult. The shepherds are worried that people will freak out and leave their services. Instead of being faithful to God's Word, their agenda is to increase the number of those attending each week, rather than making disciples (disciplined learners).

Let's take a look at the onslaught of witchcraft with this rise of Wicca and some of what is happening in Europe today:

Narrator: *"Today in England, witchcraft and its more modern incarnation, Wicca, are pagan religions. Wiccans worship the gods and spirits of nature. In return for their faith, the spirits grant them the power of magic. It was this power that first drew Galiese Cod to Wicca. Now she's studying to become a full-fledged witch."*

Galiese: *"I like the name, witch, and I suppose, in a way, I'd like to reclaim it as being a good word and standing for all the things that I believe in."*

Narrator: *"She has her husband's complete support."*

Galiese: *"He sees my pentacle that sits by me. And I have a great belief that it should be next to my body as opposed to on show."*

Narrator: *"Once a month, Galiese meets with her coven; a group of like-minded witches who bolster one another in their faith. They call themselves "The Raven and the Rose." When witches gather in a circle, they believe they can weave stronger magic. Tonight, will be Galiese's first time participating in a secret ritual."*

One of the members brings out red sandalwood (for passion) and grinds it up with a pestle and mortar.

Narrator: *"It's April 30th. Tomorrow, witches all over England celebrate what they call the first day of summer: Beltane. As high priestess of The Raven and the Rose, Jeanette Ellis will lead her coven's Beltane ritual."*

Ellis: *"We're cooking up an incense for Beltane. Making an incense is a spell. The different ingredients go into it. Like making a cake you blend them all together and they all have specific jobs within the cake, or the incense, in this case. And we'll burn that tonight."*

Narrator: *"On Beltane, the coven will thank the gods for the earth's renewed fertility. For witches, only Halloween, 'All Hallows Eve', is more sacred."*

Ellis: *"We take the energy of the goddess and god of earth and air and fire and water. The energies of the universe, I place within."*

The witches hold hands and walk around in a circle as they sing to their gods.

Narrator: *"Homage paid, the witches can ask for their gifts from the gods."*

The witches jump over a small fire and ask for things such as wisdom and luck.

Narrator: *"Then, as with holy day celebrations everywhere, it's time for the party to begin. For most in England, Beltane is known as May Day; an ancient feast still celebrated widely. Witches participate in May Day festivals across England. The Raven and the Rose coven seizes the opportunity to march proudly through the streets. Their public walk shows that prejudice is beginning to wane."*

And that is just in time for the Seven Year Tribulation to hit the world. God said it will appear on this planet when we are living in the last days, which is demonstrated by the fact that witches are proudly out marching in parades. And it is not just in Europe. This is going on all over the United States, as well. We're going to get into the history of this modern Wicca movement, but before that, if you saw the video that goes along with the transcript, I just gave you, you'd see their occult parade included people dressed like a Jolly Green Giant. Because that character was there with the witches, I did the research to find that the Jolly Green Giant has its roots in witchcraft. I kid you not! How crazy is that?

You see the history of the Jolly Green Giant goes back to 1928. He started as a white guy, so where did the change to green come in? Here is that explanation from a secular article:

"The Jolly Green Giant's original incarnation was reportedly influenced by illustrations from 'Grimm's Fairy Tales', a collection of German fairy tales from the early 1800's."

That is kind of wild, but let's get into the history of Wicca that explains why we've had this explosion of witchcraft practices. Again, I am giving you information about Europe, but it's also over here in America.

"Wicca is a modern-day, nature-based pagan religion."

Can I translate that for you? It is old-fashioned witchcraft.

"Though rituals and practices vary among people who identify as Wiccan, most observations include the festival celebrations of solstices and equinoxes, (the positioning of the moon and stars,) the honoring of a male god and a female goddess, and the incorporation of herbalism and other natural objects into the rituals. Wiccans practice their religion according to an ethical code and many believe in reincarnation."

Their philosophy says that they should do whatever they want as long as it doesn't hurt anyone. But if that is true, why are witches, right now, attempting to place hexes on us for producing this study? I thought you said you won't hurt people. That is called hypocrisy. As you saw there, they also believe in reincarnation. Is that biblical? No! We saw that many times in three of our studies: *New Age & The Last Days Deception, Hinduism and the Dangers of Yoga* and *Buddhism.* **Hebrews 9:27** makes this definitive statement:

"Just as people are destined to die once and, after that, face judgment."

Wiccans also pride themselves on supposedly being "pre-Christian." They say we need to listen to them because Christianity came along after their beliefs, so they are really the first early religion "pre-Christian." But, of course, they are not. And that is why I wanted to methodically go through those many chapters we just covered about witchcraft history, from the Tower of Babel to the point where it has been and still is permeating the planet. Again, where did it start? It originated at the Tower of Babel. Does that pre-date the scriptural account? No! There is the whole Genesis account way before that. Before the birth of witchcraft and other occult practices at Babylon, there was Adam and Eve, the days of Noah, with the worldwide flood and many generations between Adam and Noah. So, witchcraft certainly did not pre-date the Christian account. That is a lie. But it is how they seduce people to join them.

Wicca can be practiced individually or in groups they call, "covens." We Christians would say we are gathering at Church services, while they get together in coven "circles."

"Wicca also has some commonalities with Druidism in its environmental component and is considered the inspiration of the goddess movement in spirituality."

We will eventually get into a hodgepodge of occult practices that include beliefs like druidism and shamanism. Also, we will see how it's not just feminism, that is a smokescreen, to get people into the occult. The environmental movement is doing the same.

"There is great diversity among individuals and groups that practice a Wiccan religion, but many are duotheistic, worshiping both a female goddess and a male god (sometimes referred to as a Mother Goddess and a Horned God)."

That said, the extent of the philosophy is really a mishmash of anyone's beliefs because the core is really, "Come one, come all!" No matter what you believe, you can join them and behave however you would like, just as long as you sign up and join them in their occult practices.

Some Wiccans are flat-out atheists, while others are pantheists, believing that "all is God." Others are polytheists with "poly" meaning "many" and "theist" refers to "gods." I think it is interesting that some are respectful of the god and goddess concept but say those entities are not real; they are only symbols. That actually parallels the fact that 65% of the professing American Church says that satan is not a literal being he's just a symbol of evil. I wonder who started that idea in the Church? Many Wiccans just happen to have the same sort of beliefs.

"Rituals in Wicca often include holidays centered around phases of the moon: solar equinoxes and solstices; elements such as fire, water, earth and air; and initiation ceremonies."

Later, we will get into the calendar they use for those rituals. The fifth element they add is the spirit and that is why they have these symbols:

That star with five points is a "pentacle," or "pentagram." In Wicca, each point relates an element: spirit, air, earth, water, and fire. I One picture we saw was very sad that someone was so proud of their witchcraft that they actually had the pentagram, or pentacle, put on their tombstone. Unfortunately, I'd say he or she knows better now. That is not something you want to advertise being a part of.

There are about equal portions of men and women in Wicca and it's crazy that 62% come from Protestant backgrounds. That's a failure of the Church. People are looking for real spiritual truth just as I was. You can hear about that in my testimony with the video message called "Get A Life!" at our website: www.getalifemedia.com. Prior to being a born-again Christian, I was searching for truth in the occult New Age movement because so-called Christians seemed to demonstrate hypocrisy and baloney. I looked for a spiritual path and found it with New Age. I didn't know they were demon spirits. I got involved with the occult, and it was horrible. But it's an example of how people are hungry for the spiritual truth and we have the privilege of showing them the only true spiritual path, which is the Spirit of God through His truth in the Bible. If we don't do that, they're going to go somewhere else. And that is backed up by the statistics, which tell us that 62% of Wiccans come from a Protestant background. It's crazy!

Joanne Pearson surveyed Wiccans in England and found out that the average age was 35 years old with the mainstay of the organization being 25 to 45. So, the younger generations have been getting into it.

"Pearson's survey also found that half of British Wiccans featured had a university education and that they tended to work in "healing professions" like medicine or counseling, education, computing, and administration."

They are all throughout society. Someone might go to a medical professional there, to get his or her back fixed, and the next thing they know witchcraft is being performed on them. That can even happen here in America, so we need to pay attention. Now, that is some of the European stats, but what about North America? Here is some of that:

"In the United States, the American Religious Identification Survey has shown significant increases in the number of self-identified Wiccans, from 8,000 in 1990, to 134,000 in 2001 and 342,000 in 2008."

In North America, the numbers tripled from 2001 to 2008. Hey, I wonder why that was? When did *Harry Potter* come out in the movie theatres? It was 2001. As Warner Brothers, the producers of *Harry Potter* and Disney know, movies have a huge influence on people. If you don't think so, you're fooling yourself.

And here's something crazy: Believe it or not, Wicca is the largest non-Christian faith practiced in the United States Air Force. This video transcript goes into why there has been such a huge surge with witchcraft in the military:

Narrator: *"Halloween may mean costumes and candy for you, and for us, but for those out there who are witches, this is their most sacred holiday."*

Sarah Lucero, news anchor: *"In San Antonio there's a Wiccan coven touting the largest weekly service for the study of witchcraft in the world. Where they meet and who is in the class, may surprise you."*

Jeff Goldblatt, news anchor: *"Marvin Hurst has their story."*

Music is playing as a woman sings about the earth, fire, and water.

Marvin Hurst: *"Mention the word, witch, and, instantly, most conjure up thoughts of black magic rituals in the belly of seclusion."*

Military commander inside an air force-base gathering building: *"Just keep the line progressing."*

Marvin Hurst: *"Now, come inside the Arnold Hall Community Center at Joint Base San Antonio Lackland. It's a different picture."*

Witch, a high priest, talking to a crowd of seated soldiers: *"I am Archer and I'm a witch."*

Marvin Hurst: *"Archer, a.k.a., Tony Gatland, is the high priest of this coven. A packed house of basic military trainees are studying witchcraft in his circle."*

High Priest being interviewed: *"When we come over here on a Sunday, oftentimes there are 300 or 400 attendees."*

Marvin Hurst: *"There are around 320 this day, who are taking part in Samhain, the witches' New Year's celebration on Halloween. They honor the dead and the rebirth of their god. Trainees literally lined up, by choice, to learn about Wicca. Fantasy reading and 'Harry Potter,' peaked trainee, Atreyu Cannon's, interest in Wicca five years ago."*

Cannon: *"There is nothing wrong with Wicca and, of course, that's why we have this service here on an Air Force base."*

How did he say he'd been influenced to go that route? It was through *Harry Potter*. At least he was honest enough to admit that. How many people do we know who have given the same old excuses for letting their kids read and watch the witch-glorifying programs like that? They say, "Hey, it's helping my kid read," or 'It's just entertainment." We're now seeing the fruits of that compromise giving rise to Wicca in these last days. It's very unfortunate.

Now, let's take a look at where Wicca started. Again, it is just old-fashioned Witchcraft that has been around ever since Babylon, but this particular repackaging of it is credited to one woman:

It started with Margaret Murray in England, who was a famous "first-wave" feminist. That first wave of feminism is said to have been in the 1800's and early 1900's. Later, we will get deep into feminism and show you how the roots of it comes clearly from the effort to seduce ladies into witchcraft. And it still has that aim today, with their ideas on female empowerment that rely on worship of the goddess. That is flat-out witchcraft and feminism is still steeped in it. Murray was one of the most prominent feminists at the movement's origins. She was an anthropologist, a folklorist, and also an Egyptologist. She studied and wrote many books about Egypt, which we learned was a country deeply involved with witchcraft and other occult practices. So, we can easily see where she most likely came up with the idea to rebrand witchcraft.

"She wrote several books on medieval religion centered around witch cults in medieval Europe that inspired British seekers to create their own covens and structure worship around her descriptions, starting with 1921's 'The Witch-Cult in Western Europe.'"

That book really began to influence people to start being bold about coming out as witches and openly practicing their witchcraft. I don't have time to go through all the books that she wrote, but the woman lived to be a hundred years old and wrote a ton of books on Egypt. Ten years after writing that book, she wrote another one called, *The God of the Witches*. But historians say it was that first book that cracked open the door to helping witchcraft become more palatable. Murray was also the first woman in the United Kingdom to be appointed as an archeology lecturer. So, she was plugged into the college circuit. Luckily, America doesn't have problem college professors today, who are involved in occult practices. They never attempt to brainwash our young people into following the same dark path, right? Yes, that was sarcasm. Actually, that sort of indoctrination happens on a massive scale today in our universities. And we pay big bucks for it to be done to our kids.

Again, Margaret Murray was an early feminist-movement figure, but her influence, conditioning, and encouraging of people to get involved with witchcraft, and to bust out of their secret witchcraft and be proud witches. That is why they call her the "Grandmother of Wicca." Murray never married. Instead, she devoted her life to her work. Murray's biographer said she was deeply committed to public outreach:

"She wished to throw open the doors and invite the public in."

Unfortunately, that invitation was not to a good life. And here is another example of the sad pattern: By her mother, this grandmother of modern Wicca was raised as a devout Christian.

"Murray had initially become a Sunday School teacher to preach the faith, but after entering the academic profession she rejected religion."

Her turning point occurred when she went to secular college. I've shared this statistic many times, and it really seems to show up in the stories that get more plentiful every year: After the first year of college, over 80% of kids that have grown up in Christian homes, reject the Christian faith. It is a war zone out there and even our Christian children are not being equipped for the fight because our Churches are not preaching the whole Bible to make disciples of those young men and women. If they are not taught this important information, churches are throwing them to the wolves, and they are going to be eaten alive. Apparently, that is also what, somehow, happened to Margaret Murray. Here is more about her and remember Wicca's supposed code of ethics, which is, their empty promise not to harm anyone with their practices:

"She was also a believer and a practitioner of magic, performing curses against those she felt deserved it; in one case she cursed a fellow academic, Jaroslav Černý, when she felt that his promotion to the position of Professor of Egyptology, over her friend Walter Bryan Emery, was unworthy. Her curse entailed mixing up ingredients in a frying pan. It was undertaken in the presence of two colleagues."

Yet, they always want us to believe their witchcraft harms no one and they only want to peacefully worship nature. Well, then what's with the curses?

"Murray's witch-cult theories provided the blueprint for the contemporary Pagan religion of Wicca, which 'formed the historical narrative around which Wicca built itself,' for on its emergence in England during the 1940's and 1950's, Wicca claimed to be the survival of this witch-cult. Wicca's theological structure, revolving around a Horned God and Mother Goddess, was adopted from Murray's ideas."

I'm convinced that she got a lot of her beliefs from studying the Egyptians, who were steeped in witchcraft, as well as the European folklore aspects of her society that we saw a lot of in the last chapter. The name Wiccan groups use for their groups of witches, a "coven," comes from Murray. That is part of the reason they call her the Grandmother of Wicca. And apparently, she was popular in England. In fact, about three years before she died, she is seen in a 1960 BBC (British Broadcasting Corporation) interview.

Those television people seemed excited to have her on. They loved this lady who started the witchcraft movement in Europe. It's crazy!

"She died on 13 November 1963, and her body was cremated."

After that grandmother of Wicca, where did the movement find more leadership? It came from Gerald Gardner.

The picture I found while doing my research is, that dude certainly has a witch or warlock hairdo. He has it going on from both ends of his head: the pointy hair and a pointy beard. Gerald Gardner is credited for Wicca being spelled with an extra "c." For that and other innovations to the movement, Gardner is considered the "Grandfather of Wicca." He carried the torch forward, so now we want to take a look how he got involved. He was an Englishman, civil servant, and an amateur archeologist, who was interested in the occult and magick. The dark arts were obviously his passion as he got his hands on anything he could regarding witchcraft. He joined the New Forest coven that was practicing witchcraft based on Margaret Murray's writings, after which he was introduced to a guy you have most likely seen before, Aleister Crowley.

Gardner was influenced by Margaret Murray to start his witchcraft career and then had it furthered along through Aleister Crowley. If you've read or seen our extensive study called, *Scientology and the Occult Teachings of L. Ron Hubbard*, you'll know that Hubbard was deeply involved in the occult where he got a lot of his ideas for Scientology, including the levels in their organization, which each cost money to obtain. That whole system came from Crowley, who charged followers for information to get to each new witchcraft occult level. L. Ron Hubbard's Scientology system also charges its occult followers to get to each new level in their organization. And it is expensive! The whole foundation of Scientology came from Aleister Crowley. And on the garb Crowley wears he has the triangle and pyramid, as well as Egyptian clothing. Egypt and Crowley were both deep into the darkest evil witchcraft. We will get more into Crowley in our future Satanism study.

Gardner was an occultist and ceremonial magician. He was born into a wealthy family, and I bet you can guess what is coming next: His parents were fundamentalist Christians in the Plymouth Brethren faith. Gardner obviously rejected that, and I don't know why, but I will say this: Even in secular society, the guy he was following, Aleister Crowley, is called "the evilest man that ever lived." Crowley was immersed in the darkest evil and that is the guy Gardner was chumming up with. Crowley's own mother described him as "the Beast," with a capital "B." I know our kids can get unruly, but there was something very wrong going on there.

Gardner's father was a particularly devout traveling preacher. Every day at breakfast, Gardner's dad read a chapter from the Bible to his wife and young Gerald. Yet, somehow, some way, Gerald still rejected Christ. After his father's death, he inherited his family's wealth and just went nuts. He was deep into the occult as he traveled the world. As part of the counterculture in that day, he was a social critic, who was bisexual and into drugs.

He was also into occult sex magic, which we don't have time to look at here but it was the same practice that Scientology's founder, L.

Ron Hubbard, and the inventor of rockets, Jack Parsons, where doing with all their occult activities at Jack Parson's house that they called "The Parsonage." They were involved in occult studies and rituals learned from Crowley, one of which involved sex magic. They were actually working to bring in the Antichrist. As freaky as it sounds, Jack Parsons, the guy who created JPL (Jet Propulsion Laboratories) was deeply into occult practices with Hubbard and it was all from Crowley's evil lessons. Crowley performed occult rituals involving drugs that helped him achieve an altered state of consciousness, so that entities would appear. Of course, those were demons. But this is what is wild: There is a picture of Crowley's drawing of one that he said contacted him:

He called that familiar spirit (demon), "Lam," and it is just one of the demon spirits that gave Crowley his occult ideas, which made him the evilest man to ever live. What does that picture look like?

It's very similar to how we often see supposed aliens depicted by those who've had encounters with them. So, wait a second. Do you mean to tell me that maybe this whole UFO thing is a bogus cover for the real spiritual (demonic) element behind that whole phenomena? Is it just demons duping people to lead them away from Jesus Christ, which is their first priority? If you want more information on that whole premise, get the book or documentary we produced: *UFO's—The Great Last Days Deception.* We put that out a few years back to expose the truth behind this alien issue and how it relates to the Bible's warnings.

I'll give you another nail in the coffin of that deception: How do we know these so-called aliens are really just more demons? Besides looking exactly like "spirits" that appeared to Aleister Crowley and led him astray (by him getting into an altered state of consciousness to connect with them), secular researchers are saying the one thing that freaks aliens out is the name of Jesus Christ. Do you know why? Folks, it is because they are demons. Let's read more about that from a video transcript with a dialect that requires a few brackets to clarify what this UFO researcher said:

"All of these secular researchers, interviewing people who've had encounters with so-called aliens, are told this about those aliens: 'They're deceptive. They lie to people. They're deceptive.' But people never questioned it during the experience. Suddenly, afterward, when asked, 'Were you told this? Were you told this?' They answer, 'Yes.' And someone tells them, 'But that's not true and the other is not true. Doesn't that make you a bit suspicious?'

I've met, literally, hundreds of people who've had this one: They are lying in bed, they see a black cloud or entity in the room, it moves or hovers, they lose control of their voice, and they're paralyzed. The skeptics try to explain it away as sleep paralysis. However, people call on the name of Jesus, for example, and even something like that stops. I myself had that same experience. I haven't told many people this: As a baby Christian, I think I'd been saved a matter of days and didn't know anything about spiritual warfare, I was lying in my room and I had this experience but I was so excited about my newfound faith that I managed to squeeze the words out: 'Jesus, help me.' I was being pressed against the bed and choked. It stopped in an instant.

We have testimony after testimony after testimony. Guy Malone is a researcher in Roswell, New Mexico. He says, 'Well, think about it: If these really are advanced entities flying millions of years across space, with that type of technology why would they be frightened of the name of Jesus, a supposedly deceased religious figure?'

Joe Jordan, who's cataloged over four hundred cases now, has recently been promoted. He lives in South Korea as the national director for MUFON (Mutual UFO Network), the world's largest UFO investigative group. He, as a nonbeliever, first stumbled upon this. He said, 'So, what is it about Christians that aliens don't like?' That was what he thought. And then he realized, like all other researchers who come to study, if they are open enough to take the evidence for what it is, they realize they're not dealing with aliens. They are dealing with spirit beings. He said he came to understand that the Bible was the only thing that could explain the spirit realm adequately.

The only permanent solution is the authority of the Creator. He is the only one that obviously can have authority over those beings. They are not Neverland aliens visiting us from a galaxy far, far away. They are deceptive supernatural entities emanating from another dimension. Any serious expert will tell you that these are what they would describe as inter-dimensional beings that should have stayed in the spirit realm but crossed over into ours."

That is interesting, and it's just in time for the Seven Year Tribulation; a time when the enemy, by simply repackaging witchcraft as Wicca, has also convinced people to get along with old-fashioned witchcraft. Along with that deception he is indoctrinating people into the idea that aliens, old-fashioned demons, or familiar spirits, can be contacted by occult practices, are benevolent, more-ancient, and superior-intellect entities that have come from far away to help us by sharing wonderful information that will save our planet. But as demons, those entities are liars, and it is all the same bucket of baloney. I just had to hit the alien subject a bit after seeing Crowley's demon-alien drawing.

But let's talk more about Gerald Gardner, the grandfather of Wicca. He had two important influences with Margaret Murray, who kind of kickstarted the Wicca movement, and then also his involvement with Crowley. Gardner wrote out Wiccan rituals that were strongly drawn from Crowley's rituals. So, that was Gardner's hybrid witchcraft education that he put together from Murray and Crowley.

"Crowley had, in 1914, proposed the idea of forming a new religion that would pull from old pagan traditions worshiping the earth, celebrating equinoxes and solstices and other hallmarks of nature-based worship."

Apparently, Gardner thought that was a great idea and started running with the practice of Wicca. In 1951, after England's repeal of their three-hundred-year-old laws against witchcraft, witches were then protected. So, all the restraints came off and it was cool to be a witch again. Gardner took that opportunity to come out in public as a witch and started giving interviews as one. Two years later, he met Doreen Valiente, a person we will look at in the next chapter. She was initiated into his coven as the high priestess. Valiente admitted that Gardner's *Book of Shadows* was highly influenced by Aleister Crowley's horrible occult rituals.

The *Book of Shadows* is a collection of spells and rituals. It is the most prominent book used by modern Wicca as their workbook of spells, rituals, calendars, and other witchcraft practices. That came from Gerald Gardner, who put it together in the 1940's and 1950's. It was written by hand and, originally, there was only one copy that existed for each coven and that was only to be held by the high priestess or high priest. That scarcity became unreasonable, so copies eventually became more plentiful, allowing every witch to have one.

Other information provided by the book are invocations, herbal concoctions, runes, rules for the covens, traditions, symbols, poems, chants, and anything else witches need to practice witchcraft. I don't want to say it is their "bible", so I'll just call it their handbook. Everything a witch would need to know is in Gardner's *Book of Shadows* and Wiccans still use it today. Early on when the book had fairly new information, an initiate had to hand copy one from the high priest or priestess' copy. But with modern technology they have been able to scan, and mass produce them. Now, that material is easily found on the Internet. In fact, you can look online for videos that show pages from the book. Here are some of the captions from a witch showing how a person can make his or her own binder containing their own copy of the *Book of Shadows* pages:

"A 'Book of Shadows' is a collection of recipes and learning material. I use printer-friendly parchment paper to get a nice vintage look. Many of the Beginner resources from Spells8 are Wicca-oriented. A 3-ring binder is perfect to start a 'Book of Shadows!' Never miss a sabbat! Celebrate the cycles of nature in solitary or with a group."

Hey, everyone can get a copy, though I don't recommend it. Unfortunately, the practice of witchcraft has been much more easily spread by online access to this *Book of Shadows* that can be easily downloaded or printed out. It is all over the internet now but was somewhat kept at bay back when it had to be hand copied. Not only that, our media has been highly promoting this material as some sort of cool information for people to distribute and own. In fact, CBS has a television series called, *Charmed*, which features the *Book of Shadows* with its spells and rituals. Because of watching that show, some are searching for the information, finding it is real witchcraft instead of just make-believe stories, and getting involved in the occult.

A movie that helped spawn the *Charmed* series was the 1996 film, *The Craft*, which also had the *Book of Shadows*. And you may remember *The Blair Witch Project* that had a sequel called, *Book of Shadows: Blair Witch 2*. Of course, the latter one showed the *Book of Shadows*. In 2011, there was a television series called, *The Secret Circle,* about a family who had their own self-styled book of shadows with its unique spells passed on from generation to generation.

Unfortunately, another big promoter of occult practices is the video gaming industry. Video games are heavy into the occult. A Japanese horror-adventure game is simply called, *Corpse Party: Book of Shadows*. The sequel, *Corpse Party: Blood Drive* goes even deeper into the book.

An Australian television series, *Nowhere Boys*, has two characters that acquire a *Book of Shadows*. Even the fifth edition of the roleplaying game, "Dungeons and Dragons," shows how anyone can get a copy of the *Book of Shadows,* to learn more spells and other witchcraft practices. All this promotion in the media has led to huge growth in what is called, "Gardnerian" Wicca.

Eventually, we'll see that Wicca has many branches. Again, we have been following the history of the same old repackaged witchcraft, now called, Wicca that was collected and put into writings by Margaret Murray, the grandmother of Wicca. Then Gerald Gardner, the grandfather of Wicca, combined that information with Aleister Crowley's stuff to form Gerald Gardner's line of teachings that is referred to today as Gardnerian Wicca.

A couple of those branches of Wicca are Alexandrian Wicca, Dianic Wicca (feminism), Celtic Wicca, the Church of Wicca, Georgian Wicca, and on and on it goes. Later, we will get into some of those and how they got started. To use a very loose vernacular that has nothing to do with the Christian Church but helps us think about the organization of Wicca, they could be said to have different denominations in Wicca, just as we in the Church do. There are different flavors and blends of beliefs and practices depending on the branch. Unfortunately, though, it is all the same sorts of evil practices.

With Gardnerian Wicca, a high priestess rules the coven and the high priest and priestess have the titles of "Lady" and "Lord," with their given name following. They work in couples while some forms of Wicca do not have couples. Instead, other versions are open to homosexuality, bisexuality and all kinds of sexual immorality. They believe in the idea that members can do whatever they want, supposedly as long as they don't harm anyone. Of course, we saw how that is a false claim and hypocrisy because they actually cast spells to harm others.

All over the world and even here in the United States, witches are getting bolder about proclaiming that they are Wiccans, and even witches. Many today are proud of it and don't care who knows. The term they use for those deciding to reveal themselves, is "coming out of the broom closet." That means the witch wants to let people know that they are now involved in Wicca or that he or she is a flat-out witch. Homosexuals would call their revealing of a same-sex partner preference to be, "coming out of the closet." So, these witches are just adding "broom" to that. And many of today's witches are getting extremely bold about it. In fact, I think it has permeated the United States even more than we want to believe. Here are a couple of girls who have come out of the broom closet:

Melissa Madera: *"I didn't always identify as a witch. I used to be a pastry chef. I feel like, in capitalist America, we always identify with our occupation first. So, now that I'm a professional witch, I'm doing witchcraft a lot harder and a lot more than I ever was. I'm one of the owners of Catland Books, and we are an interfaith occult shop and event* *space, meaning we hold community events, rituals, talks, and classes. We also sell pretty much everything you'll ever need for witchcraft."*

Sarah Lyons: *"Magic is something that I do. Witchcraft is something that I practice. And being a witch in the modern world; it's a little bit rebellious."*

Madera: *"I'm a witch because it's something I grew up with and something that made a lot of sense for me as an adult as a practical approach to spirituality."*

Lyons: *"So, one of the first things I learned about witchcraft was about the Wheel of the Year and, sort of, the seasons changing and the festivals that go along with the seasons changing. You've got Samhain, which most people know as Halloween. You've got the winter solstice, which is Yule. But that was the first sort of thing that I acknowledged in terms of like living magically. Dreaming is very important in witchcraft. A lot of my magic revolves around dreams and dream magic. Every morning I wake up, and I pour a glass of water for my ancestors and I leave it at their altar. And that is just a way to honor them and to thank them for where I am right now. And at the end of every day, I always say thank you to four things. I say thank you to the land. I say thank you to the gods, spirits, and animals of the place that I'm living. I say thank you to the mighty dead. And I say thank you to the living people. So, those are my two daily practices. And then it's kind of like what I need to get done in between."*

Madera: *"My practice revolves mostly around spirit contact and trancework. I do a lot of work with certain spirits that, like, I think I can get a practical result out of and going into trances and, like, dealing with them there."*

So, she is going straight to the demons. But, apparently, she believes it's something good to do and she's so proud of it. She's coming out of the broom closet just in time for the Seven Year Tribulation, when people's hearts will be so hard that they can go through the worst time in the history of the world, and still not repent and get right with God. That is a major sign that we're living in the last days. We are watching that happen now. It's crazy!

In 1964, at the age of 79, Gardner suffered a fatal heart attack at breakfast. Unfortunately, he knows better now, which is very sad. Believe it or not, in 1973, much of Gardner's extensive witchcraft artifacts were sold to this company: Ripley's Believe It Or Not! The rest went to his immediate witchcraft buddies, one of which was the lady we saw earlier, Doreen Valiente.

As we get further down the history trail away from the grandmother and grandfather of Wicca, Murray and Gardner, we'll see that Doreen Valiente is considered the "Mother of Wicca." She revised Gardner's *Book of Shadows* to make it much more popular and palatable for public consumption. She then split from the initial coven she had been in with Gardner. Through starting her own, she began to widely spread those witchcraft practices and it eventually hopped over to America. We will get to that in the next chapter.

Chapter Thirteen

The History of Wicca Part 2

For a quick recap of what we've learned so far, we saw that Wicca means witchcraft, and it's just the same old occult practices since back at the Tower of Babel. There are many types of witchcraft and it is practiced all around the world. The only protection from witchcraft is given by God to Christians through the authority of Jesus. Wicca or witchcraft has been the same evil for thousands of years, moving from its origin in Babylon to Egypt, Greece, Rome, Asia, India and the islands of that region, Africa, Latin America, and Europe.

In the last chapter we saw the repackaging of witchcraft by Wicca, which is the modern-day version. But it is still old-fashioned witchcraft that has, in large part, come out of European witchcraft. Margaret Murray is considered the grandmother of Wicca's witchcraft remake. She was an Egyptologist, and we know that Egypt was heavily into witchcraft. She brought that Egyptian witchcraft to Europe, beginning with her book, *The Witch-Cult in Western Europe*. That began to revive witchcraft's popularity in the U.K. and eventually led to Europe's ban on witchcraft being lifted. From Murray, Wicca, witchcraft, spread through Gerald

Gardner, who was considered the grandfather of Wicca. He got in contact with Murray and was influenced by her, as well as another icon of occult witchcraft, Aleister Crowley, who even secularists say is the evilest man that ever lived.

Gardner wrote a book called, the *Book of Shadows*, which today is considered one of the greatest resources for witches; it is a handbook used worldwide. Obviously, that book is packed with horribly evil practices, and it is the reason that, today, there is a branch of witchcraft called Gardnerian Wicca. As we continue to trace the history, what we will see is that Wicca witchcraft spread across the world through different fingers, or branches, like Gardnerian and Alexandrian Wicca; each putting their own spin on it. And I think that is why a lot of people get seduced into Wicca. The belief system puts the individual into the driver's seat. There is a large pot of Wicca practices from which followers can take whatever they would like and leave the rest; whether you want the version that Gardner, Alexander, or any other witch came up with. A witch can pick and choose.

Now, what does that sound like? It is the same philosophy in the New Age movement that we covered in our study, *New Age & The Last Days Deception*. New Age allows followers to grab a bit of Hinduism and some Buddhism, along with beliefs from many other systems. And it feels so good to the flesh because every New Ager gets to play God, which is the same lie from **Genesis 3:5** that the devil told Eve:

"For God knows that in the day you eat of it, your eyes will be opened, and you will be like God."

Just like the lie that New Age offers with the idea that you can be your own god, in the Wicca belief system you get to decide between what's right and what's wrong. Likewise, Wicca split off into branches that allow witches to just pick and choose what they want. And Wicca continues to split today. Some witches keep their practice on more of an individual basis, while others meet together in covens. After Gerald Gardner's founding of Gardnerian witchcraft, the next person in line to pick up and run with his branch of Wicca was Doreen Valiente.

This lady began to make witchcraft sound poetically witchy with a Shakespearean feel. That made it more palatable for the public, and some historians even say, if it were not for her work, Wicca may never have gotten off the ground. We are going to take a look at that but before we do, let's see if we can find another passage in the Bible that tells us not to get involved in witchcraft. Of course, we can because there are a huge number of them. Another of those is **Isaiah 47**, which is God's judgment on Babylon. This passage shows God's harsh words for Babylon and tells us why he judged those people. We already know how they were steeped in witchcraft because they were the beginning of those evil occult practices. History shows us it eventually spread across the planet and all that agrees with the biblical account.

Now, let's take a look at what Babylon was involved in with their witchcraft practices all over that society. You don't have to find an ancient Bible version, that has some sort of secret southern Hebrew to find out why God judged Babylon. He makes it very plain in **Isaiah 47:8-14**, where He calls people wanton creatures, which is a pretty obvious sign that they are in trouble with God:

"Now then, listen, you wanton creatures, lounging in your security and saying to yourself, 'I am, and there is none besides me.'"

God tells us these people, who were deeply involved in the occult and witchcraft, are claiming they are also gods. Excuse me?! There is only one God. In fact, many times, God tells us, "I am God. Besides me there is no other." He says that repeatedly in the Bible. So, these people have the audacity to equate themselves with him. God goes on:

"Now then, listen, you wanton creature lounging in your security and saying to yourself, 'I am, and there is none besides me. I will never be a widow or suffer loss of children.' Both of these will overtake you in a moment, on a single day: loss of children and widowhood. They will come upon you in full measure, in spite of your many sorceries and all your potent spells. (They are involved in witchcraft and the occult.) *You have trusted in your wickedness and have said, 'No one sees me,'* (as if God is

blind.) *Your wisdom and knowledge* (i.e., witchcraft and the occult) *misled you when you say to yourself, 'I am, and there is none besides me.' Disaster will come upon you, and you will not know how to conjure it away.* (They can't just make it go away by witchcraft and sorcery.) *A calamity will fall upon you that you cannot ward off with a ransom; a catastrophe you cannot foresee will suddenly come upon you."*

God is saying there is no amulet for them to use. Do you see what God is doing there? He's playing on their own words and letting them know that none of their sorcery (witchcraft) or other occult practices are going to stop God's judgment from coming. And God says they will get a catastrophe they could not foresee with their evil divination. They claim it tells them the future, but God is saying they are not going to see this coming. It will suddenly be upon them.

"Keep on, then, with your magic spells and with your many sorceries, which you have labored at since childhood. Perhaps you will succeed, perhaps you will cause terror. All the counsel you have received has only worn you out! Let your astrologers come forward, those stargazers who make predictions month by month, let them save you from what is coming upon you."

On social media these days, it's crazy that even so-called Christians are asking for people's horoscopes and giving theirs. Supposed Christians are quoting horoscopes but, as we saw in our New Age study, that is not something you want to mess with because it is another part of the occult. Notice how God talks about those astrologers making predictions month by month. It is just what the occult does with their calendars to this day, as we will get into that a bit later. God goes on about these occult people:

"Surely they are like stubble; the fire will burn them up. They cannot even save themselves from the power of the flame. These are not coals for warmth; this is not a fire to sit by."

Can I translate that for you? You are in big trouble with God! You have gotten involved with witchcraft to the point where you think it has given you security with some sort of so-called godlike powers. And you had the audacity to say that you are God. But God is letting you know that false feeling of grandeur has put you against the One true God. God alone is God; He alone is all powerful; and only He can provide true safety and security. God warned about occult practices long ago, but people still went ahead and persisted in their witchcraft. God is patient but only up to a point. And what happened in this biblical case at the Tower of Babel? Bang! The hammer came down and He took Babylon out.

Now, here's my point: From this Old Testament passage on through the New Testament, do you think God changed his mind about how he feels about the occult and its witchcraft? Absolutely not! If God had strong words for Babylon back then, what do you think he has got for people who get involved in this evil today? It is the same today and it's on a nationwide level. Every nation that goes down this route long enough, is going to have God taking them out. Folks, that is a clear warning we need to heed.

With that understanding, let's take a look at why our own nation is being infiltrated with the occult; specifically, with witchcraft. Believe it or not, that started with Doreen Valiente. Earlier we had the grandmother and grandfather of Wicca. Now we see the woman considered the "Mother of Wicca." That is Valiente, who met Gardner in 1952 and, under his direction, revised his *Book of Shadows* with its spells, rituals and calendars. She did so to make it more appealing for popular consumption.

That is something often needed, and I think it can be especially so with us men. You know us guys; we are maybe not the most artistic, including myself. There are many who clean up what I write. As they heard that, I am sure those involved in the process just laughed, heartily. But that is okay, I swallowed my pride long ago.

Gardner had pieced together and whipped out his *Book of Shadows,* so, Valiente came along to clean it up, making something more poetic and (using their word) "witchy" sounding. What that accomplished was to make the book much more palatable and it went on to be a huge influence. Here is Doreen's story from a secular article and keep in mind that a mystical experience, even one that gives you goosebumps, does not mean it came from God, which is what we hear in the charismatic community all of the time:

"Doreen Valiente, the mother of modern witchcraft, was nine years old when she had what she called an indescribably mystical experience and saw the veil of reality tremble. On a balmy summer evening in the 1920's, she crept into her south London garden at twilight and was consumed by the feeling that her surroundings were fabricated to hide something else; something 'very potent.' Her parents were probably right to wonder whether she was interested in the occult when she began running around her neighborhood on the household broomstick, so they packed her off to a convent school."

That is like jumping from one fire into the next. Roman Catholicism is not going to fix you. We dealt with that in our large study, *Roman Catholicism & The Coming World Religion*. Catholicism is a false, pseudo-Christian, and works-based gospel. Being put into a convent was not going to help her. Instead, it normally makes the spiritual life worse and in this case it apparently did. She ran away and, frankly, I would have too. The sad aspect of her story is the thought of what might have happened if she had been plugged into a healthy evangelical church that preached the Bible. Maybe her life would have been different. Unfortunately, a lot of people were led astray by her material because they chucked her into Catholicism and that did not work. Even back then, this is what young Doreen was able to come across in the area that she lived in:

"Aged 15, she left the school and refused to go back. Inspired by the books she found in her local library; she became fascinated by witchcraft."

Good thing we don't have to deal with our kids finding that kind of material today, right? Wrong. Libraries are taking out and banning good

Christian classics while allowing the occult to infiltrate on a massive scale. And don't think that doesn't have an effect on kids. Of course, that's just the local library, which people don't use as much anymore because they now have the Internet, which is everywhere. And on that worldwide library, conservative Biblical Christian ideas are being called hate speech and blocked, as users can access anything they'd like about witchcraft and the rest of the occult. That new pervasive library in our pockets is promoting the occult on a massive scale. No longer is it just small influences like Valiente's old low-tech local library, that had a major influence on her, resulting in her becoming fascinated with witchcraft.

"Decades later, Valiente was one of the most important figures in Wicca. Believed to be the first fully-formed new religion to appear in England and spread across the world, by writing down much of its liturgy, and helping to lift a ban on witchcraft, which had been in place for over two centuries."

Two big promoters of witchcraft happened around the same time: Valiente cleaned up Gardner's material to make it widely palatable and, at around the same time in 1951, the ban on witchcraft in England, that was over two hundred years old, was lifted. From that point it began to spread on a massive scale, demonstrating that the reverse of the ban was a huge mistake! Here is some about an exhibition of Valiente's witchcraft:

"A new exhibition at Preston Manor, in her hometown of Brighton, exploring her role in Wicca, is particularly timely for contextualizing now ubiquitous symbols and 'witchy' fashions. The exhibit also showcases her extensive collection of Wiccan and occult artifacts that is believed to be the most important of its kind in the world, which included Tarot cards, a witch's ceremonial knife called an Athame, and two glass curse bottles."

That house is a sort of tribute to the "wonderful" role she played in the development of modern-day England. There are also items included from Gerald Gardner.

Who would have thought people would celebrate witchcraft with a museum? Well, it's not just there that it's been done. A bit later, we will get to how they're doing the same thing here in the United States. So, Valiente had an experience that was not from God, she got information on witchcraft from her local library, and then eventually connected with Gardner. But how did that last one happen? It was through the media of her day: a magazine. Media was an early promoter of witchcraft, greatly facilitating its rapid spread. In the 1950's, after England's ban on witchcraft was lifted, Valiente read a magazine about Gardner and contacted him. Apparently, their relationship went well because Gardner made her the high priestess of his coven.

Eventually, she broke off from him, but before that he encouraged her to help with the rituals and ceremonies. Pretty soon he was promoting her as the face of Wicca, which is why she was given the opportunity to revamp his *Book of Shadows*. Maybe Gardner was concerned that his pointy beard and hair would frighten folks away, while Valiente looked more the part of an aesthetically appealing witch; kind of like our long-running 1960's sitcom: *Bewitched*. With all due respect to our ladies, for that show, those *Bewitched* producers didn't pick some ugly, stooped-over, and pimply old spinster-looking lead actress. They choose an attractive woman to help popularize the show, and in so doing, increased the appreciation for witchcraft. Here is what a founding trustee and curator of the Valiente exhibition said:

"She gave the modern craft a robust religious litany and a logical framework. It was this that allowed it to be more easily passed on through initiation and is probably the reason it spread so firmly and rapidly and continues to expand across the world today."

That is how influential Valiente was. One university lecturer on religions says this about her cleaning up Gardner's work to make it more witchy and poetically palatable for people to get sucked into:

"Had Valiente not been Gardner's High Priestess, Wicca would almost certainly be very different and may even not have survived into today's world."

Unfortunately, she played a huge role in the spread of witchcraft; she was pivotal figure. Valiente wrote a bunch of books. Here are three of them, including *An ABC of Witchcraft, The Rebirth of Witchcraft and Witchcraft for Tomorrow*:

The Charge of the Goddess was one of her most important books.

The keyword there is "goddess" because she focused on and encouraged the worship of the female goddess (deity), which almost all Wiccans still do to this day. Eventually, we will get into the female goddess and their male horned god. The female goddess began to usurp the male god, as far as being the prominent deity. And it was because Wiccans came to emphasize the goddess as the womb, from which all things supposedly come. About the same time those beliefs started launching, guess what else came along to promote this stuff with the Wiccans? It was feminism. Later, we'll have an entire chapter demonstrating how feminism comes out of witchcraft and is all about promoting witchcraft. As a supposed way to show women what they can do better than men, the ladies are being sucked into so-called women's rights and women's power that is just witchcraft with a goddess-worship mentality that is embedded in the practices of Wicca.

"Certainly, Doreen was a strong supporter of women's rights and wrote about feminism in her witchcraft books as well as speaking up for feminist issues throughout her life."

"Such attitudes, therefore, attract young women, in particular, to the religion of Wicca."

And why is that? It is because female Wiccans are told that a witch is the ultimate image of feminine power and that they should not let a man tell them what to do. It is the same message that feminism is running on and that parallel is not by chance. For both philosophies, that idea is just a step to get women seduced to come their way and then indoctrinate them into witchcraft and goddess worship. Here is more about Valiente and remember that their philosophy is, "come one, come all," so they accept everyone:

"Her final public speech was in November 1997; here she urged the Wiccan community to accept homosexuals. Valiente's health was deteriorating as she was diagnosed first with diabetes and then terminal pancreatic cancer."

Valiente died in 1991, and her legacy is that she really helped spread Wicca (witchcraft) in the United Kingdom after revamping it. But how did those practices come to America? That was through Raymond Buckland.

Buckland had also contacted Gardner and was also influenced by Margaret Murray. He brought Wicca over to the U.S. by founding what was considered the first Wiccan coven here. In fact, we have already seen the grandmother, grandfather, and mother of Wicca. By their own terms, Buckland is considered the father of modern American Wicca. This was written before he died:

"Raymond (Ray) Buckland is a prolific author and Witch who was responsible for bringing Gardnerian Witchcraft to the United States in 1964. Ray has been a leading spokesman for Wicca in the United States for more than five decades. An Englishman by birth, Buckland was born in London on August 31, 1934. Ray's father was of Romany (Romanian) Gypsy heritage, which is probably where he got some of his witchcraft practices. It was in London that he would meet his first wife and magical working partner, Rosemary."

"At some point, Ray had a more than passing interest in the occult, reading with great interest many books, amongst which were two that would transform his participation in the occult. In the late 1950's Ray

read Margaret Murray's 'The Witch-Cult in Western Europe' and Gerald Gardner's 'Witchcraft Today.'"

So, the grandmother and grandfather of Wicca influenced him. In fact, he began to communicate with Gardner and kept that up even after moving to Long Island, New York. Gardner set Buckland up to establish a branch of Wicca in the U.S. So, it started spreading like a franchise. Buckland and his wife expanded their Wiccan coven on Long Island. It grew at a steady pace, and Buckland began to develop an Americanized form of Wicca. Just as Valiente made it more poetically palatable and witchy sounding, Buckland made the version for us a bit more independent so Americans could do it their way. It was the democratic approach. He came up with what he called, "Seax-Wica," which is Wicca for the American mindset. Here is a video transcript about that:

Title: *"Types of Witches: Traditions & Paths"*

"At first glance, it may seem that a witch is a witch. But the further you go into learning about the craft, the more you realize there are lots of different types of witches. And since Wicca is an ever-changing religion that adapts to the practitioner, it is ever evolving to meld with the needs of its adherence. With so many possibilities, how do you know which type of practice is best for you? Even if you have already chosen your path, it is always a good idea to learn about other possibilities. And if you have not chosen a type of practice, here is a great list of possibilities to begin thinking about which one is right for you.

Seax-Wica Witch: Raymond Buckland moved to New York from Britain and brought with him a version of Gardnerian Witchcraft. His practice adapts Gardnerian practice for an American culture. Within the practice of Seax-Wica there is an emphasis on herbs and divination. This tradition does not include oaths of secrecy, rigid hierarchical structures, or a Book of Shadows. There are no degrees, so, a democratic approach to coven leadership is established. Self-dedication and open mindedness abound within this practice."

Again, Buckland allowed Americans to do it their own way with his Americanized Wicca he called, Seax-Wica. He also wrote a very popular book about it called, *The Tree.*

The Tree became the guide to Seax-Wica and was originally published in 1974 and republished in 2005 under the title, *The Complete Book of Saxon Witchcraft.* If you want a Crone translation on that title, just call it, *"Buckland's Book of American Witchcraft."* After years of Buckland telling people they did not need to follow the rigid dogma of Gardner's *Book of Shadows*, Buckland basically wrote his own book of witchcraft dogma that he called *The Complete Book of Witchcraft.*

In the witch community they call that the big blue book and in the witchcraft world it is looked upon as essential. But again, witches get to pick and choose whatever they want and that is what sucks people in with the same sort of relativistic mindset as the New Age movement. Followers of either philosophy, witchcraft or New Age, get to be their own god, deciding what is true or not true. If a witch wants to use the *Book of Shadows*, that's great. However, if they would rather follow the big blue book, or maybe use both, that's fine too because each individual gets to pick and choose their own truth, regardless of what the real God says. That is never going to work out for anyone.

"'Buckland's Complete Book of Witchcraft' has influenced and guided countless students, coven initiates, and solitaries around the world. One of modern Wicca's most recommended books, this comprehensive text features a step-by-step course in Witchcraft, with photographs and illustrations, rituals, beliefs, history, and lore, as well as instruction in spell work, divination, herbalism, healing, channeling (communicating with demons,) dreamwork, sabbats, esbats, covens, and solitary practice."

So, again, Buckland said American witches did not need to follow the doctrine of the *Book of Shadows*, and then he wrote a book of doctrine to tell witches exactly how to do everything. Here is more about his book:

"The workbook format includes exam questions at the end of each lesson, so you can build a permanent record of your spiritual and magical training. This complete self-study course in modern Wicca is a treasured classic, an essential and trusted guide that belongs in every witch's library. Never in the history of the craft, has a single book educated as many people."

Unfortunately, Buckland's blue book was a landmark work for witchcraft. He then set up a museum in 1968, which was the first museum of witchcraft and magic in the United States. And again showing the Bible's decree that there is nothing new under the sun, Buckland's museum was only because he was talking with Gardner who'd already started doing the same thing in the U.K. Buckland's museum started in his basement as a private showing but then began to grow until it got media attention, including a documentary. All that press makes things more popular so more and more people have wanted to go see the place. And it's just crazy how many people are drawn to see the tools of those dark, evil occult practices, including ritual knives; as if that's something cool. It is just gross. And unfortunately, we are going to see more of the truth that those knives are to not only be used to kill animals; sometimes they are used to kill people. This is sick stuff! Here is a bit about Buckland's museum from a guy who talks and walks with a camera while visiting it:

"Well, my friends, welcome to the Buckland Museum of Witchcraft and Magic. This is pretty cool. Basically, the basis of this museum was that there was a man named Raymond Buckland, who was kind of looking for some sort of spirituality. He found out about witchcraft, the Wiccan, and got with the man who named Wiccan [Gardner.] That's actually Raymond right there, Raymond and his wife. And then this is Raymond Buckland's ceremonial robe. Now, in this case, you can see that is a wine jug that they used for ceremonies. And then here is a silver cuff bracelet. There is his wand; Buckland's ritual wand used in the Long Island coven in the 19th century. He made that ceremonial helmet; the high priest ceremonial horned helmet made in 1970's. And then here's some more of the U.S. initiation knives, over here."

"Now, in this case, it says, in the 1970's, a ceremonial magician friend of Buckland's said that he was having his life ruined by a demon in his apartment in Manhattan. And so, he said somehow this demon was released. You can see there is a box in there and it says, he asked for Raymond Buckland's help to capture this demon. And it says it took him three days to trap the demon in the box through incantations. It says that he found a grimoire, magic book, that helped Buckland trap the demon. And it says the box has not been opened since. There you can see a Ouija board. And then, in this case, they have all kinds of tarot cards and zodiac things. These are 'I Ching' coins that belonged to Aleister Crowley. Wow. That's what those coins are right there. Huh."

Once again, who do we see again that even comes into the history of American witchcraft? It's Aleister Crowley, who is a common thread we will also see throughout our future study of satanism. But that whole idea of the Buckland museum is disgusting. And that guy's tour of it goes on and on if you want to find it online. Here in Las Vegas, we might go explore and celebrate some history at the Atomic Museum, or you and I might want to visit our nation's capital to see museums about founders like Abraham Lincoln. But even in America, people are actually going to see the history of witchcraft like it's something cool. And that is not the only witchcraft museum in the U.S. It tells us that attitudes are turning, and that tide is moving in a negative direction.

Buckland published many other books, including *A Pocket Guide to the Supernatural, Witchcraft Ancient and Modern,* and *Practical Candle Burning Rituals.* It is one thing to write a bunch of books, but it turned out that people were buying them big time!

"By 1973 he was earning enough money with his books that he could take over the running of his museum full time. Until 2010, he published a book almost every year since. His health began failing in 2015, as he suffered first from pneumonia and then a heart attack. After recovering, he experienced more heart and lung problems in late September 2017, which resulted in his death on 27 September."

So, Buckland popularized Wicca in the United States, and this is the lady that also helped.

Sybil Leek wrote a book that really catapulted her into "celebrity" witch status. As we will see shortly, that was in a twofold sense. She was considered a celebrity and she shared her craft with celebrities, which is something her family had already been doing over in England. Leek started out in the U.K. and eventually came to the United States, setting up shop in Los Angeles. So, Buckland was on Long Island to build out the East Coast and Leek landed in L.A., which meant the U.S. was then dealing with coast-to-coast witches, as well as the influence of both the male and female kind. Those factors helped it spread on a massive scale. Part of that was because Leek also wrote many, many books on all aspects of witchcraft and even had a regular column in the "Ladies' Home Journal" magazine. It makes you wonder how many ladies got indoctrinated into witchcraft from these sorts of women's magazines. They actually allowed a witch as a regular columnist that used the opportunity to promote that stuff! I'm sure that doesn't continue today, right? Wrong! Women's magazines can be a prime way to draw our ladies away from Christianity and into occult practices. And I am sure there are plenty of guys' magazines that do so too.

By 1969, Sybil Leek was "the world's most famous witch" and part of it was the book *The Diary of a Witch*. That really catapulted her into celebrity status. She was born in the U.K. in 1923. When the witch ban was lifted in the late 1950's, she came out to confess what she had been doing as a witch. But she didn't want to freak people out, so she called herself a "white" witch or a "good" witch. But that was just more of the deceptive-color words for witches that makes no difference because it is all the same evil occult witchcraft. From her confession, people were kind of intrigued by a person who would actually admit it right off the bat after the ban was lifted. And by saying she was a "good witch," Leek had associated herself with that good witch, Glinda, in *The Wizard of Oz*. Maybe partially from the popularity of that book (1900) and movie (1939), people began to flock to Sybil Leek. A massive number of tourists visited the U.K. village she lived in. In fact, her landlord refused to renew her lease, so she decided to pack her bags and head to America to promote her books. That's how she ended up in L.A. where, locally, it's all about Hollywood and the media. They and others picked up her story and promoted her.

The media helped to influence society by promoting Leek's witchcraft and they still champion witchcraft today; again, showing the Bible is right when it says there is nothing new under the sun. In 1964, a radio presenter named Annie England was one of the first to interview Leek and help build her celebrity status. Listen to this quote from Annie:

"Everyone wanted her on their show. She rubbed shoulders with all the celebrities of her time, like Gypsy Rose Lee, a famous burlesque dancer and Neil Diamond."

Besides Hollywood, the music industry also got involved to promote Leek. This is from a secular article:

"But the best legacy for Sybil is the fact that witchcraft is thriving in America and the U.K. She was a pioneer of her time and she is an inspiration to modern-day witches."

So, she played it up for the media, and that involved something she carried on her shoulder. It is a crow she trapped.

This lady actually walked around with that crow on her shoulder all the time. She named it, "Mr. Hotfoot Jackson." In fact, this is the video transcript of an interview where she has that crow on her shoulder while explaining why Halloween is good for witches, and it gives us another reason why we shouldn't be messing with that occult stuff:

Narrator: *"Halloween, well, for most of us, that's an excuse for a party; an excuse to get dressed up and have a good time—the traditional time when spirits walk. But if you believe in witchcraft, then Halloween is one of the most important times of the year. I am in the heart of the New Forest, Southern England; a forest that is absolutely steeped in witchcraft.*

In the forest there are covens of witches, each of them with thirteen witches and they all take Halloween very seriously, indeed. This is the room of one of them, Mrs. Sybil Leek. She is a housewife and mother, she's forty-one, she's an antique dealer and a self-confessed white witch. She says that she could do all the frightening things like sticking pins in effigies and bringing curses down on people's heads, but tonight, the witches and the warlocks will be meeting at such a sabbat. What will they be doing and why?"

Sybil Leek: *"We will be taking part in just one of the four great sabbats witches have always done for thousands of years. We shall be doing it because Halloween is quite important to us as a religious ceremony. It is the time of the year when the power of the sun is dwindling and, of course, we don't want this to happen. And this is also the time when we ourselves will be feeling a great need to renew the energy of our occult past within our self to carry us through for the rest of the year."*

Narrator: *"Are there very many witches about?"*

Sybil Leek: *"Well, I think you will be very, very surprised if you knew how many initiated witches there are in the whole world and, not only that, there's a very great following in witchcraft."*

As we'll see in a minute, that big increase in witches has been greatly facilitated by Leek, her family, and other witches in the world of celebrities and political people. Now, I don't know if that crow on her shoulder was just a gimmick, but I would assume her dry cleaner was not very pleased having to clean up after it. Sybil Leek's book opened the general U.S. public to the occult, while the same promotion of witchcraft was happening through her male cohort on the opposite coast, Buckland. And the media was there at both ends of our country (especially with Leek) to encourage and promote their witchcraft, just as it does today.

"Sybil left many articles and magazine columns, as well as at least sixty books on astrology, numerology, crystals, mediumship, herbalism, Tarot, gypsies, predictions, dreams, and ghost tracking (a prominent subject in

our media today). Sybil traveled the world and hobnobbed with many celebrities. She was bedridden at the time of her passing at age 65."

Leek died of cancer in 1982. As far as the celebrity issue, not only did she hobnob with celebrities like Neil Diamond and Gypsy Rose Lee, she even admitted that her mother, (who was also a witch like most of the rest of her family), also hobnobbed with all kinds of famous people over in the U.K. Apparently, it's nothing new to be sought out by the media and other people in power when a person gets involved in the occult. Celebrities and others of influence will come seek out occult people. Here is Leek admitting her family's practice of seducing celebrities and other important figures from around the world:

Interviewer: *"When we come back, I'd like Sybil to really tell us, she's a legend in her own life and she has met legendary figures. She has written a book called, 'My Life in Astrology'. We will be back in just a few seconds. (After a commercial break, the interviewer questions Leek.) Sybil, I found your book, and I've read three of them. How many books have you written?"*

Sybil Leek: *"Thirty-nine, I've had published. I've written more, but thirty-nine have made it."*

Interviewer: *"Thirty-nine books. It's an interesting title: 'My Life in Astrology.'"*

Sybil Leek: *"I'm purely dedicated to research in astrology. I love it."*

Interviewer: *"You're a prolific writer. Now, you are also a medium."*

Sybil Leek: *"Um humm."*

Interviewer: *"I have seen film of Sybil Leek taken into a setting where there were supposedly, or many believed to be, either poltergeists or restless ghosts. How did you start in this? Was this part of your whole background?"*

Sybil Leek: *"Well, I always accepted reincarnation as a fact; that the spirit is indestructible. I think to release these troubled spirits is part of my life."*

Interviewer: *"Tell me now: Your mother was involved in some area of psychic phenomena, wasn't she?"*

Sybil Leek: *"All my family. My two sons are far better mediums than I am."*

Interviewer: *"Who are some of the people that you saw, as a child, in England, or at your home, that came to see your mother?"*

Sybil Leek: *"Oh, I had the most fantastic childhood because we were born in England but spent a lot of the time in the south of France. My father was a very scholarly gentleman and people like H.G. Wells would visit us."*

Interviewer: *"H.G. Wells?"*

Sybil Leek: *"Um humm, and Lawrence of Arabia and the Sitwells (British writers.) And I really didn't know anyone when I was a child, unless they were famous."*

Interviewer: *"And it became a natural part of your everyday life?"*

Sybil Leek: *"It became a part of my everyday life."*

Apparently, on a regular, constant, and nonstop basis, during her whole childhood, celebrities, political figures, writers and other famous people were coming to her family of witches for who knows what. And, of course, she just continued that way of life when she got to America. But I'm sure that's not going on today, right? I'm sure we don't have celebrities involved in witchcraft. Well, folks, that does go on and you may not know this but some people you never imagined are involved with witchcraft and no one makes a big deal about it because it's been so downplayed in our culture here in America. In fact, do you know that the wife of Tom Brady (six-time Superbowl champion quarterback for the New England Patriots) is a witch? You might think that is crazy but here is Tom admitting it in this video transcript:

"I've learned a lot from my wife over the years. She's so about the power of intention, you know, and believing things that are really going to happen. And she always makes a little altar for me at the game because she just wills it so much. So, she put together a little altar for me that I could bring with pictures of my kids, and I have these little special stones, healing stones and protection stones, and she has me wear a necklace and take these drops she makes and I say all these mantras. And I stopped questioning her a long time ago. I did. I just shut up and listened. And at first, I was like, 'This is kind of crazy.'

And then about four years ago, we were playing the Seahawks and she said, 'You better listen to me. This is your year, but this is all the things you're gonna have to do to win it.' I did all those things and, my God, you know it worked. It was pretty good. And then in 2015, it was about early January and she said, 'You know how much I love you?' And I said, 'Yeah.' And she said, 'I just want to let you know this is not gonna be your year.' And of course, we lost. I said, 'What does 2016 look like?' She said, '2016 is gonna be your year.' So, it was early January this year, and I said, 'Babe, I'm asking, do we have a chance?' And she said, 'Yeah, but you're gonna have to do a lot of work and you're really going to have to listen to me.' So, man, I listened to her. And right after the game she said, 'See, I did a lot of work. You do your work. I do mine.' She said, 'You're lucky you married a witch. I am just a good witch.'"

Straight from his mouth he admits that she says he married a witch, a good witch. And if you could see the video, you would notice that our society no longer shrinks back from that kind of behavior. The audience he was talking to laughed all through what he said. They thought it was hilarious, which shows you just how far acceptance of witchcraft has advanced in our country. A major sports star with a lot of valuable endorsements on the line is easily able to admit that his wife is a witch, and he's involved in the rituals she recommends, helping him to win games. Of course, he's not worried because the audience just laughed their way through it. What did God say to Babylon? He let them know that, even though they may think their occult practices are keeping them safe and secure, and they may think they are so cool, destruction is going to come on them and they won't be able to predict when. Do you think God is pleased with any of those witchcraft practices? No! And its nuts that our culture just thinks it's funny. Here is more from Tom Brady in a New York Times interview in 2015:

"Brady said his family has space for multiple faiths, stating, 'I think we're into everything. I don't know what I believe. I think there's a belief system, I'm just not sure what it is."

Well, apparently, it involves witchcraft. At least that's what your wife is pushing, and you're going along with her. Now, I want to show you something else that is disturbing. And before that, just to recap what we've seen so far, we looked at the two major influencers with American Wicca, who were a male and a female with one on the east coast and one out west. And part of their technique was to hobnob with and influence the media, key figures in media, and those with power like celebrities and politicians.

Now, on top of that, and hang with me at the beginning here because this may sound crazy, I've got a Crone theory to share with you: I think we're seeing a major influx of the occult into the Democrat Party. And I want to demonstrate that to you because it goes right along with this tactic of influencing people in power as a way to eventually permeate a country with whatever movement is being pushed. The reason I want to point this out is because, like me, we all know people who are or have been a Democrat. And when you ask how they could vote for the Democrats with all the non-Biblical things they stand for these days, sometimes they will justify it with something like, "Well, I'm just trying to hold on the best I can because they have changed a lot and especially recently." We also hear some say, "It's not like it used to be back in my dad's day with Democrats like President Kennedy."

So, they will admit that the party has radically changed, but they're still trying to hang on to their affiliation with it. My point is, even longtime Democrats admit their party has changed and recently changed radically. And why is that? Well, I think it's because the Democrat Party is involved in the occult. The occult has infiltrated the party, and I want to demonstrate that to you. Here is the title of a secular article about a woman that recently ran for the 2020 Democrat nomination for President of the United States:

"Marianne Williamson Reveals the Democrats Are a Cult."

But how could running for president help her realize that the Democratic Party has turned into a cult? Well, the article poses that question because, if you know anything about her, she's a New Ager who is involved in the occult. And how could someone involved in the occult be running for president of the United States? Well, the article says the answer is obvious: She's been with the Democrats for a long time because they are also involved in the occult. In fact, we know about some of that and dealt with it in our New Age study. This infiltration by the occult started with Hillary Clinton holding seances in the White House. What party is Hillary Clinton from? It's the Democratic Party. It's well-documented that Hillary was overseeing those seances in the White House, that involved Jean Houston, who was there to supposedly try contacting the spirit of Eleanor Roosevelt. Of course, she did contact something, which might have even been posing as Roosevelt, but it was a demon. The other famous person supposedly contacted was Ghandi. So, this was going on in the White House with Hillary Clinton, who is a Democrat.

Well, guess who was there at that time? Marianne Williamson participated in Hillary Clinton's White House seances. So, mention of these occult ties is nothing new in the Democrat Party but these days the practices are coming more and more to the surface, gaining momentum in the party, and changing its makeup. Here is more from the article:

"When Hillary Clinton wasn't trying to commune with Eleanor and Ghandi, she appeared to share the obsession of Marianne Williamson and John Podesta, her campaign chair."

      We won't get into all the weird, wacky activities with Podesta and Hillary that came out with those WikiLeaks emails, uncovering their spirit cooking and other occult practices. The right words to describe those practices of theirs are "rotten" and "sickeningly evil." What party is John Podesta a part of? Again, it is the Democrat Party. And this has been going on for a long time. It is not just seeping in to influencing the party like the scenario with Tom Brady being coached with it by his wife. The occult is changing that party's belief system. And I think that is why people are saying the party is not like it was back in the days of Kennedy. The occult has taken over. Listen to these beliefs of the current Democrat Party and you tell me if they aren't leaning toward the occult:

"Democrats were twice as likely as Republicans to think that astrology is 'very scientific.' Liberals were more likely to believe in astrology than conservatives. Only 48.6% of Democrats were able to correctly answer that the earth revolves around the sun. 35% percent of Democrats believe they experienced the paranormal. 69% of Democrats believe in ghosts. That's why Marianne Williamson is up there on the debate stage."

      Marianne fits right in because that is their party now. They have not only changed, but it's been toward an alignment with occult witchcraft beliefs. And that is why you can have a hardcore occultist actually be running for the President of the United States under the banner of the Democrat Party.

"At the 2020 debates, the Democrats are letting their leftist freak flag fly. They are coming out of the closet. Why shouldn't they come out of the closet about their New Age beliefs? 70% of Republicans believe in the God of the bible. Only 45% of Democrats do. 47% of the Democrats say that religion isn't really important in their lives. What do they believe in? Spirituality. Auras. Energy forces. Karma. Battling dark psychic forces. Being attuned to the universe."

That is an occult mindset! Here is more from the article:

"After Trump's election, tens of thousands of women like Marianne Williamson swarmed the streets wearing pink hats to shriek at the sky and repel the dark psychic forces. They believe in everything, ghosts, auras, energy forces, UFOs, and even angels, but not God."

In fact, they're not just being overtaken with the occult mindsets, beliefs, people, and influences, but this is also why their party has become, and I'll use this word, <u>godless</u>. They stand against everything that we believe, not just as conservatives, but also as Christians. And I think it is because they've been overtaken. You may remember 2012 at the Democratic National Convention when they had taken God and Jerusalem out of their platform. Do you remember that? Why, of all things, would you take out God? And you can see the video on the internet where convention leadership tried to add God back in but the people on the convention floor were going nuts, booing and hissing. They were angry at putting God back in the Democrat platform, along with acknowledging Israel's Jerusalem. Why would you do that? How did you get so godless?

That was back in 2012 and it is still building today; not only with the occult influences and beliefs, but toward the Democrat party becoming flat-out godless. In fact, this transcript is of a recent incident where the video shows them wearing Covid masks. Here are Democrats leading the Pledge of Allegiance in our U.S. House of Representatives and this commentator picks up what they conveniently left out:

Commentator: *"Here's the Democrats leading the Pledge of Allegiance in Congress."*

House Clerk: *"The Chair will lead the House in the Pledge of Allegiance."*

Democrat House Chairperson: *"I pledge allegiance to the flag of the United States of America and to the republic for which it stands, one nation...indivisible, with liberty and justice for all."*

Commentator: *"Hmmm...something was missing there. Oh, you removed God. They removed God from the Pledge of Allegiance."*

Why would you do that? I mean, think about it: Why would a political party specifically be so anti-God, including anything to do with Christianity and the Bible? I think it's because they've been infiltrated with the occult mindset, belief system, and frankly, people who are involved in the occult in that party. I really think that's why.

Now, let me give you a couple other examples. We dealt with this next one in our study, *Abortion: The Mass Murder of Children.*

Every one of over twenty Democrats running for president in 2020 were pro-abortion and the bulk of them even want to murder children outside the womb after they are born alive. They say we should not give help to a live baby struggling to live. Those advocating that, include Kamala Harris who is running right now on the Democrat ticket for Vice President of the United States. How did they become a "murder the children" party? That is what they have become. Being a Democrat means you are pro-abortion, which is the murder of babies. How did that happen? Well, to use Sybil Leek's word, I think it is because of who they have been "hobnobbing" with for a long time now. It has been steadily rising to the surface. In fact, they are also bringing the killing to the other end of the spectrum, wanting to murder adults, as well.

Under their socialistic universal healthcare, anyone who costs the system too much has a duty to die. And if you do not want to accommodate them, they'll just have a death panel make you die. That headline reads, "Democrats have become the party of abortion and euthanasia." So, from both ends of the spectrum, they want to kill babies and adults. Is that just their "alternate ideal?" Well, I do not want to stretch this too far, but what's something similar that happens with witchcraft and other occult practices? People who go down that road far enough, end up ritually sacrificing, (murdering), children and adults.

On top of all that, when we look at the Democrat Party's agenda, everything they now stand for is the complete polar opposite of the Biblical and even constitutional values of our country.

The leader of the Democrats right now, Joe Biden, wants to kill babies. Trump supports letting the babies live. The Democrats want riots and violence, defunding of our police and gun control. We want law and order, support for the police and gun rights. They want illegal immigration, higher taxes, and a weak military. We want legal immigration, tax breaks, and a strong military. They want over-regulation while we want support for job-creating small businesses. They want to let anyone vote. We want voter I.D. They want a welfare state, poverty, big government and suppression of free speech. We want a working class, prosperity, small government, and free speech. They want liberalism and we want conservatives. They want communism while we want to follow the constitution. They want socialism. We want capitalism. They want defiance. We want patriotism. Every single thing, tit for tat, it's the exact polar opposite.

Do you remember when the two party's beliefs used to blend a bit? Now, I am not giving the Republicans a free pass! This is not about picking a party that is Biblically pure. I'm just saying something has radically happened to the Democrat Party. This research has opened my eyes, even more than they had been, to the realization that the occult has taken over the Democrat Party. And I am going to give you even more proof. With this current 2020 presidential election, people are asking this question:

"Why do the witches only pray against and cast curses or hexes at the conservative president and not the Democrat?"

First, in the United States of America, the thought that witches would be openly out in mass, gathering together and working through the community is bizarre enough. But, on top of that, they are continually putting out demonic prayers against our conservative president. Why do they never pray against a Democrat? Why is it only the other side? I think it is because that's a practice by Democrats, who would not want to pray and hex against themselves. I want to give a video transcript about that, and it is something that is still going on today. And it didn't just happen one time against President Trump. These witches meet every month to try working their hexes and curses on him. In fact, this witch takes credit for their efforts at supposedly helping get all those fake news stories out there about Trump:

Narrator: *"Melissa Madera is a self-proclaimed witch and she's been casting spells for New Yorkers for years. But since the election of President Donald Trump, she says she's been using her magic a little differently."*

Melissa Madera: *"I am very, very pleased with the results we've been getting."*

Narrator: *"She hasn't shared how the witches cast the hex, but she believes the spells are helping to expose injustice in the Trump Administration."*

Melissa Madera: *"Every time we've done it. We've seen new information come out about whether he's been engaged in tax fraud or Russian collusion or fraud with the election and stuff like that. Every time we do it, more and more comes to the public eye."*

So according to that witch, where is some of the impetus coming from for all this baloney with the constant negative media coverage that will not stop and gets crazier as time goes by? I'll say that also helps explain some of why the period leading up to and since that 2016 election, and especially this whole year leading up to this 2020 election, has been such a battle. In fact, we use this phrase, and I think it is exactly what we face with all that: It's a "spiritual battle." This isn't normal politics anymore, and it's because there is something spiritual going on in the Democrat Party. I believe it's been taken over by the occult. In fact, that party is coming out with a new logo that is very interesting, though a lot of people would vehemently say it's just a coincidence. Now, I'm not going to say, "Thus saith the Lord," but a lot of people are starting to wonder about their logo:

That's a bit weird. Of all the possibilities, why choose that logo? Now, people might accuse me of making too much of this, but when we look at this whole background of what's happening with the current Democrat Party, including their behavior, what they are involved in, and their present beliefs, could the logo be a message they are sending to their supporters? I don't know but it makes you wonder. I can't necessarily prove it, and I don't think they'll ever admit it, but, man, all that seems to support my conclusion not being far off base. In fact, here is another interesting article for those who think I'm crazy to believe that the Democrat Party has been taken over by the occult mindset:

Here's the headline takeaway from this survey. The finding is that 98% of Americans who support socialism over capitalism reject the Biblical worldview. That tells you it is a godless agenda being promoted by the Democrat Party.

And it's not just that they are involved with and being influenced by the occult, promoting occult ideals, have a background involving the occult and occult practices, and that witches are only working with their party. On top of all that, the latest socialism agenda we are dealing with here from the Democrat Party is also a godless path. What has the Democrat Party become? Is it the party of socialism? In fact, on tape, Joe Biden said him being elected would make him the most socialist president in the history of the United States. That is why George Barna from the Cultural Research Center said this:

"The 2020 election is not about personalities, parties, or even politics. It's an election to determine the dominant worldview in America."

President Trump has accused Joe Biden of being a Trojan Horse for socialism. And again, the mindset of socialism is from the occult. George Barna's survey also showed this:

"When you look at the Democrats, for instance, I would say they're leading the curve in moving toward the perspective that 'Life is about me.'"

Now, you've heard me say this multiple times and after this witchcraft study we're going to get to this in massive detail in our next study on satanism: What is the number one law of satanism? It is, "Do what you will, shall be the whole of the law." Do you know where that comes from? It was from Aleister Crowley. And the Democrat Party is moving us towards a perspective that says, "It's all about me, myself, and I," which is an unholy trinity and another aspect of the occult.

"Barna sees the "remnant" of those who hold a biblical worldview as the linchpin to turning the American culture around."

In other words, if we Christians with a biblical worldview don't speak up, if we don't get engaged in our culture, then this vision for America from the Democrat Party is what will come to our entire country. And it is not just what President Trump has been warning about, as far as socialism knocking at America's door. It is also an occult mindset, which means a godless mindset would take over our country. It feels like a spiritual battle because it is one!

Let me give you one or two more quick examples to prove this point that everything that the Democrat Party is now promoting is coming straight out of witchcraft. Here is one that parallels the big issue going on right now with the riots:

It's racial division, and guess who is promoting that? It is witchcraft. And again, I don't want you to think I'm just whipping this out of thin air as a convenient theory. This is what secular folks are saying, including a mention of "wokeness," which is an often-heard term these days:

"Fighting Racism in Academia with Witchcraft: Self-declared witches are well known by now for their wokeness and their hexing of enemies, including Brett Kavanaugh and the Confederacy."

Of course, the latter one is talking about their attempt to erase history by pulling down statues. And witches are the ones promoting this through the Democrat Party. Even in our colleges and universities, witches are playing politics with the practices:

"Witchcraft in colleges is not unknown, and now self-declared witches are invoking satan and hexing the leader of the young conservatives."

Again, it's the conservatives that occultists are working against. Here an interesting quote:

"Magical thinking is a hallmark of leftist thought."

Do you get it? It's not just that the Democrat Party has gone left, or even that they've gone so far as socialism, but where is this whole attitude coming from? It is the occult. And that quote was from a self-declared witch that was at least being honest about it. So, even the witches admit that is where this is coming from, and it's now determining the direction of the Democrat Party.

I want to give you one more related troubling development with the Democrat Party, and it involves their latest agenda. It is not just the racism, the statues, socialism, burning down our cities, and blah blah blah. What is the other big push happening right now? It is their Black Lives Matter movement (BLM). Guess who is running that movement? It is Witches.

BLM leaders practice witchcraft and summon dead spirits. One guy says he's calling on Christians right now, who have allied themselves with the Black Lives Matter movement, to "rethink your decision." Now, if you think that BLM leaders contacting demons is a crazy statement to make, here they are themselves, admitting they're involved in witchcraft to summon the spirits of their dead ancestors and that's what is supposedly driving their movement:

Narrator: *"Do witches run Black Lives Matter?"*

Melina Abdullah (co-founder of BLM Los Angeles): *"And maybe I'm sharing too much, but we've become very intimate with the spirits that we call on regularly. Right. Like, each of them seems to have a different presence and personality. You know, I laugh a lot with Wakisha, you know. And I didn't meet her in her body. Right. I met her through this work."*

Patrisse Cullors (co-founder of BLM and trained Marxist organizer): *"It's a very important practice. Hashtags, for us, are way more than a hashtag. It is literally almost resurrecting a spirit, so they can work through us to get the work that we need to get done. I started to feel personally connected and responsible and accountable to them; both from a deeply political place, but also from a deeply spiritual place. In my tradition, you offer things that your loved one who passed away would want, you know, whether it is like honey or tobacco, things like that. And it is so important, not just for us to be in direct relationship to our people* *who've passed, but also for them to know that we've remembered them. I believe so many of them work through us."*

Bishop Larry Gaiters, host & moderator of Global Spiritual Revolution Radio: *"Black Lives Matter is run by three witches who are lesbian witches: Alicia Garza, Patrisse Cullors, and Opal Tometi; she's of Nigerian descent. All three are part of the Black Boule Secret Society. And there are witches and warlocks in the entire spiritual dogma or doctrine of Black Lives Matter. It is from the West African religion called Odu Ifa. But over three thousand different religions in Africa are rooted in witchcraft and divination."*

And BLM has merged with the Democrat party. So, when we take a look at all these things the Democrat party has partnered up with, it's just a natural slide, because they've been indoctrinated into the occult.

Now, knowing all that about the Democrat Party, one guy asks how we can reconcile what we just saw with what the Word of God says. As Christians, we have to evaluate everything through the Word of God. Let me translate that, and I'll just be blunt: Knowing all we just looked at, and I don't care who you are, if you claim to be a Christian and you continue to vote for the Democrat party, you're going to stand accountable to God. They have been infiltrated by the occult, so they are no longer the Democrat Party of old. And if you are putting a vote with them, you are helping the occult take over the United States of America. Do you think God is going to bless that? Did he bless Babylon when they went down that road? No! In fact, he destroyed what they were doing and scattered them. So, you might want to think twice if that is you. We still hear Christians today saying, "I don't care. I'm going to vote Democrat anyway." Wow!

In the next chapter we are going to look at another guy who advanced Wicca even further. His name is Alex Sanders.

Sanders founded a strain of Wicca called Alexandrian Wicca and was catapulted to fame as a witch because he wrote an autobiography.

Again, a book was the way to gather a following. But guess what else he did that was innovative for the time and a big breakthrough for his notoriety? He got into film. So, now witchcraft started doing movies and his was called, *The Legend of the Witches*. He began to promote that a bit before Hollywood disconnected from their longtime-Christian influence that determined who did the scripts, what movies were made, and what ratings were given to them. Do you remember when Hollywood, (believe it or not), had to submit all their scripts to a religious authority? That was why shows used to have rules against people kissing for more than four seconds, as well as husband-and-wife bedroom scenes always showing two beds. Remember that? I don't know why but Hollywood stopped that. Personally, I think it was a spiritual thing. But it added movies to the books and magazine that were already promoting witchcraft and other occult practices. And as we will see in the next chapter, that movie fame for Alex Sanders led to him being called the "King of the Witches."

Chapter Fourteen

The History of Wicca
Part 3

So far, we have seen that the definition of Wicca is "witchcraft" and it's all over the world. The only protection from it is for Christians alone, through the power of Jesus Christ. Through our look at the history, we found out that Wicca witchcraft is nothing new, even though they pitch it as nature lovers appreciating the outdoors. Instead, it is the same old rebellious occult behavior that's been going on ever since the Tower of Babel. From Wicca witchcraft's origins, we saw it spread across the world to Egypt, Greece, Rome, Asia, India and the nearby island countries, Africa, Latin America, and Europe.

Europe is where the Wicca version of witchcraft was birthed, after which it came here to the Americas. But all they did was change the name of old-fashioned European witchcraft. How did that name change cause so many to fall for it, even here in the U.S.? Well, it was through the efforts of a couple of people in Europe, starting with the grandmother of Wicca, Margaret Murray, and then the grandfather of Wicca, Gerald Gardner. The latter founded Gardnerian Wicca.

In the last chapter we saw the mother of Wicca, Doreen Valiente, was promoted by Europe's media, becoming popular with the British people at a time after England's ban against witchcraft was lifted in 1951. Valiente wrote a lot of books and even exhibited her witchcraft tools. Her biggest effort that resulted in a huge increase for European Wicca, was her revamping of Gardner's *Book of Shadows*, which is a pivotal witchcraft manual that she made more palatable for public consumption. In fact, she was such a big influence that it has been said Wicca may never have really gotten off the ground without her contribution.

From those people Wicca spread to America through Raymond Buckland on the East Coast (Long Island), the father of American Wicca, who worked with his wife to Americanize Wicca into what he called Seax-Wicca. Buckland wrote many books, including his own witchcraft dogma book like Gardner's *Book of Shadows*. His is known as the big blue book or the *Complete Book of Witchcraft*.

The other who brought European Wicca witchcraft to America was a lady that showed up on the West Coast (Los Angeles). Her name was Sybil Leek, and she came from a family of witches in Europe. Leek was made into a celebrity by the American media and influenced a lot of other popular and powerful people, just as her family had back in Europe. She really helped popularize Wicca, especially through the many books she wrote. *Diary of a Witch* was the breakout book for this lady, who traveled around with a live crow (Mr. Hotfoot Jackson) on her shoulder. Just as Leek became a celebrity who then influenced other celebs toward witchcraft, we see the same today with examples like Tom Brady, the many-time Super Bowl champion, being influenced into witchcraft rituals through his wife, who admits to being a witch.

Then we asked the question of whether the Democrat Party here in the U.S. has been taken over by the occult. Over recent years people have joked that it should be called the "Demoncrat" Party. Based on what we saw in the last chapter with the massive occult infiltration of that party, that label is probably more accurate than people realize. The Democrat Party is being taken over by the occult, and the evidence includes their latest movements with the riots and BLM (Black Lives Matter). In fact, we saw all of that is being run by witches. It sounds crazy but we saw the evidence.

Now, we want to take a look at where Wicca went from that point, on up to our modern day. The next big step was through Alex Sanders.

Sanders came up with what is called Alexandrian Wicca. Again, we're going to see that there are a lot of Wicca branches. You could also call those branches "denominations", but I use the term lightly because it's really our Christian term. As a new Christian we would set out to find a Church and that normally involves deciding on a denomination. There are so many. Well, if we use that term very loosely for Wicca, that is really what's going on with those seeking a method and group in witchcraft. Even with the branch of witchcraft called, Wicca, there is not just one clear way of practicing. If someone wants to make the unfortunate choice to become a witch and follow Wicca, the next decision is which "denomination," or branch. Do you follow the path of a traditional witch, the Gardnerian route, an eclectic witch, or something like the guy we are going to look at here with his Alexandrian Witchcraft or Alexandrian Wicca?

Alex Sanders was the self-proclaimed "king of the witches." So, now we've seen Wicca's grandmother (Murray), grandfather (Gardner), mother (Valiente), father (Buckland), celebrity (Leek), and king (Sanders). But before we get further into what Sanders did, let me ask you a question: Do you think I'm having any trouble finding enough Bible verses for each chapter that tell us to stay away from witchcraft and other occult practices? No! We are not even getting close to exhausting them yet. That is why we're studying this. The warning against this evil are all over the Bible and, as Christians, we are supposed to study all of it; not just some.

Our warning for this chapter is in **2 Chronicles 33**. We're going to take a look at the unfortunate history about a certain king of Judah. As you probably know, **1 and 2 Kings**, as well as **1 and 2 Chronicles**, record the true account of different kings and kingdoms. There was the Northern

Kingdom that split off from the Southern Kingdom with ten tribes in the north and two tribes down south. Some were good kings, but a lot were bad, including most of the northern kings. The southern kings had more honorable ones, but they too went downhill and eventually both of them went into captivity.

So, the record of the rulers is in those Bible books, and we are going to read about a real king back in that day. Imagine if this was you and your life was talked about for the whole world to hear, century, after century, after century. And his true-life story is not virtuous. But notice why God has strong words for him. You know, we always hope people would write a favorable report or glowing eulogy about how we were some sort of wise and benevolent credit to humanity. That does not happen for this guy! The report comes from God about what evil and detestable practices he was involved with right out the gate after becoming king. From there, it continues straight downhill. Here is **2 Chronicles 33:1-6:**

"Manasseh was twelve years old when he became king, and he reigned in Jerusalem fifty-five years. He did evil in the eyes of the Lord, following the detestable practices…"

So, what Manasseh was doing was detestably evil in the eyes of the Lord. Wow, what was he getting involved with that caused God to use such strong words?

"He did evil in the eyes of the Lord, following the detestable practices of the nations the Lord had driven out before the Israelites. He rebuilt the high places his father, Hezekiah had demolished."

Of course, Hezekiah was a good king, but something didn't transfer to Manasseh in that next generation. The high places God talks about are where they went and worshiped the false gods. Hezekiah did the right thing in tearing those down to get rid of them but then his own son came along and rebuilt it all. Oops! There is mistake number one.

"He rebuilt the high places his father, Hezekiah had demolished; he also erected altars to the Baals and made Asherah poles."

Scripture tells us that, behind every idol is a demon. So, this involves demonic practices, including false worship and idols. It gets even worse:

"He bowed down to all the starry hosts and worshiped them."

How about those Christians, who are into astrology? Does it sound like God's okay with that? No! As we have seen, astrology is occult practice. And listen to what Manasseh not only did outside, but then had the nerve to bring into this place:

"He built altars in the temple of the Lord."

That is kind of like what we saw with so-called, "Christian witches." What are they doing right now, today? It is the same attempt at merging occult practices with Christianity. But you cannot do that! It is profane!

"In both courts of the temple of the Lord, he built altars to all the starry hosts. He sacrificed his sons in the fire in the Valley of Ben Hinnom, Gehenna."

And then he killed his own sons in these occult practices. Does that go on today? Yes, we saw that and it's unfortunate, but it still happens. Gehenna was the section of Jerusalem that was a dumping ground for all manner of trash, so it continually burned. In the New Testament, Jesus uses that place as an example when he is asked what hell is like. He tells them it's like Gehenna, where "'the worms that eat them do not die, and the fire is not quenched."

"He practiced sorcery, divination, and witchcraft, sought omens, and he consulted mediums and psychics. He did much evil in the eyes of the Lord, provoking him to anger."

If you are going to be in a position of power, would you say that's not the epitaph or eulogy you'd be wanting, especially since it's coming from God? I think it is pretty obvious. Here's the thing: In His character, God is the same yesterday, today, and forever. So, if He considered it detestably evil then, no matter what spin man wants to put on it through the media or whatever, how does God feel today about people involved in sorcery, divination, consulting mediums, spiritists, and witchcraft (Wicca)? It is still detestable to Him! It is an evil thing in His eyes today, just as it was back then.

Now, let's again take a look at why people, even here in America, are still increasingly getting involved in this detestable practice called, witchcraft that has been relabeled as, Wicca. Well, again, this guy's legacy will include the major advancement of what God considers detestable evil:

As mentioned, Alex Sanders came up with the Alexandrian tradition and I want to give you this quick video transcript to break down some of the many, many branches of Wicca. Sanders and his wife started their own coven (group of witches) and then proceeded to put their own spin on witchcraft with his Alexandrian Wicca.

"Traditional Witch: A traditional witch practices from a historical perspective in following the old craft that came before the modern adaptation of Wicca. Many traditional witches study their ancestry and the folklore attached to it. They want to honor the old ways of worshiping and most often choose a pantheon that aligns with their cultural backgrounds."

"Gardnerian Witch: The father of Wicca, Gerald Gardner, developed this practice in Britain during the mid-20th century. From his original coven, Bricket Wood, he passed on his interpretation of witchcraft. As an initiation tradition, only another Gardnerian coven can bring in a new practitioner. This is done in order to trace the lineage of practitioners back to the very first coven. In this practice, covens have thirteen members and are led by a high priestess and priest. The Gardnerians adhere to the story of the horned God dying and being reborn each year as the mother

goddess remains eternally alive. Their rituals are highly elaborate, and many of the orthodox covens still practice ritual nudity. Gardnerian covens are quite secretive, so it can be a bit difficult to figure out as a new practitioner."

"Alexandrian Witch: Alex and Maxine Sanders created the Alexandrian tradition as an offshoot of Gardner's practice. While the two practices are similar in many ways, they are on very different paths. Alexandrian witches are initiated and organized around a high priestess. The Alexandrian tradition focuses on the ancient archetypes of the oak and holly kings who battle and win, then battle and lose to bring out the light and dark, warmth and cold. While not as secretive as their Gardnerian counterparts, Alexandrian witches still place emphasis on tradition and following protocol."

So, again, these branches or denominations of Wicca are just spin-offs from the same old witchcraft practices. There are a lot of similarities between them and a few unique aspects. Different groups focus more than others on particular rituals and hierarchical structures versus more of a freewheeling organization. Some of the Gardnerian witches have said that Sanders created his Alexandrian Wicca when he refused initiation into a Gardnerian coven. From there he got a copy of Gardner's *Book of Shadows* and basically went off to start his own version. Here is more about Sanders:

"A gifted psychic with a flamboyant style, he was for years the most public witch in Britain, gaining headlines for his reputed sensational acts of Magic. Sanders was born in Manchester, the oldest of six children. His father was a music hall entertainer and suffered from alcoholism. By Sanders' own account, he was seven when he discovered his grandmother, Mary Bibby, standing naked in the kitchen in the middle of a circle drawn on the floor."

Imagine being a seven-year-old kid and walking into the kitchen to find your grandmother is naked, most likely sitting on a pentagram in a witch circle and doing some ritual stuff. Now, that is bad enough, but listen to this explanation that she came up with when her young grandson caught her being strange and naked in the middle of the floor:

"She revealed herself as a hereditary Witch and initiated him on the spot. She ordered him to enter the circle, take off his clothes and bend down with his head between his thighs. She took a knife and nicked his male body part, saying, 'You are one of us now.'"

His own grandmother did that to him! Wow.

"According to Sanders, Mary Bibby gave him her 'Book of Shadows', which he copied, and taught him the rites and magic of witches. He discovered his own natural psychic gifts for clairvoyance and healing by touch."

So, he felt he had special powers to heal people. I'll give you some examples in a little bit, but I want to answer this question: Can witches, satanists, sorcerers, and other people involved in the occult, actually do healings? Well, let's take a look at that. To use a good analogy, God does miracles, and satan has power, but only so far as performing some magic. Satan's power is not like God's, but what he does have he uses to deceive people. Let's take a more detailed look at that:

"You will be hard pressed to find someone who has never heard of some kind of religious miracle. Many Catholics are convinced of the validity of various sightings of the Virgin Mary around the world, stigmata (people's palms appearing to have blood on them like they have been pierced as Jesus was,) weeping or bleeding statues, and even 'incorruptible bodies' (corpses that undergo little, no, or delayed decomposition.)"

In our *Final Countdown* study, we mentioned a story about how people were flocking to one of those supposedly bleeding statues. But then a local guy said he guessed it was probably bird droppings because they like to eat from a large nearby tomato patch. That was so funny. Besides Catholicism, which is not Biblical Christianity, other religions have seen the same sorts of experiences.

"There are reported miracles in other religions as well. Hinduism, Buddhism, and Islam all claim to have documented miracles."

And it is the same in witchcraft. Witches recruit by claiming to have powers and even being able to heal. But is that really going on? We dealt with this in our Hinduism studies with a guy that could make "holy ash" appear on his hands, which just looked to me like dirty hands. He also did sleight of hand to appear as though he made little trinkets appear. That is the kind of thing that goes on. We also know that, over time, the body will often heal itself from many issues. Here is more on demonic and satanic miracles:

*"Satan has the power to perform miracles. While his power is limited, he can and does perform miracles in order to deceive. **John 8:44** says that satan is a liar and the father of lies. Satan can make himself appear as an angel of light, **2 Corinthians 11:14**. He does this to draw people away from God."*

When Catholics and others go to see an apparition of Mary, does that draw them closer to God? No, it endears them to Mary, which is an experience outside the Scripture; instead of one with God. Someone might find a weeping or bleeding statue and then start throwing money at its feet or praying to it, but is that drawing them to God? No. In Hinduism and Buddhism you have these guru guys that can supposedly perform healings and make candy appear. But is that drawing them closer to God? No. In our earlier look at Egyptian witchcraft, we saw this:

*"When Moses and Aaron confronted Pharaoh, they performed a miraculous sign to confirm their message from God (**Exodus 7:8–10**). The magi of Egypt were able to perform the same miracle "by their secret arts" (verse 11). God's miracle was shown to be greater (verse 12), but the fact is that the magi were able to perform a satanic miracle in the king's court."*

God's snake ate the snakes from Pharaoh's witches, thereby sending the message that those occultists have no power compared to God.

And after that miracle, Pharaoh's witches could not replicate any of the other miracles God performed with the judgments in Egypt. So, what's the point? Again, yes, they did have power to do some things that could deceive people just as witches contacting demons might also be able to pull off today. In fact, I believe this is why **Revelation 9** tell us that people in the Seven Year Tribulation will not stop worshiping demons and practicing their pharmakia (drugs), sorcery, witchcraft, and other occult behavior. It is not surprising that Witchcraft is on the rise today because that's going to be part of the Seven Year Tribulation with the Antichrist tapping into that occult community. Those looking for signs and wonders, which is even big with the charismatic movement inside the Church, are going to be duped.

*"During the tribulation, the Antichrist 'will use all sorts of displays of power through signs and wonders that serve the lie' (2 **Thessalonians 2:9**). These miracles are explicitly said to be empowered by satan. Jesus warned that the end times will be characterized by the treachery of counterfeit prophets who 'will appear and perform great signs and wonders to deceive' (**Matthew 24:24**)."*

The Bible tells us how to handle people that point to something and say, "Wow, that's an incredible miracle." We are to quote **1 John 4:1**, which says,

"Dear friends, do not believe every spirit, but test the spirits to see whether they are from God, because many false prophets have gone out into the world."

And if we have any doubt, we are to go back to the Scripture to see whether it lines up with the Bible and points people toward God and Jesus. And that cannot be only somewhat; it must be 100%. I want to bring that up because this little bit of power, including supposed healings through witchcraft techniques, is how people have been seduced into the occult. That evidence of some supernatural power does not mean it's from God. Here is some of what Sanders said he could do:

"Sanders reportedly got rid of warts by 'wishing them on someone else, someone who's already ugly, with boil marks I can fill up with the warts.' He claimed to cure a man of heroin addiction, and cure cystitis in a woman by laying his hands on her head and willing her affliction away. He also said he cured a young woman of stomach cancer by sitting with her in the hospital for three days and nights, holding her feet and pouring healing energy into her. He effected other cures by pointing at the troubled spots on the body and concentrating. Pointing, he said, never failed."

This next one from him tells you where all this is coming from and he boasts here about supposedly doing evil:

"He claimed he gave magical abortions by pointing at the womb and commanding the pregnancy to end."

That tells you where this is coming from. Satan is not just a liar. As **John 8:44** tells us, the devil is also a murderer and has been one from the beginning. Here's another of Sanders supposed famous abilities:

"One of Sanders' more famous alleged cures concerned his daughter, Janice, who was born in dry labor with her left foot twisted backwards. Doctors said nothing could be done until the child was in her teens. Sanders received an 'impression' from a familiar-spirit demon posing as Michael to take olive oil, warm it, and anoint Janice's foot. Sanders did so, then simply twisted Janice's foot straight. The foot remained corrected; Janice walked normally, except for a slight limp in cold, damp weather."

Well, that's not really getting healed then, is it? When God does miracles, the outcome is perfect. Give me a break! And that was supposed be one of his most famous ones, whatever. Here is some of Sanders' history starting at the age of twenty-one:

"He worked as an analytical chemist at a laboratory in Manchester, where he met and married a 19-year-old coworker, Doreen, when he was

21. They had two children, Paul and Janice, but the marriage rapidly disintegrated. Doreen took the children and left Sanders when he was 26. "Sanders then entered a long period of drifting from one low-level job to another, drinking and indulging in sexual flings with both men and women, according to his account of his life."

Then he decided to really ramp up his witchcraft:

"He decided to follow the left-hand path and use magic to bring him wealth and power. "

Let's talk about that a bit, and we'll probably get into it more in our study of satanism.

"In Western esotericism the Left-Hand Path and the Right-Hand Path are the dichotomy between two opposing approaches to magic (witchcraft.)"

That's why that Baphomet has one of its hands going in different directions; one is on the so-called Left-Hand path, and the other is on the Right-Hand Path. Here is how they break that down:

"In some definitions, the Left-Hand Path is equated with malicious black magic or black shamanism, while the Right-Hand Path is equated with benevolent white magic."

Excuse me? It's all coming from the same beast and it's all bad! So, Sanders went to so-called black magic, the Left-Hand Path, to get power. And on top of what he or she is already doing, a person that goes the Left-Hand Path is rejecting the status quo of everything, including embracing all that goes against the norm of morally honorable and correct behavior. Left-Hand Path's do the exact opposite of anything virtuous and they purposely do so. They believe that performing taboo behaviors, the opposite of what is right, like killing when God says not to kill and committing adultery against God's decree, will give them more power. That's a Left-Hand Path person.

"They often question religious or moral dogma, instead adhering to forms of personal anarchism. They often embrace sexuality and incorporate it into magical ritual."

That Left-Hand Path was originated in the West by this lady, who we saw in our study, *New Age & The Last Days Deception:*

From a family with wealth, after traveling around the world, Madame Blavatsky founded the Theosophical Society. She went to Asia, which we already saw had a lot of witchcraft. Likewise, she traveled to India and Tibet where they too had much witchcraft and other occult practices. This talks about where she got the information and how she Americanized it:

"The Western use of the terms Left-Hand Path and Right Hand-Path originated with Madame Blavatsky, a 19th-century occultist who founded the Theosophical Society. She had traveled across parts of southern Asia and claimed to have met with many mystics and magical practitioners in India and Tibet. She developed the term Left-Hand Path as a translation of the term Vamachara, an Indian Tantric practice that emphasized the breaking of Hindu societal taboos."

So, Left-Hand Paths do the opposite of societal norms and, like Valiente did with Gardner's *Book of Shadows*, Blavatsky cleaned up the information for public consumption. Then, like Buckland Americanizing Wicca witchcraft, Blavatsky revamped and introduced those South-Asian occult practices to America.

"Tantric practice emphasized the breaking of Hindu societal taboos by having sexual intercourse in ritual, drinking alcohol, eating meat and assembling in graveyards, as a part of the spiritual practice. The term Vamachara literally meant "the left-hand way" in Sanskrit, and it was from this that Blavatsky first coined the term."

Blavatsky bringing that witchcraft to America, was one of the many reasons it spread quickly across the country and her method was one of the many aspects of witchcraft that Alex Sanders got involved with. His early influences were through coaching from his grandmother, the *Book of Shadows* and its Gardnerian Wicca, and Blavatsky's Left-Hand Path. And he was still not done, as we will see. But all of his efforts developed into a unique branch of Wicca that is still going on today: Alexandrian Wicca.

Sanders also admitted that he worshiped the devil. But wait. Stop right there. You will often hear those involved in Wicca claim they do not worship satan. There is a misnomer that the horned god has to be satan and I'll give them that. We will eventually see who this horned god is, but that said, make no mistake that the Wicca practice of witchcraft, any other occult practice, and any practice that falls outside and contradicts the Bible, is inspired by satan. That is the first point. Second, there are people involved in witchcraft and Wicca witchcraft, who outright admit to worshiping satan. And I am going to show you that in a minute, because Wicca will often claim they have nothing to do with satan and only worship Mother Earth (the goddess of nature). But that is not what they are worshiping in the spiritual world that includes demons and satan. Before I get into that proof, I want to mention something else that Sanders was into. Again, this guy was picking up all kinds of evil practices for his own religion. Another area he explored was the *Book of the Sacred Magic of Abramelin The Mage*.

"The Book of Abramelin tells the story of an Egyptian (they were steeped in occult witchcraft) mage named Abraham, or Abra-Melin, who taught a system of magic to a Jewish guy in Germany, presumed to have lived from c.1362—c.1458. The system of magic from this book regained popularity in the 19th and 20th centuries."

So, Alex Sanders also got involved in this aspect. The book is written more like a novel or autobiography and describes this guy, Abraham, going from Germany to Egypt, where he learned occult techniques and brought them back home. Here is a description of the book and remember that their guardian angel is really just another demon:

"The text describes an elaborate ritual whose purpose is to obtain the 'knowledge and conversation' of the magician's 'guardian angel.' After the preparatory phase has been successfully completed, the magician's Holy Guardian Angel will appear and reveal magical secrets."

Of course, an angel from God is not going to do that, so it tells you what you're dealing with, a demon. But that's what's in this book.

"Once this is accomplished, the magician must evoke the 12 Kings and Dukes of Hell (Lucifer, Satan, Leviathan, Belial, etc.) and bind them."

Have fun with that! You're the one that's now bound to this satanic stuff. So, Sanders got into that and it is going to get even worse as we trace more of his history:

"He apparently attracted people who supported him financially. He formed his first coven, began getting media attention, attracted more followers and by 1965, claimed to have 1,623 initiates in 100 covens who then "persuaded" him to be elected king of the Witches."

The media helped him get to those numbers and ran with him being labeled king of all witches. And, boy, did his ego get a huge welcome boost from that!

"He claimed to create a flesh-and-blood 'spiritual baby.'"

What is that? Well, this idea takes us back to our study, *Scientology and the Occult Teachings of L. Ron Hubbard*. We got into the occult practice of "sex magic" that Hubbard and Jack Parsons were practicing. But let's get back to Sanders:

"He claimed to create a flesh-and-blood 'spiritual baby' in a rite of ritual masturbation, with the help of a male assistant."

So, that was what those guys were doing.

What is sex magic, which is sometimes spelled, "magick?" It's basically using sexual arousal in your demonic ritual practices because they believe that state will facilitate more power. So, Sanders also got into that. And where did he take it to from there? To the same guy we keep seeing pop onto the scene spreading evil: Aleister Crowley. Again, according to the secular media and embraced by Crowley himself, he is called the evilest man that ever lived.

Only God knows who the evilest man has been, but Crowley is the one who popularized sex magic in the Western world. Crowley is credited with taking sex magic and turning it into something that can achieve results through a set formula. For those involved, certain sexual acts, combined with specific rituals, will supposedly produce power to do particular things. I'm not going to give you the list of the different so-called "sexual acts" because they're abominations. But we will probably get into some of this perverse stuff in more detail with satanism. Even the modern-day *Satanic Bible*, written by Anton LeVey, has these same sexual rituals to perform for people to start connecting with Satanism, as a way to gain power. But that mindset of sex magic comes from Crowley and, as I said, it was also something Scientology's L. Ron Hubbard was into:

Hubbard wasn't just involved in sex magic. He also worked with a lady named Marjorie Cameron and Jack Parsons, who was the inventor of rockets and founder of JPL Laboratories. Those three were doing a ritual called "Babylon Working," where, through sex magic involving whatever they were doing with Marjorie Cameron and rituals, they were attempting to bring the Antichrist into our reality.

It sounds crazy but that kind of practice was something else this Sanders guy got involved with. So, now, let's go back to that supposed flesh-and-blood baby that Sanders claimed to make appear through sex-magic rituals. And by the way, does any of this sound like something we ever want to get involved with? Does it seem healthy enough to teach to your seven-year-old grandson? These are some sick debaucherous activities! Yet how is Wicca portrayed through our media? They make it sound wonderful with wholesome people worshiping nature in another form of acceptable spiritualism. No! This is deeply satanic and seeing the behavior it leads to, it's no wonder God says Wicca witchcraft is detestable and evil in His eyes. We are to stay away from it!

"Sanders said the baby disappeared shortly after its creation, and 'grew up' as a spirit (demon) that took him over in his trance channeling. Michael, as the spirit was called, supposedly was responsible for 'forcing' Sanders to carry on at wild parties, insult others and otherwise act abominably. Eventually, Sanders claimed Michael became a valuable spirit familiar, offering advice in healing matters. Sanders also channeled a familiar entity (demon,) Nick Demdike, who said he had been persecuted as a witch in the Lancaster trials of the 17th century."

Apparently, Sanders was possessed by multiple demons in his life. Despite that, he married this lady:

"In the 1960's, Sanders met Maxine Morris, a Roman Catholic and 20 years his junior, whom he initiated into the craft in 1964. Maxine became his high priestess. In 1968, They married..."

Again, part of the reason Sander's witchcraft took off in popularity was because he got favorable press. Unfortunately, the media has huge power to help anyone they'd like to get his or her message out, whether good, bad, or really ugly. And this stuff Sanders was into was ugly with a capital U!

"Sanders was catapulted into the national public spotlight by a sensational newspaper article in 1969. The publicity led to a romanticized biography, 'King of the Witches', and a film, 'Legend of the Witches.'"

Now, I'm not going to give you the transcript of that entire movie because it's an hour long, but I will give you a couple of minutes so you can get an idea of what was in this film. Again, it came out in 1969 and its Sander's own documentary. Read this and then tell me who this guy really worships:

Narrator: *"In the beginning was the moon, Diana; sad, silent, alone, she wandered—the waves, her sighs, and the tears of solitude. She searched everywhere for a companion but found only reflections of herself. Lonely, Diana desired a lover. That desire became the dawn. And from the dawn, came the sun, Lucifer, the god of light."*

Alex Sanders: *"Hail Lucifer, from the abodes of night. Pour forth thy store of praise. I lowly bend before thee. I adore thee to the end. With loving sacrifice, thy shrine adorned. My lips are to thy feet. My prayer, upon the rising incense smoke, up born. Then descend to aid me. Without thee, I'm lonely and forlorn."*

Narrator: *"It must be noted that, in this ceremony, Lucifer is not the devil, but the bringer of light. Bring light into darkness, oh lord."*

So much for the idea that Wiccans don't worship satan. That's as blunt as you can get. If you were to watch the actual movie, you would notice how spiritual their music makes their practices seem. But the whole thing is sick, heavy-duty, occult-witchcraft practices and Sanders was pledging his allegiance to Lucifer. After that movie came out in 1969, Sanders popularity really took off like a rocket. And as I said, he was hugely helped along by our secular media:

"Sanders was given numerous appearances on media talk shows, and public speaking engagements. Sanders enjoyed the publicity and was adept at exploiting it..."

Now, if you are rightly thinking that the media's whole promotion of his witchcraft is crazy, here is a factor I want to bring up to explain some of the reason why this promotion happened. Again, his movie came out in 1969 after something significant changed in 1968. Movie's needing approval from the Motion Picture Production Code, was done away with.

If you're not familiar with this history of Hollywood and the media, that code was in force from 1934 to 1968. When movie pictures first came out, they were extremely graphic, lewd, and even pornographic. They called it the "roaring 1920's" for a reason, it was an immoral time. It got so bad that folks banded together to create this Motion Picture Production Code that censored rotten content and it put a stop to the problem. Afterward, we got what people called the 'heyday' for films with those like *The Ten Commandments* that promoted the Bible. I'm not saying they were Biblically accurate, but it's not like what we have today with outright New Age, witchcraft, and other occult material.

Again, this was still in effect all the way up until 1968. During that time, the heyday of Hollywood, when you could actually watch a movie with your kids in the room and not flinch at some of the content, here are those aspects that you could not have in a movie: No profanity; no mention of God, Lord, or Jesus Christ without it being in the proper Biblical context; no curse words; no nudity of any kind, even in a silhouette form; no illegal drug trafficking; no sexual perversion; no sex hygiene; no venereal diseases; you couldn't even show the actual birth of a child and not even in silhouette; and you couldn't ridicule the clergy. They made it mandatory to portray certain things correctly, like the U.S. flag. And they had to honor the country. But these days, that moral discretion is all gone!

The movies also could not portray deviant or dangerous behavior as if they were promoting it. They also could not show anyone how to do things like theft, robbery, safe-cracking, or dynamiting of trains, mines, and buildings. They didn't want people to replicate those things. Today our media even shows us how to get away with the perfect crime and how to kill people step by step. Before 1968, movies could not show brutality, gruesomeness, a technique of committing murder by any method, and they could not give sympathy to criminals. Do you remember when the good guy always won? Movies had to have a positive attitude toward public characters and institutions, as well as not glamorize sedition (inciting the public). Boy, is that needed today?

Movies could not show cruelty to animals or children, women selling their virtue, rape or attempted rape, "first night" scenes, a man and woman in bed together, or seduction of girls. You had to honor the institution of marriage, couldn't portray drugs in a positive light, had to have a positive portrayal of law enforcement and law enforcement officers, and there was no excessive kissing. All that sounds antiquated today, but it kept a lid on a lot of attempts to break down the walls of decent morality.

Here's the point: What came out in movies all changed in 1968 when we abandoned the picture production code where movies had to submit their scripts and be under threat of not having their film released if they violated sound principles. The switch they made at that time was to the rating system we deal with today. It's not by chance that happened in 1968 and Sanders' film, glamorizing luciferian witchcraft came out the very next year. The restraint was lifted, and it's been downhill ever since. And while we are on the subject, I have to give a swift kick to Hollywood:

"The name, "Hollywood" was carefully chosen as the name for the newly established motion picture industry in the 1920's. In ancient witchcraft, the most powerful wood for a witch or wizard to make a magic wand with was from the Holly tree. Thus, the most powerful magicians always used a hollywood magic wand. And one of the things that they used the wand made of hollywood for, was to mesmerize people."

And Hollywood is still doing that today, including mesmerizing people to think witchcraft and other occult practices are desirable.

But getting back to Sanders, he was a flamboyant guy who always appeared in robes while everyone else was naked. He said he did so to let people know who the leader was. And here is no shocker: Alex Sanders was a con artist! He passed off the writings of others, (like Gardner, Valiente, and other occultists), as his own. He was just picking and choosing other people's work to present as his own. He was a liar, which makes sense because he was following the ultimate liar, satan.

"Sanders died on April 30, 1988, after a long battle with lung cancer. His funeral was a media event. Witches and Pagans from various traditions attended to pay their respects."

And that launched Alexandrian Wicca, which is practiced in many countries today and many people might never have been introduced to witchcraft if not for Alex Sanders. Hey, if you thought King Manasseh was bad, do you think this guy is in trouble? I don't know what he did with his last breath, but I hope he got right with God through Jesus. However, understanding his life, that possibility is not looking good.

Now, that brings us up to modern-day Wicca and the major promoter of it now:

Laurie Cabot was born in 1933, is still alive today at 87 years old, and continues doing her unfortunate deeds. She has come up with a couple of her own different branches of witchcraft, including the "Cabot Tradition."

"She's a witch, author, artist, businesswoman, civil rights watchdog for helping witches be accepted, and founder of two traditions of contemporary witchcraft. She is known as 'the Official Witch of Salem' in Salem, Massachusetts…"

Speaking of Salem, let's quickly deal with the witch trials.

Non-Christians have often falsely criticized Christians because we supposedly committed those horrible atrocities during the Crusades. However, first of all, I wasn't there, I didn't do that. Second, those were not Christians. They were Catholics under direction of the popes. And I'm not defending that behavior because it was wrong, so I don't need to even respond to that, and you should not accuse me of it.

Not accusing me of it, should also apply to the Salem Witch Trials. How many of us Christians have heard this accusation thrown in our faces: "You Christians are a bunch of dangerous hypocrites. You killed all those women at the time of the witch trials." Well, first, two wrongs don't make a right. Now, that barbarity really did happen, and I'm not going to defend it because what happened was unthinkable. And let me give you a couple of reasons why that happened with hundreds of people arrested, imprisoned, tried, and found guilty of practicing witchcraft. Nineteen of them were hanged, one was crushed under heavy stones, and five more died in prison. So, it was bad!

But is that something God condones? No! Why? Those people convicting the witches and carrying out those death sentences made two mistakes. First, the witches were tried in court during this Christian age with a New Testament, a New Covenant of grace. Those handing out the punishment for the convicted witches were applying the Old Testament standard that is not applicable for this past two thousand years of the Christian Church age. For their wrong sentencing, the courts went back to Old Testament passages like **Exodus 22** and **Leviticus 20**:

"Thou shalt not suffer a witch to live."

"A man or woman that hath a familiar spirit (demon,) or that is a wizard, shall surely be put to death: they shall stone them with stones: their blood shall be upon them."

So, the people in that day cited Bible verses like those as the reason to give the death penalty to some of the convicted witches. But, if that were the true way to handle it, then why does **Acts 19** show Paul not doing the same? We saw this earlier when Paul was ministering to Ephesus and caused the new Christians, who had been occult people, to burn their expensive witchcraft books and confess their sinful deeds. Instead of stoning them according to the Old Testament, what did Paul do? He welcomed them when they confessed and repented of their sins. Why? Because today and throughout the New Covenant under the New Testament, we do not kill witches; we witness to them. That does not mean we condone occult behavior. But we do want to witness to them.

The New Testament has another example of the New Covenant as it is applied to witchcraft. That is a passage we already discussed in this book, **Acts 8**, with Simon the Sorcerer, who was not stoned by Peter but only rebuked. If we are still supposed to kill witches, as the Old Testament prescribes under the Old Covenant, then why didn't Paul, or Peter, do that? It is because the death penalty was Old Testament civil law. However, God's moral law with the Ten Commandments is in force for all time with its prescriptions for a certain moral character. But the civil, priestly, and dietary laws are for the Jewish nation, not the Christian Church.

So, those people passing out the sentences at the witch trails made a mistake. They misapplied Old Testament passages to say they were applicable for the Church age. And that is a whole other can of worms with religions today still attempting to enforce that outdated Old Testament covenant that does not apply to Christians. They try to bring those laws into today with all their legalism and they cite the Bible as their proof text. But, again, that is the old covenant, which is not for us Christians today.

And to use a modern term, the other issue in the Salem Witch Trial days was that those people were suffering because of "fake news." They created an ongoing hysteria, and the evidence became just hearsay: one person's word against another. People got worked up into a frenzy. Is that how we are to move forward on issues that come up? No! It is about the rule of law and not gossip, slander, and hearsay. If we are going to pursue anything, let alone something involving prison and the death penalty, we need to make sure we have the facts right because people are innocent until proven guilty. Instead, back in that day, they ran with fake news and, boy, isn't that applicable for us today; especially the hysteria it constantly fuels?

Here's my point: I'm not going to defend the Salem Witch Trials, and I don't need to. You cannot throw that in my face because I didn't do that, don't condone it, and will admit it was wrong. However, that does not mean that witchcraft is honorable, acceptable, or a positive influence and lifestyle for people to follow. And I have the right to speak up against that.

In fact, in love, I am commanded by God to witness to them, so they can, hopefully, get out of witchcraft. Do you see the difference? So, we Christians need not shy away from the Crusades accusation or the Salem Witch Trials. I will say this though, because it does still happen today: If witches do kill people, what do we do? We take them to courts of law, just like any other murderer and we deal with it according to the law. Now, let's get back to Laurie Cabot.

Still to this day, in her 80's, Cabot is famous for dressing in all-black garments and makeup, as well as wearing her pentagram, (or pentacle). She claims to come from a long line of witches, supposedly even as far back as 4,000 years ago, which would put the first witch in her family at around the time of Babylon. I don't know if that's true or not, but either way it sounds like she has a long line of unfortunate witchcraft in her family. In 1933, she was born as an only child in Wewoka, Oklahoma.

Just as Buckland got into witchcraft as a young boy through his naked grandmother doing the witch thing in the kitchen, Cabot also started very young. She was six years old. Her father was a science-orientated man, who did not believe in the devil. That science influenced her to do some tweaking of the witchcraft message, just like Valiente made Gardner's *Book of Shadows* more poetic and palatable or how Buckland Americanized it to not be so ritualistic and demanding of followers. Cabot is the one who is responsible for trying to paint witchcraft as a science.

So, she set out to make it more sciency and less occultish. That's the same tactic employed by Hinduism when they first tried evangelizing the West. Hinduism tried to come over here with that approach in the late 1890's but at that time America rejected their yoga and meditation. We still had a pervasive Christian mindset at that time so Hindu beliefs and practices could not gain ground. But they re-strategized and came back at us again later. This time they got people involved by claiming their religion was a science. People meditating and practicing yoga were hooked to monitors that confirmed how these Hindu rituals lower brain waves, heart rate, and stress level. Hey, that may be true, but it is still a false and dangerous Hindu practice. So, Cabot did the same science makeover with witchcraft through the help of her dad's science.

Still at a young age, three witches performed Cabot's witchcraft initiation ceremony. As this explains, she had met them through the media of that day, the library:

"When she was 16, the Witches initiated her in a profoundly transformational experience. She was anointed with oil and dubbed with a sword. She took the sword, impaled it in the earth, and said, 'I return to earth my wisdom and I call myself Witch.'"

After that was when Cabot branched out to create her witchcraft-science angle. She married twice but both failed. After her second divorce she took her daughters and moved away.

"She made a vow that she would live her life 'totally as a Witch': she would wear nothing but traditional Witch clothing (which she says is long black robes), wear her pentacle displayed, and would emulate the Goddess by outlining her eyes in black makeup, according, she says, to an ancient tradition."

I can't prove this, but what she claimed got me thinking as far back as Egypt and how their artwork often depicted people having major black lines, or coloring, around the eyes? And we know their background with the occult. I don't know if that's where Cabot got it, but it could be. Of course, telling ladies they should not wear black makeup is getting into unneeded legalism. I'm just saying that was very interesting. So, Cabot was big on black and, even today, witches generally wear a lot of black makeup and clothing. Why is that? Well, this is according to Cabot and is basically what other witches believe:

"Black absorbs light while white reflects it; this absorption of light facilitates psychic power. To further augment power, practitioners wear gold jewelry for psychic strength, usually in the form of a pentacle pendant."

Here is more on Cabot trying to make witchcraft into a science:

"In 1955, Cabot founded the Cabot Tradition of the Science of Witchcraft (originally called Witchcraft as a Science) In addition to witchcraft basics and history, instruction includes parapsychology; physiology; astrology; geometric structure; sociology; anthropology; meditation; aura reading, balancing and healing; the use of crystals; and the psychic arts."

Now, what does that sound like? It's just a big old pile of New Age! If you've seen our study on the New Age movement, you know that belief system is a hodgepodge of diverse practices, including many that are from the occult. Recruiting efforts for both witchcraft and New Age stay away from freaking people out by accidentally admitting that they are occultists, who create their own spiritual reality and worship Lucifer. Instead, with New Age, they attempt to project that they are all about some wonderful enlightening New Age for man. It is the same with Wicca: People are told it is just a nature science to alleviate stress and have a happy life. And for women, they like to claim it is so much better than living with those mean and awful men. We will get more into that in the next chapter on the subject of feminism.

Cabot also follows what is called, "The Wiccan Rede," which tells a witch that he or she should do all they would like but harm none. Turn to someone, or your pet, and snicker with your hand over your mouth. With all due respect, that's serious hypocrisy! As we initially put this study out from the pulpit, we were informed that witches were tuning in and getting on their witch chat boards, working together to try putting curses and hexes on us for informing Christians about occult witchcraft. Yet, they supposedly follow a creed that tells them to harm none? I think we all see the duplicity there. In fact, here is another example from a British news show recently where the lady actually demonstrates how to get rid of somebody, which again brings up the question about what happened to not harming others? Here is the transcript:

Caption: *"The witch who wants you to live your best life."*

Female Interviewer: *"You were about seventeen, weren't you, and it was through a friend, who was doing Reiki to begin with, that you had this* *conversation, you got into that. But how did that lead to you becoming a witch?"*

Semra Haksever, (full-time witch): *"I think that just kind of opened the path, like my spiritual path, and like just all the people I met through doing that back then...and all the years, and all the synchronicities, and all the crazy people; I don't know, incidents that happened in my life have really led me to where I am now."*

Female Interviewer: *"So this isn't like, sort of, witches on broomsticks with cats."*

Haksever: *"No."*

Female Interviewer: *"This is very different stuff. So, what type of witch are you?"*

Haksever: *"I call myself an eclectic witch. So, I take, you know, different little bits of magic from all over the place. And it's all about self-empowerment and doing rituals to help you manifest, connect to the moon, and make you feel really good about yourself."*

Female Interviewer: *"So, you have cast spells where they've been so powerful that the result has been brilliant, right?"*

Haksever: *"Yeah, amazing. The most recent one that was crazy, was that I manifested a holiday. I did a spell for a holiday. It was a little spell with a bay leaf and a sacred symbol, and I got a free two-week holiday to Bali, all expenses paid."*

Female Interviewer: *"And you're gonna show us some of these now, aren't you?"*

Male Interviewer reads a viewer's question for the Haksever: *"Have you got a spell to get rid of people?"*

Male Interviewer: *"Lacy said she's like to get rid of her lazy husband."*

They show a picture of the lazy husband sleeping on the coach.

Haksever: *"She needs to make some black salt."*

Male Interviewer: *"So, he's gone to sleep, and he has things to do. So, what would she do? She needs his shoe for this, doesn't she?"*

Haksever: *"She needs some black salt, and she can write it down and just rub the black salt all over the paper because it's powerful stuff."*

Haksever shows a small jar of black paste.

Haksever: *"This is black salt. So, it's a mix of burnt sage, which is really great for protection, and old charcoal from spells that I've used. So, if you are making spells, you can have the charcoal and salt. And so, what you would do is just take a little pinch of it, like that, pop it in there (a bowl) and then if you want it to work fast you can use cayenne pepper. Pepper speeds it up; makes things happen really fast. So, you pop a little pinch in there like that. And then what you do is you pop it into the pestle and mortar, like that. And then you can blend it. If you're blending stuff, to make something go away, you mix counterclockwise. If you want stuff to come in, you go clockwise. So, you can just do a blend."*

Male Interviewer: *"What about the shoes?*

Haksever: *"Put this concoction in the tip of the shoes. Make their shoes face the front door and then put a pinch in each, in the tip."*

Female Interviewer: *"And then in seven days that lazy guy will be gone?"*

Haksever: *"Yeah, and it works fast."*

Where do you even start with this? First, when did we get rid of standards for demonstrations on television? They are showing witchcraft techniques as a life hack! They are actually presenting it as a way to improve your life and they are outright glamorizing it. And what really blew me away was how television programs like that one are showing step-by-step, occult-witchcraft rituals that we can do at home! And if you watch that entire show, they demonstrated a bunch of other concoctions and spells. I just gave you the one example. And did you catch that tag line at the very beginning? They introduced her as a witch that just wants to show you how to live your best life!

Who else does that sound like? That's what Mr. Joel Osteen pitches with his messages all about self, self-empowerment, and self, along with more self. As we have seen multiple times now, what's the number one law of satanism? It is, "Do what thou wilt shall be the whole of the law." That came from Aleister Crowley and that selfism is satanic. So, why is that witch doing her witchcraft? It is because she thinks that will help her live her best life now and it's all about her. Again, the philosophy is, "It's all about me!" And believe it or not, even Osteen's wife admits their form of worship is all about self and not God. But that's flat out Satanism, folks. Here's what Osteen said:

Commentator: *"Attention, all Christians. When you go to church next Sunday, you might not be doing it for God; but to satisfy your own selfish needs. Can you believe that? That is what some people are saying. At least, that's how people are interpreting the remarks that were made by popular Lakewood Church co-pastor, Victoria Osteen. Check this out."*

Victoria Osteen talking to a stadium-size crowd of followers: *"I just want to encourage every one of us to realize, when we obey God, we're not doing it for God. I mean, that is one way to look at it; we're doing it for ourselves because God takes pleasure when we're happy. That's the thing that gives Him the greatest joy this morning. So, I want you to know this morning, just do good for your own self. Do good because God wants you to be happy. When you come to Church, when you worship Him,* *you're not doing it for God, really, you're doing it for yourself because that's what makes God happy. Amen?"*

Video switches to a group of satanists seated in a circle.

Narrator: *"Founded in San Francisco, California, by Anton LeVey in 1966, the Church of Satan sees belief in God or hell as delusional. And so, they choose to practice self-reliance and self- worship."*

Interviewer questioning Priestess Lilith Sinclair of the Temple of Set: *"If a Christian said to you, you're just really worshiping yourself, what would you say?"*

Sinclair: *"In a sense, they would be right. It is a form of self-worship."*

Interviewer questioning ex-satanist, Mike Leehan: *"You were a satanist for how long?"*

Leehan: *"Twelve years."*

Interviewer: *"What does it mean to be a satanist and to have satan as a god?"*

Leehan: *"To adore satan. You're serving satan. You're serving self. More than anything else it's egocentric, self-centered, serve me, always me, immediate gratification. That's all it's about."*

Magus Peter H. Gilmore, High Priest, Church of Satan: *"The Church of Satan has chosen satan as its primary symbol because, in Hebrew, it means adversary, opposer, one to accuse or question. We see ourselves as being the satans; the adversaries, opposers, and accusers of all spiritual belief system that would try to hamper enjoyment of our life as a human being."*

Anton Szandor LaVey, Church of Satan founder: *"This is a very selfish religion. We believe in greed. We believe in selfishness. We believe* *in all of the lustful thoughts that motivate man because this is man's natural feeling."*

I had to share that because people might think I'm crazy to say that is satanism. Well, there you heard it straight from the satanist's mouths. When your belief is that life is all about self, that's satanism and now it's even in the Church. And it follows that witchcraft, which also comes from satan, is also all about self, just as Osteen preaches self-enhancement, self-improvement, and whatever focuses on self.

Now, let's get back to Laurie Cabot, who taught continuing education classes at Salem State College for seven years. Hey, I thought we weren't supposed to have any religions or Christianity taught in schools. That's what they tell us. Apparently, witchcraft is okay, and you can even have a practicing witch teach it. Cabot also opened up a couple witchcraft shops in Salem that were called, "The Witch Shop," and "Crow Haven Corner." The latter was extremely successful as a tourist attraction.

In the 1970's, she gave her shop to her daughter to run. Then in 1973 she began an annual tradition called, "Witch's Costume Ball," which is a costume party that still goes on today, celebrating Samhain, or All Hallows' Eve (Halloween), one of their prominent high, unholy days in Salem.

That ball attracts a growing international community, and part of the reason is all the unfortunate media attention they get. I'm sure many of us remember this guy: Michael Dukakis, who ran for U.S. President in 1988, was the Governor of Massachusetts in 1977 when he signed a citation making Cabot, "the Official Witch of Salem." Is that a good thing for him to promote? What party is he a part of? Again, it's the Democrats.

"In 1986, she founded the Witches League of Public Awareness to serve as a media watchdog and civil rights advocate for Witchcraft."

Right after that, the U.S. saw witchcraft begin to greatly increase in the public view. Wicca also became a religion around the same time:

"In 1986, Wicca was recognized as an official religion in the United States through the court case Dettmer v. Landon. In the case, incarcerated Wiccan Herbert Daniel Dettmer was refused ritual objects used for worship. The Fourth Circuit Court of Appeals ruled that Wicca was entitled to First Amendment protection like any other religion."

I wonder if they have to wear Covid masks when they gather as Christian Churches have been made to, just sayin'.

"In 1998, a Wiccan student in Texas enlisted the aid of the ACLU after the school board tried to prevent her from wearing Wiccan jewelry and black clothes. The board reversed its view. In 2004, the Indiana Civil Liberties Union fought to reverse a judge's decision that divorcing Wiccans were not allowed to teach their faith to their sons. In 2005, U.S. Army Sgt. Patrick D. Stewart became the first Wiccan serving in the U.S. military to die in combat. His family was refused a Wiccan pentacle on his gravestone. As a result of a court case initiated by the Americans United for the Separation of Church and State, Wiccan symbols are now accepted by the Veterans Administration."

All that launched an increase in practicing U.S. Wiccans that has led to the number today being in the millions. And part of it was Laurie Cabot taking it on as a civil rights issue.

She even ran for Salem mayor in 1987 after people made derogatory comments about witches. She was kind of like a watchdog for witchcraft. Before that, in 1980, Cabot served as a board member for the Salam Chamber of Commerce. So, she got involved in the schools, businesses, and politics. Cabot is still alive and active today. She also found a way to act as some sort of a so-called pastor:

"In 1988 she established the Temple of Isis, a chapter of the National Alliance of Pantheists. Through the National Alliance of Pantheists, she was ordained Reverend Cabot and may perform legal marriages."

"Cabot's books include 'Practical Magic: A Salem Witch's Handbook' (1986); 'The Power of the Witch, with Tom Cowan' (1990); 'Love Magic, with Tom Cowan' (1992); 'Celebrate the Earth: A Year of Holidays in the Pagan Tradition, with Jean candles 49 Mills and Karen Bagnard' (1994); and 'The Witch in Every Woman: Reawakening the Magical Nature of the Feminine to Heal, Protect, Create and Empower, with Jean Mills' (1997)."

She's all about feminine power and certainly doesn't like using the term, "mankind." She likes to use "humankind." Maybe that is more baggage from her unfortunate history involving contentious run-ins with men in her life, which doesn't mean all guys are bad, but that's where she went.

"Cabot maintains a full schedule of teaching classes, giving readings and making public appearances. She is active in community work, including a tree-planting program for the Salem area."

Of course, the tree-planting involves being out there in nature and worshiping the creation instead of the Creator.

Here's the point of understanding Laurie Cabot's experience: Unfortunately, she's still going on today, having a huge hand in recruiting people to think that witchcraft is just a science and an alternate way; a life hack. She wants you to try different aspects of witchcraft and, if those don't work for you, try something else that witchcraft offers because it's supposedly going to help you. It's all about yourself. But the reality is that those getting involved are taking on a demonic, satanic, luciferian practice. This is why we need to witness to people, including this lady, who is still alive at 87. She can still come to Christ. You might be thinking she's too far gone, but we are not to write anyone off. My heart's cry is not just to gain knowledge about witchcraft, which is all over the Bible. As a Bible Church, we study it because God wants us to learn all of His Word, not just pick and choose for ourselves. Our focus in studying this, or any of the other studies in our series, *World Religions, Cults and the Occult*, is to get equipped so we can feel confident enough to reach anybody for Christ, especially those trapped on this dark path. And Jesus can save them like he did with this lady in a video transcript called, The Story of a Former Witch:

Former witch, Sheila: *"I think I wanted to have power over the things that scared me. I thought that it would give me that."*

Narrator: *"Growing up, Shalom was known as, Sheila. As a teen she began searching for truth. Her fascination with the occult and her love for nature led her to Wicca."*

Sheila: *"I was always very much in love with nature, and so it was a natural thing to worship nature. So, it was easy for me to get into that."*

Narrator: *"As Sheila became more involved with Wicca, she became very outspoken about the religion. She felt it was her duty to let the world know that witches were nothing like the normal perception."*

Sheila: *"You know, I thought of myself as a good witch, kind of like Glinda. But that's kind of the way I looked at it for myself."*

Narrator: *"Despite thinking she was a good witch; Sheila began to delve deeper into the occult lifestyle. Drinking, drugs, and sex became a way of life."*

Sheila: *"I didn't believe in sin. You know, that opens the door pretty easily for you to get into just about anything you want to."*

Narrator: *"Even though Sheila practiced magic and attended pagan gatherings, she still felt hopeless. At 25, the man she was engaged to marry walked away from her after his family learned she was a witch. Devastated and alone, she turned to her magic, hoping to find peace."*

Sheila: *"And I just thought, well, you know, I'm not really in harmony with nature enough yet."*

Narrator: *"Sheila searched everywhere for answers. She spent time worshiping her favorite tree, doing spells, and appealing to the god and goddess for answers."*

Sheila: *"I really, really thought I was on the right track. I thought I was really getting somewhere. I thought I was becoming enlightened. But things were still a mess."*

Narrator: *"A few years later, another man came into her life: Kevin. Before long, the two fell in love and decided to marry. But just like before, his family found out she was a witch and wanted the relationship to end."*

Sheila: *"So I was really angry that, once again, Christians had interfered with my love life. So, I decided I'd have a little talk with Jesus because I still believed that Jesus had existed, that he was, you know, a really smart guy. I said, look, you know, I'm really suffering here so I need your help. You're supposed to be the Prince of Peace; I need some peace here. And it was really strange because I actually experienced peace at that point."*

Narrator: *"She began reading the Bible and studying Christianity. She wanted to understand the peace and power that came over her after she had prayed."*

Sheila: *"I had so many viewpoints that had to change, that it was a process. I mean, I literally felt like scales were being dropped from my eyes, like Paul's experience."*

Narrator: *"Sheila and Kevin got back together and began studying the Bible and going to Church. The couple gave their lives to Jesus and soon married, this time with the blessing of his family."*

Sheila: *"The first thing that I felt was, boy, what a lot of wasted time that I could have been happy, and I could have been sober; that I could have been worshiping the right God."*

Narrator: *"Now, her duty has changed a little. She no longer seeks to educate the world about who witches really are, but instead who Christ is."*

Sheila: *"After practicing magic for over 20 years, I never encountered any power like what I've encountered since I've been a Christian."*

Narrator: *"With the peace she's always longed for, Shalom is hoping to help other pagans and Wiccans find it, too."*

Sheila: *"You can, you can find forgiveness. It does not matter what you've been into. It does not matter what you've done. He's gonna still forgive all of that and there's hope, there is hope."*

Amen! That's why we're studying what we're studying. It's not just in case we get on Jeopardy, and the Daily Double involves the witchcraft category with some question like, "Who founded Wicca?" This time of getting equipped is for sharing the information with unfortunate souls who have been duped into the occult and its witchcraft. And if you are reading this book and are currently any part of witchcraft, or were in years past, listen to that lady. What she is testifying to is true. There is hope! The one that you are or were worshiping is false, and it will destroy you. But Jesus Christ can forgive you, give you hope, and make you whole. And I know there's a dark hole in your heart that your witchcraft and occult practices are not filling. It is a God-shaped void that only God can fill. That starts when you call upon the name of Jesus Christ. Wherever you are, if that's you, do that tonight.

Now, speaking of bad relationships and awful men, as well as female-goddess worship that is pushed on our ladies through Wicca, in the next chapter we'll talk about Dianic Wicca.

Besides the introduction to that topic in this book, Lord willing, eventually, we will have a lengthy study of feminism and how it's just a smokescreen to get women of all ages into straight-up witchcraft.

Chapter Fifteen

The History of Wicca
Part 4

By way of review to better learn the information, we've seen that the definition of Wicca is witchcraft. Those practicing it want us to believe it's not witchcraft, but it is! There are many types of witchcraft and it is all over the world. The protection from it is only through Christians relying on the power of Jesus to exterminate evil. Witchcraft is nothing new, as we've seen in our exploration of its historical journey, as it spread around the world. It's the same old-fashioned occult behavior that began after Noah's flood at the Tower of Babel. Those occultists and witches were dispersed when God confused the language. That migration led to witchcraft infecting Egypt and then Greece, followed by Rome, Asia, India and the nearby island countries, Africa, Latin America and Europe.

Europe is where North America got a lot of our modern witchcraft that was relabeled and repackaged as "Wicca." We looked at the history of Wicca witchcraft and how it got to be commonplace in the United States. It was begun by the grandmother of Wicca (Margaret Murray) and then advanced by the grandfather of Wicca (Gerald Gardner), who came up with his *Book of Shadows* and Gardnerian Wicca. His cohort, Doreen

Valiente, who is considered the mother of Wicca, carried it forward, after which Raymond Buckland, the father of Wicca, established Wicca on the East Coast. Around the same timeframe, Sybil Leek, known as the celebrity of Wicca, moved to the West Coast and helped popularize it there, as well as across our country through the willing promotion of our media.

We saw how celebrities from television, movies, sports, and politics have also advanced witchcraft. Just as Super Bowl football star Tom Brady has done through his wife's witchcraft, like the Demoncrat (Democrat) Party does every day. That's because they've been so heavily infiltrated with occult practices. Then we talked about Alex Sanders (Alexandrian Wicca), who is considered the king of witches. Sanders was representative of the eclectic nature of witchcraft practices, similar to the New Age movement because of how witches can pick and choose from a huge variety of methods, beliefs, and spiritual reality, playing God while ignoring the real God.

Frankly, the Alexandrian version of Wicca witchcraft is extra rotten! All witchcraft is bad, but we saw him flat out worshiping satan on film with his "Left-Hand-Path," (verses the Right-Hand Path), of witchcraft that gets into black magic. He combined Abramelin Magic with Aleister Crowley's methods that included sex magic. Sanders came out with his witchcraft documentary right after the Motion Picture Production Code was scrapped, in favor of our present-day movie-rating system. From that point when Hollywood became unfiltered, we saw a massive influx of occult movies and that's when Sander's popularity began to take off.

From there, Wicca witchcraft was advanced by Laurie Cabot, who is still alive and, unfortunately, continues to promote witchcraft. She burrowed deep into witchcraft after two failed relationships with men, deciding to promote witchcraft as in a sort of earth science. Through that approach, she has been successful in convincing many that witchcraft is just a science, which supposedly contributes to the good of "humankind" as she does not like to say "mankind." However, no matter how they are described, these occult practices are still evil witchcraft. Cabot has a huge number of books she has written to promote occult witchcraft. She has also been involved in the business of witchcraft shops and an annual international event called the Witch's Costume Ball. Cabot also started the Witches League and even advocated witchcraft in politics through her post on the Salem (Massachusetts) Chamber of Commerce board and running for mayor of Salem. Democratic presidential nominee, Michael Dukakis, called her the "official witch of Salem" (like that is an honorable title). All that helped the practice of witchcraft to really grow in the United States as a lot of anti-witchcraft court cases and rules were loosened or done away with. Now, in her 80's, Cabot is still advocating for witchcraft today.

In this chapter we are going to take a look at the Dianic Wicca movement, which is another way witchcraft is being promoted today. We are going to see that Dianic Wicca came straight out of, and is synonymous with, the feminist movement. You might think that is too strong of an accusation but wait until we get through the details that I'm going to give you in this chapter. Dianic witchcraft is all about the feminist movement. And the proof comes straight from witches themselves. The feminist movement is a smokescreen to, not only suck women into anti-God and anti-biblical teachings, but also with the ultimate goal of having them practice witchcraft.

Before we get into that proof, can you imagine how hard I have been praying, fasting, and greatly struggling to find another Bible passage that warns against witchcraft? It was no trouble at all because warnings against witchcraft are all over the Bible! Let's go to **2 Kings 17:7-20**, which is yet another passage from God that tells us not to get involved in this stuff. What we are going to see in this passage is the reason why God exiled the Northern and Southern kingdoms of Israel, all twelve tribes. The ten Northern kingdoms of Israel went into exile at the hands of the Assyrians, while the Southern two, Judah and Benjamin, stayed around a bit longer but eventually saw the same fate through their Babylonian exile. With **2 Kings 17**, we're going to see the reason God eventually sent all the tribes of Israel off their land and took everything away from them. Let's take a look:

"All this took place because the Israelites had sinned against the Lord their God, who had brought them up out of Egypt from under the power of Pharaoh King of Egypt."

From our earlier study of Egypt, what were they heavily involved with? Unfortunately, they did not let it go.

"They worshiped other gods and followed the practices of the nations the Lord had driven out before them, as well as the practices that the kings of Israel had introduced. The Israelites secretly did things against the Lord their God that were not right."

Isn't that just like the enemy? You think you are getting away with something, as if God is blind or can't see in the dark or when you close a door. Now, what was it that these people did in secret? Here it is and, remember, the high places were where they worshiped their false gods:

"From watchtower to fortified city, they built themselves high places in all their towns. They set up sacred stones and Asherah poles on every high hill and under every spreading tree. At every high place they burned incense, as the nations whom the Lord had driven out before them had done. They did wicked things that aroused the Lord's anger. They worshiped idols, though the Lord had said, 'You shall not do this.' The Lord warned Israel and Judah through all his prophets and seers: 'Turn from your evil ways. Observe my commands and decrees in accordance with the entire Law that I commanded your ancestors to obey and that I delivered to you through my servants the prophets.' But they would not listen and were as stiff-necked as their ancestors."

You don't ever want to be stiff-necked against God. If He tells you to do something, remember that all of his commands are for our good. Name one command in the Scripture that works against our better interests. How many are there like that? It rhymes with "none!" So, if God says it, why in the world would we not listen?! Yet, these people not only didn't listen, but they also repeatedly refused to and actually told God, "No."

"But they would not listen and were as stiff-necked as their ancestors, who did not trust in the Lord their God. They rejected his decrees and the covenant he had made with their ancestors and the statutes he had warned them to keep. They followed worthless idols and themselves became worthless. They imitated the nations around them although the Lord had ordered them, 'Do not do as they do.' They forsook all the commands of the Lord their God and made for themselves two idols cast in the shape of calves and an Asherah pole. They bowed down to all the starry hosts, and they worshiped Baal. They sacrificed their sons and daughters in the fire."

For their own gain, that was the time when these people were casting their live children into the burning arms of the giant Moloch idol. Unfortunately, as we have seen throughout witchcraft's history, those are the same atrocities that still go on to this day with the occult's murderous sacrifices to their demons and satan. And the motivation for individual gain is why they still do those kinds of heinous acts in our time. It's sick!

"They practiced divination and sorcery and sold themselves to do evil in the eyes of the Lord, arousing his anger. So, the Lord was very angry with Israel and removed them from his presence. Only the tribe of Judah was left, and even Judah did not keep the commands of the Lord their God. They followed the practices Israel had introduced. Therefore, the Lord rejected all the people of Israel; he afflicted them and gave them into the hands of plunderers, until he thrust them from his presence."

I think that's pretty blunt, right? Again, why did God send both the Northern kingdom and the Southern kingdoms, (all twelve tribes), into exile, causing them to lose their land and everything else? God says specifically why: It wasn't just because they sinned. God was judging them on their occult practices like false worship, demonic aspects, witchcraft, divination, and sorcery. In fact, he warned them over and over by sending the prophets. It wasn't just one prophet that passed through one day saying, "Hey, guys, you need to repent and stop doing this." God repeatedly warned those people. If you add up the years, you can see how God was long suffering for them! He is very patient. He was asking them to please turn around from their wicked ways. But they kept at it anyway.

So, they couldn't say He didn't give them enough notice. And what about Judah, who kept their land quite a bit longer? Didn't they see what happened with their brothers to the north?! Yes, they did but stiff-necked Judah kept pursuing evil.

And I hope that is not us today. Here's my point: if God didn't like those vile practices then, so much so that He sent His people into exile, losing their nation, freedom, and everything they owned, do you think He likes that behavior today? No, and I'm not saying we're Israel but as a secondary application, if our country continues to go down this route, glamorizing, accepting, and promoting witchcraft, what do you think is going to happen to us? The same outcome is what we face!

Now, I want to take a closer look at another way witchcraft, unfortunately, is being accepted, popularized, and even promoted today, which is Dianic Wicca and how it closely relates to feminism. Believe it or not, that practice is not just leading people into bondage; I think it is part of the destruction of our country. The video transcript I'm about to share with you is a short description of Dianic Wicca and it comes from the witches themselves. So, no one can say we are making an unfair comparison when we say that Dianic Wicca comes straight out of the feminist movement. They admit it themselves. Let's take a look at this short description of a Dianic Witch:

"Dianic witches predominantly focus on feminism and the supremacy of the goddess. As it grew out of the women's movement in the United States, Dianic witches are attuned to the political and social oppression of women, as well as the injustices they suffer within their gender. The hierarchical structure is quite lax and fluid, while allowing for growth along one's own path. Originally created by Zsuzsanna Budapest in the 1970's, any coven derived from the original lineage remains female only."

What is the key phrase there? It is "female only," and they use it because they view men as horrible, so they have to be excluded from their group.

Now, we are using this entire chapter to deal with the topic of Dianic Wicca's feminist movement because there is a lot to cover with it. Two of the subtopics are their basic beliefs and practices. Then we're going to look at one of their major leaders, who were the first to begin combining witchcraft and feminism. Believe it or not, Dianic Wicca witchcraft and feminism are really just one movement. Then we'll see what those aspects have to do with future events and where we're at today with this movement. First, let's talk about the beliefs and practices of this thing called Dianic Wicca, which this secular article calls witchcraft:

"Dianic Wicca, also known as Dianic Witchcraft..."

Let me repeat that again: Dianic Witchcraft. What's the huge misnomer out there about Wicca? Those involved keep trying to convince us that it is not witchcraft. We're supposed to believe it's just nice people appreciating and worshiping nature, which they claim is so important in our day because of climate change. But their description is not true. Instead, Wicca is just plain-old witchcraft!

"Dianic Wicca, also known as Dianic Witchcraft, is a neopagan religion and female-centered goddess ritual and tradition."

Dianic Wicca differs from most of Wicca because the followers will only worship a goddess and men are not allowed to join. Most of the other Wiccan covens and branches worship the dual deities of the male Horned god and the female Mother goddess. But this Dianic witchcraft is all female. And here is one lady, who promotes it.

We'll talk in much more detail about Zsuzsanna Budapest (not her real name), who founded Dianic Wicca in 1970 and named her movement after the Roman goddess Diana. Besides worship of the goddess, Diana, they will actually worship any female goddess of any culture, as long as it is a feminine deity. They claim the goddess is the source of all living beings because it is women that birth the babies. Last time I checked; they are right in that we all came from a mom. However, they go too far beyond that to claim it means women have the real power. It is the feminist message they've woven together with witchcraft.

"Dianic covens practice magic in the form of mediation and visualization in addition to spell work. They focus especially on healing themselves from the wounds of the patriarchy (male domination) while affirming their own womanhood."

So, they must band together as ladies to perform witchcraft on each other to heal themselves from the ravages of those horrible men.

"Rituals can include reenacting religious and spiritual lore from a female-centered standpoint, celebrating the female body, and mourning society's abuses of women. The practice of magic is rooted in the belief that energy or 'life force' can be directed to enact change."

Apparently, women need to rid themselves of any male-dominating influence. Here they at least admit it:

"However, it is important to note that rituals are often improvised to suit individual or group needs and vary from coven to coven. Some Dianic Wiccans abstain from manipulative spell work and hexing because it goes against the Wiccan Rede."

Remember what Wiccans claim to believe and practice: They can do anything they want, if it doesn't harm others. Yet, in the actual practice of that supposed belief, they become completely hypocritical. For example, in the last chapter we read about the witch who was on television showing the hosts and their female viewers how to get back at a guy through witchcraft. How is that not harming someone? Also, just because we have been teaching about witchcraft, the chat boards have witches purposely putting hexes and curses on us. How is that characterized as harming none? It is hypocritical but at least the Dianic version admits it. In fact, here is more of what they say:

"However, many other Dianic witches (notably Budapest) do not consider hexing or binding of those who attack women or otherwise go against their Wiccan Rede, to be wrong and actively encourage the binding of rapists."

So, they don't even live up to their own rituals.

"Like other Wiccans, Dianics may form covens, attend festivals, celebrate the eight major Wiccan holidays, and gather on Esbats, Sabbats and other events. They use many of the same altar tools, rituals, and vocabulary as other Wiccans."

Again, when compared to much of the rest of Wicca, Dianic Wiccans accept only women witches and the worship of only a female goddess. It's all about women, and men are bad. In fact, their attitude toward men is that the guys better watch themselves or the witches are going to get them. That's really what it's all about. And what does that sound exactly like? It's the feminist movement, which came out of Dianic Wicca, as we'll see in a minute.

"When asked why 'men and gods' are excluded from her rituals, Budapest stated: 'It's the natural law, as women fare so fares the world, their children, and that's everybody. If you lift up the women, you have lifted up humanity.'"

So, they are claiming any real power comes from women, which is the way it should be, instead of from men. And they even admit that this witchcraft practice of Dianic Wicca came out of the Women's Liberation and Feminism movements:

"Dianic Wicca developed from the Women's Liberation Movement and covens traditionally compare themselves with radical feminism."

That's a direct quote, so you can see that I'm not making this comparison up. I'm not trying to portray it in an unfair light. They admit it themselves. In fact, here is a witch admitting that the feminist movement came from witchcraft:

Narrator witch: *"It really wasn't until 1893 with Matilda Joslyn Gage, an American suffragist: She wrote a book called, 'Women, Church and State.' It reframed the European witch hunts as a misogynistic attempt by the church and state to police female sexuality, women's bodies, and women's reproductive function. That is, to my knowledge, the first time the word, witch, was used in a positive way. And the funny thing about her is that her son in law was L. Frank Baum, who wrote 'The Wonderful Wizard of Oz.' He was inspired, by her writing, to conceive of the witch as, not only evil, but also good. So, we have these polarities of the good witch and the bad witch, which then goes into the MGM film and sets the stage for the way we view witches forever, pretty much."*

In a scene from the *Wizard of Oz*, the Wicked Witch of the West speaks to Dorothy while Glinda the "good" witch stands behind Dorothy: *"I'll get you my pretty! And your little dog too!"*

Narrator witch: *"And then you have the movie, 'I married a Witch,' in the 1940's; a sort of a more-lighthearted view of them. There are blond witches, you know. They are glamorous. And then there was 'Bell, Book and Candle' a movie with Jimmy Stewart and Kim Novak, in the late 50's. And then 'Bewitched,' the popular television show in the early 60's, coincides right when Betty Friedan is putting out, 'The Feminine Mystique' popular book. So, 'Bewitched' is kind of, you know, talking about the plight of the white middle-class housewife, just like Betty Friedan's book, and the Women's Liberation movement is, sort of, bubbling under the surface and culture at the time. And with 'Bewitched' I think a few episodes were written by a self-professed feminist, Barbara Avidan. So, there were actual real early feminist leanings in there. And, you know, the way Elizabeth Montgomery's character from 'Bewitched' uses magic, is like the way early feminist thought could be conceived; like, Samantha's husband, Darrin, is really annoyed and always frustrated she's using this magical power. It is like something he cannot access, and he can't control. And it gives her agency. Even though, you know, it's kind* *of like a fluffy, funny show, there are some little radical currents in there that I think are picked up and expressed more explicitly in later films in the 70's, 80's, 90's, etc."*

In a scene form '*Bewitched*,' Samantha says this to her husband, Darrin: *"You're a big, dumb head!"*

Darrin says back: *"You're calling me names now?!"*

Narrator: *"My favorite representations of the witch is pretty recent, actually. 'The Witch', by Robert Eggers, was a fantastic horror film that really used period lighting and period text to inform how people viewed witches at the time. And then 'The Love Witch' movie, by Anna Biller, is a sort of saturated, colorful meditation on sex magic and female sexuality and sort of the world through the female gaze."*

A concerned-looking man asks the love witch: *"What was in that drink you gave me?"*

And the love witch, was probably thinking, "Oh, you'll find out soon enough, you bad, evil man." That narration was straight from a witch who readily admits her malevolent motivation toward men. And it came straight out of feminism. Combining the two is really a smokescreen to get our ladies involved with witchcraft. And notice how Hollywood is always there to warm us up to occult and witchcraft beliefs and practices. As far back as *The Wizard of Oz* book that was turned into a monumentally influential movie, it turns out the book's writer was a relative of the popular feminist writer. In that book, he decided to break the mold by describing some witches (and their occult witchcraft) as good. It is fiction, but he put out the idea that there are bad witches, as well as good ones. And that idea took off from there. So, once again, there is Hollywood right there in our face, helping to promote the occult. And that is not all they are promoting, as we see here:

"Dianics pride themselves on the inclusion of lesbian and bisexual members. It is a goal within many covens to explore female sexuality and

sensuality outside of male control, and many rituals function to affirm lesbian sexuality, making it a popular tradition for women who have come out. Some covens exclusively consist of same-sex oriented women and advocate lesbian separatism."

It's an all-women movement, all the way around, and all the time. That's because men are bad, which fits with the exact same feminism belief.

So, that's a bit of their beliefs and practices. Now, let's talk about one of their most prominent leaders; the one attributed with founding Dianic Wicca, which is also known as feminist witchcraft:

Again, Zsuzsanna Budapest is not her real name, which is Zsuzsanna Emese Mokcsay. You can see why she chose Budapest. Like Laurie Cabot, she is still alive today. Part of the reason she chose Budapest is because she was born in Budapest, Hungary, in 1940.

"Zsuzsanna Emese Mokcsay (born 30 January 1940 in Budapest, Hungary) is a Hungarian author, activist, journalist, playwright, and songwriter living in America who writes about feminist spirituality."

Even today, when you hear or see the terms, "women's spirituality" or "feminist spirituality," those just mean witchcraft, which is why the women sucked into following that belief system are led to witchcraft.

"Zsuzsanna Emese Mokcsay writes about feminist spirituality and Dianic Wicca under the pen name Zsuzsanna Budapest or Z. Budapest."

"Dianic Wicca began on the Winter Solstice of 1971, when Budapest led a ceremony in Hollywood, California. Self-identifying as a 'hereditary witch,' and claiming to have learned folk magic from her mother, Budapest is frequently considered the mother of modern Dianic Wiccan, feminist witchcraft, tradition."

So, she is the underpinning of feminist witchcraft. She was also the founder of the Susan B. Anthony Coven in 1971. You may know that was another woman's suffragette movement, which tells you again that Budapest was combining feminism and witchcraft. Those terms are one and the same. Budapest also founded and directs the Women's Spirituality Forum. Let me translate that for you: "the Women's Witchcraft Forum."

"Budapest was the lead of a cable TV show called '13th Heaven.' Her play 'The Rise of the Fates,' as in the mythology of witches, premiered in Los Angeles in the mid-seventies. She is the composer of several songs including 'We All Come from the Goddess.' She lives near Santa Cruz, California."

Back in the day, I'd gone to Santa Cruz several times for pastors' conferences. If you've been there too, you know it's a beautiful place right by the ocean with a lot of wooded area. And in those woods, unfortunately, there is a whole lot of witchcraft going on. In fact, I'm going to go back to the very first chapter of this book for another look at a video transcript I shared with you. It actually involved Zsuzsanna Budapest's women's spirituality movement. As you read it again, this time you'll clearly understand what is going on with phrases like, "the goddess is alive." You will know who she's talking about. When they mention the circle of women and the magic they are creating, you'll understand what they mean. So, one more time, this is Budapest in action claiming it is about women's spirituality, rather than witchcraft, which you know is untrue:

A younger Zsuzsanna Budapest speaking to the camera: *"The women's movement today is being called the women's spirituality movement in great part. And that is because it's not just concentrating on areas of social and political reform, but it's looking hard and fast at spiritual reform. Women are gathering today in circles, just as their 1960 counterparts did in consciousness-raising circles. But now, they are not just knocking down that door to a man's world, asking for entrance. Instead, they are looking at the myths, spiritual beliefs, religions, values; everything that runs our culture, everything that feeds our souls. We are* *going to take a look at the women's spirituality movement as it's been called by the women participating in it, who are weaving new stories of a returning goddess. They believe she's back on the planet, alive, and well, and she could do a lot for you."*

The video shows a witches group meeting somewhere in the woods around a female goddess figure they've fashioned out of plants.

A more elderly Zsuzsanna Budapest says: *"The goddess is alive."*

Group response: *"Magic is afoot."*

Budapest yells: *"The goddess is alive!!"*

Group yells back: *"Magic is afoot!!"*

The witches are shown dancing in a circle, clapping, and playing bongos, as well as other instruments.

Witch: *"What the goddess means to me is wholeness and peace."*

Second witch: *"The goddess means to me, my internal strength. She has come to me and shown me the beauty that is within myself."*

Third witch: *"The goddess is my voice. She is my self-empowerment. She is my self-respect. As a result, my life has really undergone some major transformations, not only creatively, but in the pathway that I have now started to take. And I have the works of Z. Budapest to thank for that."*

Budapest is shown with the witches in a half circle as she loudly proclaims: *"The goddess is alive,"* over and over. The group of witches respond each time with, *"Magic is afoot."*

Actually, the goddess is a <u>lie</u>! What was going on there? The pitch is that it is just a group of feminists getting together. However, having learned as much as you have, what is really going on there? Who's the

goddess? What is this circle they create when chanting and dancing? If
you saw the video, you'd also see candles. Those are all witch practices.
Here's more on Z. Budapest, (feminist witch name):

Her mother, Masika Szilagyi, was a medium and her grandmother,
Ilona, was an herbalist and healer. Budapest had her first psychic
experience at age three, which was an apparition of Ilona at the time of
Ilona's death. Hey, that's because television is right when it keeps
showing dead people coming back to talk with their living relatives, right?
No! That's also a lie! What did three-year-old Budapest see? It's called a
familiar spirit and that's a demon. So, here an encounter may have
happened, so I won't discount that, but that wasn't your grandma, Miss
Budapest. Unfortunately, it was a demon duping you. The Bible is very
clear: When we die, as Christians, we go to Heaven. Do we come back?
No. And if we are not Christian at death, we go to hell. And there is no
coming back from that either. We can't travel back and forth. Something
can appear to us and even look or sound like our loved one, but it is just
the same old familiar spirit, one of the demons the Bible warns us about.

*"In childhood, Budapest appreciated nature, 'playing priestess' and
conducting her own rituals. She began her practice as a solitary,
worshiping the Goddess at a home altar."*

She eventually got married to a guy named Tom and moved to
New York with him, but it ended in 1970. Like Laurie Cabot, who had
two failed relationships with men, Budapest also had a failed relationship
which became a catalyst to avoid future relationships with men. I don't
know those guys in either woman's case or they very well could have been
bad men, but that doesn't mean all men should be avoided by women for
relationships. After that, Budapest went to California and started
developing her feminist, anti-man, and female-only witchcraft.

*"Budapest saw a need to develop a female-centered theology that not only
would help women but would answer opponents of the feminist movement
who claimed that feminism was 'against God.'"*

She began to spiritualize her witchcraft feminism as a supposedly legitimate religion. There in California, it began to take off so she held sabbats where the women would gather to do their rituals.

"The sabbats were looked upon as the crushing of an oppressive and aggressive patriarchy male system."

Hey, I wish she would have met a guy to have a better relationship with, but it should not have meant her swearing off all men.

"Within nine years, membership was at 700, and sister covens had formed across the country. For 10 years, Budapest led sabbats and full moon circles, initiating priestesses and teaching women to bless each other and connect with the goddess through Mother Nature."

Speaking of so-called, "mother nature," we could do a whole study just on the Environmental movement. Over the past few years, we dealt with that extensively in our *Final Countdown* Bible-prophecy studies. The environmental movement is another smoke screen to get people involved with female goddess worship (Gaia) and many other beliefs they push, just as long as it is something that gets people away from the Biblical God. They hook you by saying you will be saving the planet but, in reality, you'll be tricked into worshiping the planet and doing what God said not to do in the book of Romans. There God tells us we already have enough proof of His existence but still people reject Him, exchanging the truth for a lie.

Romans 1:25: *"They exchanged the truth about God for a lie and worshiped and served created things rather than the Creator who is forever praised. Amen."*

That is pagan worship in a nutshell. They will worship trees, fleas, bees, rocks, themselves, and anything else, as long as it is not the true Creator of all those things, which is God. Here are more of Budapest's efforts to spread witchcraft:

"Budapest opened a shop, The Feminist Wicca, in Venice, California, and self-published a book that became a basic text of Dianic Wicca, 'The Feminist Book of Lights and Shadows' (1975), a collection of rituals, spells and lore. The book later was sold to a publisher and was released as 'The Holy Book of Women's Mysteries: Feminist Witchcraft, Goddess Rituals, Spellcasting and Other Womanly Arts' (1989). Budapest was arrested in 1975 for giving a Tarot reading to an undercover policewoman. She was put on trial and lost, but the law prohibiting psychic readings was repealed nine years later. Budapest did not form or join another coven but developed herself as a speaker, teacher, media personality, author and psychic reader. For a time, she hosted a radio program in the Bay Area."

Like Laurie Cabot, Budapest still continues down this rebellious route today.

"She also continues to lead rituals and hosts her own cable television show, 13th Heaven."

She's got a slew of other books that I'm not going to mention but her impact with Dianic Wicca is seen in all the recruiting literature from her that has been successful at seducing women under the guise of feminism and female empowerment. She even put out college courses devoted to the goddess and women's spirituality movement (feminist witchcraft). We are told we can't have Christianity in our schools and colleges but, apparently, they can teach witchcraft just because they call it the goddess, or women's spirituality, to make it appear legitimate as a class. But it is just witchcraft! That manipulation of our young women into the occult is allowed, but we cannot let our children and young people know about Christianity. Today, with just a simple name change, they slip in their witchcraft to indoctrinate our kids, while claiming the mention of a Christian option is indoctrination. Late teens and young woman go off to school and get full-on indoctrinated into this Dianic Wicca version of witchcraft.

So, that is all about Budapest, who was one of the prominent leaders and there are others advancing Dianic Wicca, who also picked up on the feminist movement that came straight out of witchcraft. Let me give you another example of what was going on during this time from another witch promoting feminist witchcraft:

"What other way are you gonna smash the patriarchy male system than with some good old-fashioned witchcraft. Led by a woman named Robin Morgan, W.I.T.C.H (Women's International Terrorist Conspiracy from Hell) is my personal favorite example of women's liberation gone weird. 'WITCH lives and laughs in every woman from the W.I.T.C.H Manifesto.' WITCH is an all-woman 'Everything' and that is 'Everything' with a capital E. It is theater, revolution, magic, terror, joy, garlic, flowers, spells!

These women were angry, they were activists, and they really did not care what anyone thought of them. But they also did not have things like Twitter and Facebook to spread their message. So, if they were going to get media attention, they couldn't make something go viral on the Internet, so they had to make something go viral on the ground. Hence, the witches cast hexes and zaps. You make your own rules. You are both free and beautiful. You can make yourself invisible or evident in how you choose to make your witch self-known. Covens around the United States would get together, put on their WITCH gear, and go a hexing. 'Double, double, war and rubble, mess with women, you'll be in trouble.' Their zaps, as they refer to their demonstrations, included things like chanting around the New York federal building: 'Assisto justice lies changed in time, we curse the ground on which she died.'

And who could forget the time when they hexed the Wall Street financiers, and the next day the Dow Jones dropped by five points. Witches have always been women who dared to be groovy, courageous, intelligent, nonconforming, explorative, curious, sexually liberated, and revolutionary. I forgot, independent; also, independent. And it's also worth noting that the Women's International Terrorist Conspiracy from Hell, WITCH and all of their zaps and hexes and guerrilla theater, is following on the heels of a very successful 1968 Miss America Pageant, which you have probably heard about, even if you don't realize that you're hearing about it, because this gathering of feminists brought their bras, and aprons, and girdles, and other artifacts of what they considered to be restrictive femininity and threw them into a trash can on the boardwalk. And they wanted to light the whole thing on fire, but the cops were like, 'Nah y'all,' and they were like, 'Okay.' Witches were the first friendly heads and dealers, drug users and drug dealers, the first birth-control practitioners and abortionists. Feminist witches? Oh, they're real all right!"

So, from a different angle, another witch is admitting that feminist witches were behind the whole Women's Liberation movement, including abortion. In fact, most every liberal belief you can name is somehow tied to witchcraft. And witches admit it!

Now, Dianic Witchcraft (Wicca) is not just being spread here in America; they want to take it global. Let me quote more of what Zsuzsanna Budapest says and it begins with her reference to the Biblical God she refers to as patriarchal monotheism:

"Patriarchal monotheism has worked to the detriment of women; it has glorified war and has permitted suffering for all. Her vision for the future is that of peace and abundance, expressed in female values, to dominate the world's consciousness. Global Goddess Consciousness means acknowledging the oneness of all as children of one Mother, our beloved blue planet, the Earth, a female goddess."

So, what's their plan? What's their panacea to fix the ills of society? They tell us we need to get rid of this male, patriarchal God and switch to a female deity that will supposedly usher in an age of utopia. As crazy as that sounds, that is what they're working towards.

And that brings us to the future aspect of this Dianic Wicca with a lot of folks wondering if it may have a bit to do with Scriptural prophecies in **Revelation 17** about the Harlot system, or one world religious system, that will work with the Antichrist. Some would say that the feminine term, "harlot," is not by chance because that might be what this one world religion will be promoting at that time of the Seven Year Tribulation. That movement might be telling us to shed our male, patriarchal God and follow a female goddess instead.

Revelation 17:3-6: *"Then the angel carried me away in the Spirit into a wilderness. There I saw a woman sitting on a scarlet beast that was covered with blasphemous names and had seven heads and ten horns. The woman was dressed in purple and scarlet, and was glittering with gold, precious stones and pearls. She held a golden cup in her hand, filled with abominable things and the filth of her adulteries. The name written on her forehead was a mystery: BABYLON THE GREAT, THE MOTHER OF PROSTITUTES, AND OF THE ABOMINATIONS OF THE EARTH. I saw that the woman was drunk with the blood of God's holy people, the blood of those who bore testimony to Jesus."*

The system is going to go after anyone who does not go along with their system, which includes those saved after the Rapture during the Seven Year Tribulation. That time will be a bloody mess with the Harlot system getting drunk on the blood of Christian people. Do we already see some of that with human sacrifice during today's occult practices? Unfortunately, yes. So, this passage is about the last-days, global-Harlot, and one-world-religion system that initially works with the Antichrist up until a point when God judges the Harlot during the Seven Year Tribulation. As we read further into **Revelation 17 and 18**, we see that God judges the Harlot and allows the Antichrist to overtake and burn her with fire. But initially, she's the one in charge because it's her that is pointed out as the one riding the Beast. At first, she is in control as she professes to be building a utopia along with a political figure out of a revived Roman Empire.

Also, some contend that there is even more here than female-goddess ("Harlot") worship. That is also an analogy used in the Bible about those times when Israel turned away from God and sold themselves to other nations' false deities. That was considered prostitution, or harlotry, which is typically a female figure. The analogy certainly fits. It is about a kind of spiritual fornication or spiritual prostitution, if you will. So, there is that element, as well.

As mentioned, some also see this future Harlot system going the way of the feminine-goddess worship, which contributes to it being so blasphemous. On top of those aspects, when we think about all this witchcraft we have been studying, (like Dianic Wicca), our world surely seems ripe to move away from patriarchal (male) God worship to a female-goddess worship. There are a multitude of angles pointing that way in our world today so I want to quickly give you a couple of those: First is the religion that makes up close to a quarter of a billion people today: The Roman Catholic Church. And leaders teach them to worship an entity they call Mary. With that in mind, do you think Catholics would go along with the idea of worshiping some sort of a female deity? I think they would slide right into it.

Some Eastern religions have a "Yin and Yang" principle that involves male and female duality. So, they are primed to jump on board. As we saw earlier, Hinduism has female deities like the goddess, Kali, that none of us would want to take out for lunch because she was all about blood and gore. She is just one of many female goddesses in Hinduism, which demonstrates a propensity toward female deities from another huge chunk of the planet. Do you think they would go along with the one world Harlot system? Absolutely!

Speaking of the Antichrist and the Woman that rides the Beast, many believe the former comes out of a revived Roman Empire, which would be Europe. The European Union has picked their new symbol, which just happens to be a woman riding a beast. Of all things they could have chosen, why specifically that? And it's not just depicted with their statues. That new symbol also appears on their magazine and coinage. The idea behind it all is to supposedly build a utopia, where all countries and all religions of the world can come together, just as this pamphlet with the European Union symbol tells us:

Their "Europe4All" star has all the different religions. That is their big plan. So, the push to bring all the world's people together under one umbrella, is not only a political effort: it's also a religious movement. And hey, if you just rotate that star a little bit, what do you have? I'm not saying it is the devil's star, but that can easily be seen in it. That's kind of interesting too.

What about the New Age and Environmental movements? What do they worship? It's another feminine deity, Mother Earth. Those huge swaths of our world's population, along with what we are seeing in this chapter on Dianic Wicca, and even general Wicca witchcraft, is all about worship of a goddess.

So, when you analyze the playing field, much of our planet and especially those open to witchcraft, are ripe for this switch-over to a feminine deity. It's almost like there has been a plan for that, just as the Bible warns us. And on top of all that, dare I say, even the Church is going along with this. We already saw witches claiming to be Christians. I'm sorry, but they are not Christian. Still they call themselves "Christian witches" as they go straight to worshiping a coming feminine deity. And that reminds me of what God's Word tells the Church about what will happen to them during the last days:

2 Peter 2:1-2: *"But there were also false prophets among the people, just as there will be false teachers among you. They will secretly introduce destructive heresies, even denying the sovereign Lord who bought them— bringing swift destruction on themselves. Many will follow their shameful ways and will bring the way of truth into disrepute."*

You might be thinking that churches openly promoting female-goddess worship, cannot happen. But we've already seen this in the Church, and I'll give you a couple of quick examples. With this first one, I'll just be blunt: these people claim to be Christians but, I'm sorry, if you really believe what I'm about to share with you, you are not Christian. And I think it is pretty apparent here with what this lady says, who considers herself to be a "Christian feminist." For those wondering, that phrase is what we call an oxymoron. Other classic examples of an oxymoron pairing are, "icy hot," "peaceful war," and "yummy chicken." These things do not exist. But let's move on to what this "Christian" feminist, Mary Daly, says about traditional Christianity:

"To put it bluntly, I propose that Christianity itself should be castrated..."

Can you sense anger here? Here's more:

"The primary focus of the 'Christian' feminist is to bring an end to what they perceive as a male-dominated religion. She continued by saying, 'I am suggesting that the idea of salvation uniquely by a male savior perpetuates the problem of patriarchal oppression.'"

Your suggestion won't change the fact that there is only one Savior, He is male, and His name is Jesus. And if you want to disagree with that Biblical reality, it means you are not trusting in Jesus, which shows you're not saved.

The apostasy gets worse with www.herchurch.org and what I'm going to mention was still on their website when I checked recently. It's from Ebenezer Lutheran Church in San Francisco where they open their sanctuary on Wednesday nights for the:

"'Christian Goddess Rosary.' They say, 'The exclusive emphasis of God as Father supports a domination structure that oppresses and subordinates women.'"

"They also encourage people to pray the 'Hail Goddess Prayer' that states, 'Hail Goddess full of grace. Blessed are you and blessed are all the fruits of your womb. For you are the MOTHER of us all.'"

That is nuts! This next quote shows how they want to deny who God is because they'd rather lie to children then tell them the truth of a male God. Jan Clanton, author of *God, A Word for Girls and Boys*, says this:

"Masculine God language hinders many children from establishing relationships of trust with God. In addition, calling God 'he' causes boys to commit the sin of arrogance... Calling the Supreme power of the universe 'he' causes girls to commit the sin of devaluing themselves. For the sake of 'these little ones' we must change the way we talk about God."

No, we must not! The truth is that He is God the Father, as well as God the Son and God the Spirit. You may not like that reality, but it won't change anything. You are entitled to an opinion but not your own facts. And God makes the rules. That is why He's called God. I don't know what your relationships with men have been in the past, and I'm sorry if they've been bad, but not all guys are undesirable and even if they all were, God is a wonderful, loving Father that you need to turn to, even now, and be rescued from the deception you're living under.

Of course, another heresy still being promoted in the Church is *The Shack*. It's one of the hottest books out there, and it's not only openly New Age in its doctrine, but actually presents God as a woman. That is in the Church, folks! So, dare I say, those espousing that are "professing" Christians, who will be left behind at the Rapture of the Church because they are not real Christians. There are a lot of people who go to church services and profess to know Christ, but they don't belong to Him. Those people are going to march right into the Seven Year Tribulation with their propensity for a female deity. So, if there is a societal change toward female (goddess) worship, even so-called "Christians" (in name only) are going to go along with that during the Seven Year Tribulation. All true Christians will be gone at the Rapture. And this whole feminine deity scenario is already being heavily promoted worldwide.

And if you don't think witches are also taking control of churches, you're wrong. This is an excerpt from a pastor warning about the influx of witchcraft into our churches:

"The Christian church is now facing a head-on confrontation with the powers of darkness, witches. The spiritual battle in which we are now engaged has sharply increased in intensity during the last few years. The

sad fact is that most sleepy Christians are so busy enjoying the world, they are almost completely oblivious of what is going on. The stark fact is that the forces of darkness, witches, are now clothing themselves in human form and sitting in our congregations, singing in choirs and working in various departments of our churches. Some witches appear content to just sit in congregations and mumble their incantations."

Hey, look they are speaking in tongues, right? Wrong! They may be spitting out their ritual-witchcraft verbiage right there next to you.

"...while others go out of their way to gain acceptance in a church and then carefully work their way into positions of influence. In fact, one practicing Satanist high priest had successfully gotten himself elected as Secretary of a Baptist church. A witch with well-developed ESP can walk into any church and immediately sum up the situation."

They know who is a real Christian, and who's not, so they can go to those who are not and manipulate them to cause destruction in that church. This is what he says is going on, and I fully believe it, especially with some of the things we have seen and experienced here at Sunrise Bible Church over the years. I do not think it's all just by chance. I think it is all part of the spiritual warfare. Here is more:

"It would not be possible to pass a 'phony' Christian off onto an experienced witch. A witch is usually quicker to pick if a person is a Christian then a Christian is to discern the fact that she's a witch. A witch with well-developed clairvoyance can discern 'lustful relationships' in a church without being told and then exploit them for satan. This is done by putting spells on the minds of people so that the people are always 'tired' and cannot think properly. They can afflict Christians with a whole variety of illnesses. Powerful witches can sometimes fix their gaze on a person and 'charm' that person in a way similar to that of an Indian snake-charmer handling a cobra. If she succeeds in doing this, she will then proceed further and get the person to do her bidding."

Remember, we are talking about what is going on inside the Church and during church services. This is not something out in the public.

"A witch will buy the loyalty of people by giving them presents, sometimes very expensive presents. By this method, witches gain a 'hold' over people. Witches can afflict people with deep oppression. This oppression can be so severe that the person concerned loses all desire to live, death is preferable. Witches can cause a 'heavy, oppressive atmosphere' in a church meeting, so that people feel 'tired' and cannot concentrate on the message."

Have you had that happen? Obviously, I have a good vantage point to see the congregation as I preach. Yes, there have been some falling asleep, as well as others heading to the bathroom again even though they went right before the service. Still others seem antsy as they are up and moving around more than usual and make me wonder what is going on that day. People can seem perky at the beginning of the service but as soon as the sermon starts, they begin to fall asleep. My point is this: Is that all just by chance or is there something else contributing? I'm not trying to get us all freaked out whenever we're sitting in church services, but I think we've got to realize this spiritual warfare can happen. We can even be in a church service where a faithful pastor is truly preaching the Word of God, but if you don't pay attention because of so many distractions, or you're just falling asleep, you're going to get nothing out of it. Week, after week, after week, after week, in many churches today, this oppression is being done deliberately by anti-Christians sitting in our midst. Here is more on that:

"This 'oppression' can only be removed by the Lord's people praying against it. If they do not have sufficient knowledge of how it is done, or how to remove it, then the 'heavy' atmosphere will remain. Witches can send demons into churches to disrupt worship services and prayer meetings. They can set Christians against each other by gossip and slander. They can break up Christian marriages by seducing spouses or maneuvering them into a compromising situation. They can easily

demoralize weak Christians and cause them to fall away. They can display psychic abilities and deceive some Christians into thinking that their powers are God-given, which happens in the Charismatic movement. A powerful witch is able to create irrational fears in a person and also to increase pain. The witch does not have to be present to do these things. They can be done from a distance. Now if all this information is 'mind boggling' and some readers find it almost too incredible to be believed, I simply remind them that things are changing rapidly. Everything is changing! The whole structure of our society is in a state of spiritual upheaval and nowhere is this change more apparent than on the spiritual scene."

Here are some keys to notify you of a witch in the midst of your congregation:

"(1) They do not possess the fruits of the spirit, love, joy, peace, patience, kindness, gentleness, self-control, etc.

(2) They sometimes, though not always, wear occult jewelry, often hidden.

(3) They 'eyeball' people by maintaining a fixed gaze.

(4) Some witches practice 'charming' and may do this by an almost continual smile."

With that last one, they are trying to charm you. Here at Sunrise Bible Church, if that goofy smile lasts for more than thirty seconds, in love, we smack them. Seriously though, that kind of smiling Christian could just be a happy Christian. I hope that is the case but that can be another technique used by witches in a church. Here are more:

"(5) They will invariably avoid the true, born-gain, and Spirit-filled Christians because such Christians are a threat to them.

(6) Witches will attempt to buy loyalty by giving people gifts, often very expensive gifts—these gifts are sometimes given for no apparent reason.

(7) Witches go out of their way to cultivate a wide circle of friends in all walks of life. This is done deliberately so that in the event of 'anything going wrong' they will have a lot of people who will stand by them and defend them—and remember the fact that many of these people are already under the witch's control or at least obligated to her in some way."

So, the witch sets up relationships to enlist possibly needed defenders, who will come to their rescue if caught pulling off their sabotage. At the time of uncovering evil done by the witch, you can imagine the sorts of responses from those who have gotten close to the witch without knowing the occult secret. They will claim, "Oh, come on. She would never do that!" or, "He would never say that!"

"(8) Witches are liars. This is only natural because of their constant association with demons."

You can confront a witch on his or her true identity, or one of their dirty deeds, but they can still lie straight to your face. At the same time, those they've been working near and made friends with will come to their rescue, sincerely believing that undercover witch that is pretending to be part of the Church, would never do or say something awful like that. And then the victim of the witch's true actions can be made to look like a goober for pointing the undercover witch out. That can happen even when it was not some mistake by the well-meaning Christian but an actual ruse by someone involved in witchcraft. He concludes with this:

"Had we understood the Scriptures better, we surely would have expected this in the last days."

He is talking about having silent-saboteur witches and other occult practitioners infiltrating our Church services. How does knowing our Bibles help us with that? It's because the Bible warns that this will happen! However, since churches today do not preach on Bible prophecy or occult practices, no one understands what is happening under their nose. They do not even know what to look for. He goes on with his conclusion:

"Large numbers of Christians have lost their Biblical balance and do not see demons as being responsible for anything. They see corruption, crime, violence, immorality, and all kinds of perversion and just accredit it all to human nature."

So, they act like it's just a psychological aberration when it's really occult mischief.

"Unfortunately, the church in these last days has become so worldly and materialistic, that it is no longer any real threat to its enemies. I constantly hear Christians talk about 'spiritual warfare' and 'putting on the armor of God,' etc., but it would appear with most, their knowledge of these things is theoretical rather than experimental. They are familiar with the 'jargon' but that is as far as it goes."

Now, if you want proof of what I'm outlining here, Becky, from our Church here in Las Vegas, happened to be at a restaurant recently and took a photo of something that speaks to this stuff spreading. This photo Becky took is of a young lady in line. What is this young woman proudly displaying in public? She is saying, "Let's summon demons." Just like people here in Las Vegas will wear, "Go Vegas," or "Go Vegas Knights," or "Vegas Raiders," what is this young witch promoting for all to see? She's telling people to connect with demons. And even worse, she is including children in the practice, depicting kids sitting around a witch's circle and even one child laying on the satanic pentagram. What?! Oh, and you know what this woman was carrying right out in the open? It's the *Book of Spells*. Just as we Christians openly carry our Bible, or at least I hope we do, she was flaunting her demonic book. That is how commonplace the practice is becoming these days. Witches are no longer hiding it. She is saying, "I'm going to display my craft, even at a restaurant. That's what's going on, and we need to wake up to this reality.

And if you do not think they're actually trying to come into the Church, you are kidding yourself. Even in our church services, we have been disrupted many times. I'm not saying it's demonic every time, but I have no doubt that some have been the result of spiritual warfare. If we look at the conflicts we have had over the years, the testing we've gone through, and other weird things that have gone on, I don't think it's all been just natural occurrences. We do not have to be afraid of that spiritual evil because, as true born-again Christians, we pray, seek God, and stand in Him. We know that "Greater is He who is in me than he who is in the world." We don't need to be afraid, but we also don't want to be foolish and act like this evil doesn't go on. When it does happen, we need to deal with it! The worst thing a Christian in the Church can do is to know that there is a conflict going on and then do nothing about it. That issue is not always natural. It could be someone trying to take you out because you are doing the right thing. We do not have to be afraid, but let's also not be foolish.

And some of these spiritual warfare issues are why we live in a time that is being considered "The Season of the Witch." Notice it is not the season of the Christian because we're long gone. Instead, some say it's the season of the Witch. Let me give you a couple of parts of an article about that:

"Rapper Azealia Banks brought witchcraft back into the mainstream by tweeting 'I'm really a witch.' But women in the U.S. have been harnessing its power for decades as a 'spiritual but not religious' way to express feminist ambitions. Then Banks joked that racism might end a lot sooner if black people could make their enemies sicken and die with a thought."

How does the media and the public allow her to get away with a statement like that? And again, where is that leftist mentality of racism coming from? It is from witchcraft. The article goes on to say witchcraft stands for girl power and notice how all these cultural aspects are getting blended together into witchcraft:

"A popular Tumblr blog, 'Charmcore,' purports to be run by three witch sisters; it gives sarcastic 'magical' advice and praise of the female celebrities it deems to be 'obvious witches.' On the more serious side, teen sensation 'Rookie' magazine has published tarot tutorials along with more standard-issue feminist and fashion advice, and 'Autostraddle,' a popular left-leaning blog for young queer women, has an in-house tarot columnist.

'To reclaim the word witch is to reclaim our right, as women to be powerful... To be a witch is to identify with 9 million victims of bigotry and hatred and to take responsibility for shaping a world in which prejudice claims no more victims.'"

They want to reshape it in the image of their goddess (feminine) worship and away from any male-dominated doctrine. Here is more from a witch about how the merge happened with feminism and witchcraft:

"In the 1970's, with the resurgence of the feminist movement, a lot of us began to investigate a feminist spirituality and the goddess traditions of Europe and the Middle East."

There is the merger being explained by a practicing witch. Here is more from the article:

"Wicca, with its focus on a goddess, instead of a male God, and its relatively open approach to creating the canon, was a natural fit for many feminist women interested in writing their own spiritual script. Not only did women make feminist tarot cards in the 1970's, but feminist psychologists also wrote books on using goddess imagery and myths as means of understanding female subjectivity."

So, as we already know well from previous studies, secular psychology works at sucking people into occult practices. The article even admits that:

"With the spells and rituals, you can participate effectively in left-wing activism."

Just as we saw in a previous chapter, over the years, there has been a huge influx of occult practices into the Democrat party. Who is behind the leftist mentality being promoted in our country today? It's not just feminism; it's feminist witchcraft! Here is the last part of this article with witches making this claim:

"I think one of the biggest conspiracies of a male-dominated society is the suppression of feminine intuition."

Now put all those aspects of feminist witchcraft together and it tells you why so many witches absolutely cannot stand President Trump. They are not just praying against President Trump because these leftists disagree with him on abortion and all the other anti-God beliefs that, frankly, much of the Democrat movement now supports. On top of that it is really the double wrong he poses against them because he dares to be an outspoken and strong manly man. The last thing you can have in feminist or witchcraft circles is a manly man who will not bow a knee to women. That is the bigger reason as to why they hate the guy. And it is why they continue to pray against him to this day as they work at putting spells and hexes on him. In fact, here are two witch-store owners from Salem, Massachusetts, who are admitting they hate President Trump because he is a strong male figure and they can't allow that in their world of women-centered witchcraft:

Erica Feldman, owner of HausWitch: *"Witches have always been somewhat feminist. We have been fightin' for the right to be treated correctly."*

Lorelei Stathopoulos, owner of Crow Haven Corner: *"Witches are what men like Donald Trump are afraid of."*

Reporter: *"'Witches,' the word alone immediately conjures up certain images in our minds. But what does it really mean to be a witch today? Salem, Massachusetts, a place known for trying and executing accused witches, is now affectionately called 'Witch City.' And it seems that a* *growing number of young women and some men are being drawn to a brand of witchcraft and it's political."*

Feldmann: *"I use the term, witch, to describe myself. I usually cite the acronym, 'Woman in total control of herself.' I am the owner of HausWitch Home and Healing, in Salem, Massachusetts. I practice witchcraft. I pull tarot cards. I have crystals everywhere. I make shrines. I cast spells. I meditate. But it's sort of a political distinction and I think it, like, speaks to my radical feminism."*

Reporter: *"Both male and female witches are studying the craft under a longtime Salem witch and clairvoyant, Lorelei Stathopoulos. You'll notice a significant difference in how the more traditional witches look and practice."*

Stathopoulos: *"I'm what you call a natural witch. I started at about twelve. My mother practiced. The thing about the new word, 'feminist': It's a great thing but it's something that we've been doing for years."*

Feldmann: *"After the election, especially...You know, I think what the witch is good for is being a force of divine feminine power. And witches are what men like Donald Trump are afraid of. So, it's like this perfect symbol."*

Reporter: *"A coven has formed around Erica's store, made up of an astrologist, Reiki masters, and healers, including Erica's fiancée, Melissa, who does Salem witch tours with a feminist focus."*

Possibly the astrologist witch: *"This isn't your grandmother's coven. It's youthful, light, and trendy. Though some are embracing the word, the term, witch, has been used to ignite fear and shame."*

Reporter: *"It wasn't until early 20th century that women's magazines started portraying witches as beautiful and desirable. This trend continued with the success of the TV show, 'Bewitched', in the 60's. The 60's also brought us a feminist group, Women's International Terrorist Conspiracy* *from Hell, or WITCH, who protested patriarchy by carrying out witch-themed political stunts. In 1985, Wicca, an offshoot of witchcraft, was recognized as a religion by the United States. In recent years, we've seen witches and non-witches publicly reclaiming the title."*

Feldmann: *"The powerful are scared of this figure, who has, like, traditionally been pretty powerless. But now that's not the case."*

Reporter questioning Feldmann: *"Whether it's Trump or all these like sexual assault cases, do you think that actually ends up creating more witches?"*

Feldmann: *"Totally! The 'Me Too' movement, that's what you're seeing. It's dark. It feels bad. And now this is the only way that we are going to start to heal it; is by, you know, ripping this band-aid off and all coming together. And to me, that sounds like a coven of witches."*

Reporter: *"As young people become less religious in this country, witches like Lorelai and Erica continue to see their covens grow."*

Their mindset comes just in time for the Seven Year Tribulation. **Revelation 9** tells us there will not only be an increase of pharmakeia that goes along with sorcery and witchcraft, but if there is a societal switch to a feminine-deity worship, these people will most likely be in favor of it. And here is what the left is saying right now that demonstrates the spiritual battle we face:

"In the coming months, the results of the 2020 election will define the country for a generation. These are perilous times. Over the last four years with the Trump Administration, much of what we hold dear has been threatened. The country is at a crossroads. The Supreme Court hangs in the balance and with it, the future of abortion and voting rights, healthcare, climate policy and much more."

They admit that is what they believe and promote, while those standing in the way are President Trump and any Christian who would stand up for Biblical values. They admit we are in a spiritual war. So, we need to wake up. And we can sure feel it going into this 2020 election as the atmosphere is really coming to a boil. They are saying this is not just an election, but it's the future direction of our country. So, as a nation, are we going to continue to limp along, hopefully more towards God or at least back that way? Or are we going to go headlong over the cliff, falling into flat-out occultism? That is what is on the line with this election.

In the next chapter we'll focus on the beliefs and the practices of Wicca. What do Wiccans believe, what do they do when they gather together in their covens with their sabbats or esbats, and what kind of spells and ritual work do they practice

Chapter Sixteen

The Beliefs of Wicca

We have come a long way in our study of Wicca and other witchcraft, which has spread all around the world and the only protection from it is for Christians through the power of our reliance on Jesus. As we have journeyed through time, we realize witchcraft is nothing new since it, and other occult practices, began around the time of the Tower of Babel in Babylon, which was a couple hundred years after Noah and his family stepped off the boat after that worldwide flood. From there, when God's judgment confused the language, witchcraft spread to Egypt, Greece, Rome, Asia, India and the nearby island countries, Africa, Latin America, and Europe.

Europe is where witchcraft got renamed and repackaged to the present version called, "Wicca." And that is what we have to deal with in our world today. But it's just old-fashioned witchcraft. Wicca started in Europe with the grandmother of Wicca, Margaret Murray. Then it progressed through Gerald Gardner (the grandfather of Wicca), Doreen Valiente (the mother of Wicca), Raymond Buckland (the father of American Wicca on the East Coast), and then Sybil Leek on the West Coast, who was the celebrity of Wicca, helping to popularize witchcraft in

America. Leek was in Los Angeles where she mixed and mingled with celebrities involved with movies, media, music, and politics.

That method of spreading witchcraft is still being used today. Then we saw Wicca advance through Alexander Sanders, the so-called king of the witches, and a woman who is still alive today, at over eighty years of age. That woman, Laurie Cabot, continues promoting witchcraft as the official witch of Salem. Unfortunately, she is still involved politically, getting restraints removed so that Wicca witchcraft can be more and more accepted across the United States.

In the last chapter we looked at Dianic Wicca, which is synonymous with feminism. We traced the trail of the Feminist movement straight back to witchcraft. The founder and most prominent witch of Dianic Wicca is Zsuzsanna Budapest (Z. Budapest). Most Wiccan witches worship the Mother goddess, as well as the male Horned God. Contrary to that Wicca norm, Dianic Wiccans only worship the feminine deity. Their beliefs and practices are all about getting rid of any male influence in our world. Budapest has promoted that through all kinds of books, media, and other dissemination channels. Like Laurie Cabot, Budapest is also still alive today and, unfortunately, continues to advance witchcraft in our society.

As we learned, the push toward a feminine deity (Mother goddess worship) and away from worship of our male patriarchal God, fits exactly with the Bible's description of what the earth will be like in the last days, in **Revelation 17**. A lot of people on our planet are already lined up to accept a global goddess. Catholicism already worships Mary and Eastern religions worship many goddesses. There are also feminine deities in modern-day movements like New Age and Environmentalism with their worship of Mother Earth, or Gaia. Even the European Union is getting in on it, and that is where many believe the Antichrist comes from, through a revived Roman Empire. In fact, as another example of Biblical prophecy coming to life in our time, the European Union has already chosen their symbol of a woman (the Harlot) riding a bull (the Beast). They put that biblically evil entity on their statues, coins, and even a magazine. It's almost like someone is following a script, which they are, and it is that which God told us about long, long ago.

With the widespread increase in witchcraft, it is now even being promoted in our apostate Christian churches today. So-called "Christians" are wanting to "castrate" Christianity, which means getting rid of our male Savior. That is from their words, and it makes them another group, who will be ripe to fall for that lie involving the Harlot. All that has led to our secular media calling this time of mankind, the "Season of the Witch." Notice it's not the season of the Christian, God's truth, or a Christian revival. Instead, this is said to be the season of witchcraft. It is taking over our country, as some Christians wonder why we are even doing this witchcraft study.

That brings us to this chapter's information, which is about Wiccan witchcraft's beliefs and the practices. Before we get into that, let's see if somehow, some way, maybe through much fasting and many prayer conferences (with food included), we can come up with at least one more verse in the Bible that warns us against witchcraft. Do you think that is possible? Well, of course it is, and you knew that because you know warnings against witchcraft and other occult practice are all over the Bible, just like my sarcasm permeates this book. I want to give you one more in the long list of passages where the Lord lets us know not to get near witchcraft. The first **10 verses of Jeremiah 27** are what we'll read this time and it relates to the last chapter's passage with God telling us why Israel's 10 Northern tribes and two Southern ones, Judah and Benjamin, are sent into exile by judgment from God. Why did they lose their nations? We clearly saw they were practicing witchcraft, sorcery, and divination.

They tried blending those occult practices into their so-called worship with God. And now we are going to see what was happening during the Babylonian reign of Nebuchadnezzar, who later gets judged by God because our Creator always has the last word. Whoever gets out of line from our Lord's wishes, has a day of reckoning to follow. But before Nebuchadnezzar's fall, we're going to see how God uses him and has a word for the secular nations surrounding Jerusalem, telling them that He has installed Nebuchadnezzar to rule at that time over those secular nations that surround Jerusalem, just like God had Nebuchadnezzar spank Israel and Judah for their disobedience in getting involved with witchcraft. So, in Jeremiah, God is addressing those secular nations, telling them they need to listen to this Nebuchadnezzar guy and stop those, who are lying to them. And can you guess what practice the liars are deeply into? Of course, it's witchcraft. That's the context so now let's take a look at God's Word.

Jeremiah 27:1-10: *Early in the reign of Zedekiah a son of Josiah king of Judah, this word came to Jeremiah from the Lord: This is what the Lord said to me: "Make a yoke out of straps and crossbars and put it on your neck. Then send word to the kings of Edom, Moab, Ammon, Tyre and Sidon through the envoys who have come to Jerusalem to Zedekiah king of Judah. Give them a message for their masters and say, 'This is what the Lord Almighty, the God of Israel, says: Tell this to your masters: With my great power and outstretched arm I made the earth and its people and the animals that are on it, and I give it to anyone I please. Now I will give all your countries into the hands of my servant Nebuchadnezzar king of Babylon; I will make even the wild animals subject to him. All nations will serve him and his son and his grandson until the time for his land comes; then many nations and great kings will subjugate him. If, however, any nation or kingdom will not serve Nebuchadnezzar king of Babylon or bow its neck under his yoke, I will punish that nation with the sword, famine and plague, declares the Lord, until I destroy it by his hand. So do not listen to your prophets, your diviners, your interpreters of dreams, your mediums or your sorcerers who tell you, 'You will not serve the king of Babylon.' They prophesy lies to you that will only serve to remove you far from your lands; I will banish you and you will perish.'"*

So, even the secular countries sent into exile had that happen because they got involved with witchcraft. Like the twelve tribes of God's people, He also warns those gentiles that they better follow His directive and not get into occult witchcraft behavior. They too were being duped by lying witches, which is the nature of witches, who follow their lying father, the father of lies, satan. And that's why God, even way back in Deuteronomy, also warns those people not to follow the ways of witchcraft because it is demonic, and demons are liars. God does not want anyone led astray and so he is even warning these secular people not to listen to those involved in witchcraft. God tells them to follow the path He's laying out, and if they do so they will be fine. But if they listen to these lying witches, who have been advocating the exact opposite, it will lead to their destruction.

Having heard that extensive warning for those thousands of years ago, do you think God would have the same warning today for those who listen to witchcraft with its divination and sorcery that promotes the exact opposite of what God says? Do you think today's defiance of God will not hurt our well-being? Or will it lead to destruction as it always has? Of course, the outcome for the modern-day witches will be the same. God will be consistent in His judgment of them, and that is what we are going to see as we get into the details surrounding the beliefs and practices of Wicca witchcraft. Wiccans believe and do the opposite of what God tells us life is all about, who He is, and how we are supposed to live our lives.

The first aspect of Wiccan beliefs for us to understand, is that it's kind of hard to codify a particular core of Wicca because it's an eclectic belief system, which means that truth is left up to each individual to decide for themselves. As we have seen in other witchcraft and so many other faith systems outside of Christianity and the Bible, Wiccans are encouraged to make up their own reality, as if our Creator would allow us to change His creation. With their deluded feelings of control over reality, it's hard to get a true consensus that can be said to represent an overall description of Wiccan beliefs. As evangelical Christians, you and I have one source of truth, which is the Bible. We can all profess our belief in the virgin birth, the deity and humanity of Jesus Christ, God the Father, God the Son and God the Holy Spirit. We all believe in sola scriptura that says the Bible alone is our authority for faith and practice.

That is what makes Christianity solid, while Wicca has no such rock of truth, so they are allowed many possible beliefs to choose from.

What I am going to do in this chapter is give you prevailing beliefs that most Wiccans would say are core to their beliefs. I say it that way because the moment you start trying to pin Wiccans down to certain beliefs, invariably, some coven will say it's not what they follow. So, that's the challenge in attempting to define the eclectic path of Wicca that is based on relativism, which means whatever you believe is true to you, whatever I believe is true to me, and there is supposedly no problem with your truth contradicting mine. And that is really how they derive their witchcraft and occult practices, as well as the belief we're going to talk about next.

Wicca's relativistic and eclectic mentality started back in **Genesis 3,** when satan tempted Eve with a couple of lies. The devil placed doubt in Eve's mind about God's Word by posing the question of whether God really said what He said. Then he got her thinking about how good the fruit looked with its pleasing appearance. Unfortunately, her flesh stoked her pride for life; the feeling that her life should be all about what she would like. Then satan dropped another bomb on her by advising Eve not to follow what she thinks God might have said and just do what satan tells her. Lucifer wanted her to become a rebel like him against God. He convinced her of that by claiming she too could be like God, deciding whether something is either good or evil.

From that one Biblical event thousands of years ago through the writing of **Genesis 3**, relativism began and has become a way of life for billions today, including Wiccans. When you see people living that philosophy in our time, they are following the same false path that caused the fall of man. Again, that mindset is the basis of Wiccan witchcraft. They make it up as they go. So, let us talk generally, even though beliefs are inconsistently scattered throughout practicing Wiccans.

Wiccans don't view their religion as necessarily a reversal of, or reaction to, Christianity. And they are certainly not, as many Wiccan's claim, a pre-Christian practice. We blew that one out of the water early in this book. As we saw at the beginning of our look at witchcraft history, it began with all other occult practices at the Tower of Babel, which was way after the first Christian history laid out in Genesis. Pagan occult witchcraft began a couple hundred years after Noah's Flood, after which wicked Babylon's sewage pipe of evil spread out to the world and gives us the witchcraft we have today. So, the Biblical account starts way before Wicca or any other witchcraft. Try as they might, their claim of being older than Christianity is bankrupt, but it is a widespread Wiccan belief.

"Contemporary witchcraft is so diverse and eclectic...that it is extremely difficult to accurately identify and define. In fact, it is almost impossible to state that all witches believe 'this or that.' No sooner will this be uttered then someone will speak up and assert that they are a witch and 'do not believe what you just stated.' There are, however, commonalities shared by most who appropriate the word 'witch' for themselves."

Most Wiccans believe in what is called the "Creed of No Creed," which is the idea that we can derive truth through experience. For determining what they hold as truth, experience is everything to Wiccans. Their creed of no creed is that they follow no dogma. Instead, it's all about what their experience tells them to do or how to feel. Experience rules the day, as their guide on the path to all truth. Hey, wait a minute, do we know any group in the Church that does the same? Yes, and it rhymes with charismatics. Yet we wonder why they are starting to slide straight into witchcraft. As we saw in our huge, detailed study called, *Charismatic Chaos*, the charismatics' whole basis of operation is exactly the same as witchcraft; truth supposedly comes from each individual's life experience.

In fact, just like charismatics, witchcraft advocates followers getting into an altered state of consciousness to have a "mystical experience," or supposedly create a "oneness with everything." Charismatics even rely on their experience over God's Word in the Bible. In fact, they say the Bible is dogma and they supposedly do not need to follow its truth because they will just let the "spirit" of God lead them through their experiences. Whether that "spirit" is really from God or demonic does not enter their equation. That process is the same with witchcraft. And since we have extensively studied both, it is apparent that their belief systems perfectly merge.

And that belief by Wiccans, that life is all about experience, leads to a second belief they adhere to, which is supposedly tolerance:

Hey, tolerance is a prominent buzz phrase for these days, right? But the definition has been thrown into confusion these days. Literal tolerance, or historical tolerance, is what you and I understand as putting up with a belief system that we do not necessarily agree with. But today's new definition of tolerance tells us that we are intolerant if we do not accept and even heartily promote everyone's belief system. We must profess that all belief systems are equally valid and admirable as our own. So, when you see or hear tolerance talked about through the media and in our school system today, that new definition is what they mean. You and I think we should be fine to put up with other's aberrant beliefs and practices. It is what we have always heard: "Love the sinner and hate the sin." But today, that is one of the most bigoted statements we can make because they tell us that means we are not accepting and endorsing everyone's choice of beliefs and lifestyle. But that is ridiculous, and it is the core of Wicca and all other Witchcraft. Their idea is that everyone can just make their own reality and all others need to accept whatever anyone claims because anything goes for everyone, no matter your background and preferences, including sexuality. It's "come one, come all!" Just make it up as you go! Here is more about how witches at least say they are tolerant:

"Tolerance is another highly touted value among witches. Diversity of belief and practice is viewed as not only healthy but essential to the survival of humanity and planet earth, and to spiritual growth and maturation as well. Independence, autonomy, and the freedom to experience, believe, think, and act as one desires are defended as if they were divine rights."

So, tolerance is a core Wiccan belief just as experience is. They say, "You have no right to tell me what to do. I can do, believe, practice, and have whatever I want. You cannot say I can't." But just like the others in our society who are hypocrites for promoting tolerance, and then not following their own principle, when it comes to tolerance of those who don't agree with them, witches do the same. Those touting this new definition of tolerance today, including witches, do not even follow it themselves:

"Witches do become intolerant, however, when they perceive intolerance and authoritarianism in other individuals and faiths (which they would term 'religious imperialism'). So we have statements like number ten of the Council of American Witches' 'Principles of Wiccan Belief': 'Our only animosity toward Christianity, or towards any other religion or philosophy-of-life, is to the extent that its institutions have claimed to be 'the only way' and have sought to deny freedom to others and to suppress other ways of religious practice and belief.'"

I didn't claim it to be the only way. Jesus did! Here is what He says.

John 14:6: *"Jesus answered, 'I am the way and the truth and the life. NO one comes to the Father except through me.'"*

Those are Jesus' words so I'm only reporting what He said. But as you can see, their core premise and basis to live their life on is supposedly accepting (from the heart) whatever anyone and everyone wants to do and believe. If you want to say your core principle is that, then why do your own words, (not mine), speak animosity towards what I believe? It is hypocritical but also common in our world today, telling us we must tolerate everyone's choices, beliefs and lifestyle, but then not reciprocating that for me? If you really believe in complete tolerance, as you say you do, then why do you have animosity toward me? As a Christian, why can't you tolerate me believing what I want to believe? But those preaching tolerance in our society today do not even live up to their own request of us, and that includes witchcraft with this aspect of their supposed core belief of tolerance.

"These beliefs stem from the notion that ultimately there is no right or wrong religion or morality. Relativism in all areas of life, including ethics and metaphysics, is the rule. Truth is what is true for you; right what is

right for you; but neither are necessarily so for me. The only absolute is that there are no absolutes."

The moment you say there are no absolutes, you just made an absolute statement. You can't get away from it. In other studies, we've blown away this whole theory of no absolutes because it's not just hypocritical and those who push it don't even live it, but those who do, base their belief in this new relativistic definition of tolerance, which is a ridiculous principle. They say we each get to determine truth because there is no right and wrong, which means they cannot tell me something different then I tell them; and vice versa. Does that even work? What if I tell them my world says $2 + 2 = 5$, and I do not care if they believe it is 4? From their heart they need to accept my math. Yet, even in our secular school system, if a child answers a test question that way, what grade would the child receive? It rhymes with "F" and they would get that every time. That answer is wrong! Would the relativists come back at that F and claim the teacher is a judgmental math bigot? You can see how ridiculous relativism is.

What if we were relativistic with our science? Hey, on my next trip to speak somewhere I think I will just jump out of the plane without a parachute, because I feel like I am able to fly. You have heard the song, "I Believe I Can Fly," right? Well, my experience with that song was so profound that my reality says I too can fly. But what would happen if I took that action based on that belief that I have from my experience? There is a scientific law that is absolute, and it is called gravity. I would find out real fast that my feeling from that experience was a lie. I can believe my own science all I want and even flap my arms, but the reality is that I would be road pizza. I can call doubters intolerant science bigots for not believing I can fly, but that does not lessen the outcome of me plummeting to the ground like a dart. So, the whole relativistic reality is ridiculous.

Can you imagine if someone used relativistic math to build an airplane? Would you fly with them even for a cheap ticket? No! So, why would we trust that method for the more important spiritually eternal matters? Do you think it could suddenly start working for that when it's not trustworthy for anything else? When it comes to any moral matters, why would we think it should work all of a sudden? But I want to say this to Wiccans: As a practicing witch, a Wiccan, you don't follow your own supposed core beliefs because, according to your own definition of tolerance (moral relativism), you are bigoted toward me and all other Christians.

So, Wiccans' core beliefs stem from their individual experience and so-called tolerance with the latter resulting in moral relativism. All that develops into their ethics. And it's no surprise those ethics from their belief system do not include the concept of sin. Of course, they don't because, in their world, there would be no sin. So, they just make that their (false) belief. Also, the reality they think they have made for themselves does not include evil. What?! We will get into that in a minute.

"Sin is viewed as an outdated concept that is 'only a tool used to shackle the minds and actions of people.' The only 'sin' or evil is that of being unbalanced and out of harmony or estranged from oneself, others, the varied life forms, and Mother Earth."

According to your definition of sin, which is not right, but I'll play your game to make a point, you are sinning when you are out of balance with my belief system and how you treat me because of it. So, since you have animosity for Christians like me, you are a sinner! And that is from your own definition, which you do not even live up to.

Here is more on their claim that sin is being out of harmony with others, including Christians, and how there is supposedly no hell:

"As there is no sin or divine retribution to be saved from, 'salvation' has only to do with attaining and maintaining harmony with the above."

Again, you're not maintaining harmony because you won't accept my belief system. Also, when it comes to Wiccan ethics, though it's hard to codify because some branch or coven might say they don't follow any particular ethic, almost all of them rely on what's called the "Wiccan Rede."

"Rede" means "advice" and it basically goes back to their claim of harming none while doing whatever they'd like. And in their rede, they even invite a stinger on themselves by vowing to live a life where they only use their occult abilities in ways that will not harm anyone. Here is what they vow:

"Any evil done to another will come back upon the perpetrator threefold or more, in some form of reincarnation."

So, they believe the harmful use of their witchcraft will mess up their supposed reincarnation afterlife, which the Bible does not teach. Contrary to reincarnation, Scripture says:

Hebrews 9:27: *"Just as man is destined to die once, and after that to face judgment..."*

So, when we die, we go one of two places: Heaven or hell; and we will not be coming back. So, we have one chance to get it right. Instead of that reality told to us by God, Wiccans follow the Hinduism belief that doing harm to others, (witches do it through witchcraft), is going to mess up a witch's karma and make him or her have to keep coming back to fix their issue. They claim they do not use occult powers for evil because of this Wiccan Rede, but is that really what they practice? This is another core area of their belief system where they are hypocritical because they do use their occult so-called powers to influence, manipulate, and try to harm people. Those are not just my accusations because their own words testify to that with their hexes and curses. What about those? How is that not harming anyone? Again, it is more hypocrisy when they won't even live up to their own belief system.

Now, let me give you another example of Wiccans doing harm to people. And remember, this is on top of the fact that we've been told. Witches are putting so-called hexes on us here at Sunrise and Get A Life

Media for doing this study, as well as what we saw earlier with the British witch on that television show who was demonstrating for anyone to replicate, how to cast specific spells to make a man go away or do whatever she wants him to do. We also saw, more than once, how witches here in the United States of America are praying against our President. Again, how are any of those instances not harming anyone? As we saw in the history of witchcraft, it is all around the world and today, witches are even networking together through the use of modern technology to hex politicians like President Trump and others, everywhere on the planet. Witches all over the earth are trying to influence the government everywhere, as this added video-transcript example shows with their efforts to cause physical harm to people:

A group of European witches hold hands and move in a circular motion inside a ring of fire.

Head Witch, Mihaela Minca: *"All politicians who are here under my spell will fall sick in their beds if they don't keep their word and banish corruption from this country. Amen."*

Narrator: *"Mihaela Minca claims to be the most powerful witch in Europe. Back in 2016 she made a political prediction that Romanian politics was going to burn. Soon after, the country exploded into some of the biggest protests since the fall of communism, with up to half a million people taking to the streets. Today, Romania is still facing challenges. Governmental corruption is the biggest. It's such a problem, in fact, that the nation's witches and wizards have had enough and are uniting to cast the most powerful spell to punish corrupt politicians."*

Witch follower of Minca: *"Mihaela is preparing the next stage of the spell and needs to borrow two goats from the house of the village's oldest enchanters. She also needs the help of the local wizards."*

Male Wizard: *"Put the goats in the middle."*

Minca: *"Good."*

Male Wizard: *"They are so cute."*

Minca: *"I've decided to have the blessing and support of three wizards. They will help and support me, during this powerful ritual. They will protect me."*

Wizards walk goats around the streets and then Minca holds up an animal heart.

Minca: *"Here we have the heart of a beaten ox, the hair of a dead man, shells I was given by a wizard from America, (Los Angeles), and black goats. We will use them, and the wizards will master them. Through these two animals we will summon the spirit of the devil. Let the animals be with power. Let us bring all the spirits. I will be supported by other wizards from the USA who will soon enter a direct transmission with us."*

On her smartphone, Minca visually connects to a wizard in the U.S.

Witch assistant: *"Hello, can you hear her?"*

Minca addressing the U.S. witch: *"Are you ready for my ritual, and to support us in our spells?"*

Narrator: *"But why are witches getting involved in politics? And do Romanian politicians believe in witchcraft? We sent Stefania Matache from 'VICE Romania' to find out."*

Stefania Matache interviewing Minca: *"Does the curse work on people who do not believe?"*

Minca: *"Yes, of course."*

Stefania: *"God help us!"*

But don't worry, they say they are all about doing whatever they want as long as no one is harmed. They claim they do not use their powers to harm anyone, so let's just pay attention to that claim and not what they actually say and do, which is the opposite. How many examples do we have to give of them practicing hard while professing not to? Even if you want to characterize their so-called Rede as their "ethics," they do not even follow that. Here is what one guy said:

"The witches' ethical code is therefore inconsistent with their metaphysical world view."

Turn to someone or your cat and say, "That is the understatement of the year." Their rede (advice) is seen in a few different forms:

"and it harms none, do what thou wilt." "and it harms none, do as thou wilt." "that it harms none do as thou wilt." and "Do what you will so long as it harms none."

And again, they violate every single one of those. Where does this Wiccan Rede come from? Well, it goes back to a familiar name. It just happens to be similar to Aleister Crowley's phrase, "Do what thou wilt, shall be the whole of the law," which also appears in literature from many other prominent witch icons of history like Murray, Gardner, and Valiente. And that is also the number one rule of Satanism, which is all about self. The idea started way back in **Genesis 3** and it is a whole mandate for living, that is followed by Wiccans.

"Whether witches realize it or not, these views raise some very problematic ethical issues."

Let's begin to analyze those problematic issues with Wiccan ethics where they claim they can just make it up as they go and no one has the right to tell them what to do, yet, they have a rede that they say everyone should follow. Here are some of those issues:

"(1) Where does the Wiccan Rede derive from?

(2) If there is 'not one right religion, way, or truth for all,' then why is this rule (the Wiccan Rede) universal? How do we know that witches are not just trying to impose their rule on us to 'shackle our minds and actions,' with the ethical rede they say you should live by?

(3) How do witches account for the origin and existence of evil and suffering?"

How do they work around their obvious hypocrisy? They do not live by their belief system with its supposed tolerance and the Wiccan Rede that they claim to follow. Instead, they use witchcraft for rotten things. But apparently that is somehow okay with them because they say there is no evil. All the destructive actions they take through their occult practices (that are meant to harm and manipulate others against their will), in theory, are not evil, according to them. Let us examine more of what this guy says:

"Does evil exist? Is evil only an illusion? Or is evil not really evil, but just unfortunate circumstances? These views are delusions. To say evil does not exist is to be blind to reality, for evil not only exists—it is all around us. From cruelty, corruption, calamity, flood and famine, disease and drought, hatred, war, suffering, misery, pain, injustices, rape, murder, and on and on—evil exists. Evil is a fact of life."

In fact, when did evil take a foothold with each witch's life? It was right when he or she gave in to satan's false claim that they can do whatever they want, even if it goes against their Creator's directives for living. That initial lie from the father of lies is where all this started, and they have bought into it. People want to lament this earth with its tragic issues, but God didn't create this fallen world with its chaos! This messed up version is what happens when people listen to satan, who was the initial rebel in **Genesis 3**. And that is what witches promote as their way of life. There is evil and he goes on to say:

"The existence of evil delivers a debilitating blow to the witches' world view."

Moving on, Wiccan witchcraft has three pillars to their world view with the first being a belief in Animism:

Animism is the belief that everything has a so-called life force, along the line of the *Star Wars* movies, as we dealt with in our *Buddhism* study.

"Animism is an important pillar of the witches' world. As used by them, the word means that the 'Life Force' is imminent within all creation: rocks and trees, deserts and streams, mountains and valleys, ponds and oceans, gardens and forests, fish and fowl; from amoeba to humans and all things in between."

According to them, even chickens have this so-called life force, as do bacteria and amoebas because animism is about all things supposedly being animated. Is it true? No! Let's take a look at what the Bible tells us about their idea of everything having a life force:

Romans 1:18-25 *"The wrath of God is being revealed from heaven against all the godlessness and wickedness of people, who suppress the truth by their wickedness, since what may be known about God is plain to them, because God has made it plain to them. For since the creation of the world God's invisible qualities—his eternal power and divine nature— have been clearly seen, being understood from what has been made (designed by the supreme Designer, God,) so that people are without excuse. For although they knew God, they neither glorified him as God nor gave thanks to him, but their thinking became futile and their foolish hearts were darkened. Although they claimed to be wise, they became fools and exchanged the glory of the immortal God for images made to look like a mortal human being and birds and animals and reptiles. Therefore, God gave them over in the sinful desires of their hearts to sexual impurity for the degrading of their bodies with one another. They exchanged the truth about God for a lie and worshiped and served created things rather than the Creator—who is forever praised. Amen."*

So, their belief in animism doesn't hold water because everything has been created by God and certainly not through some man-conceived idea of a mystical life force. And animism's supposed life force bleeds into their world view's second pillar called, "Pantheism."

As we've seen before, "pan" means "all" and "theism," or "Theos," is "God." So, they claim all has life force because all is God. Really? They are trying to convince us that we should believe God is made of all things, including trees, fleas, bees, and you and me. But that does not make sense because **Romans 1** just told us that everything came from God, not everything is God. And the created things we see should draw us to the knowledge that someone had to have designed it all. So, the Designer, the Creator, is who we should worship, not the things He made. That mistake of worshiping created things is what brings the wrath of God and it is exactly what witchcraft prescribes. They bow to things as if they are God. But there is only one God, who brought everything into existence. Contrary to that reality, here is how Wiccans take it even further:

"Divinity is inseparable from, and imminent in, nature and humanity. Since most witches teach that we are divine (or potentially so), it is clear why someone like Margot Adler, a witch herself, approvingly quotes a particular neopagan group's greeting to its female and male members respectively: 'Thou art Goddess,' 'Thou art God.'"

What does that sound like? We dealt with this same type of greeting in our study, *Hinduism and the Dangers of Yoga*. That Hindu greeting, which is even sneaking into churches, is one you are probably familiar with. It is "Namaste" and means "I bow to the God in you." As a Christian, you do not want to say that! But it is the mindset witches have. That core belief from Hinduism, which is also a pillar of witchcraft, holds no water. Both reality and common sense tell us that all is not God because there is only one God, Who is Supreme. Here is some proof of that:

Deuteronomy 4:35: *"You were shown these things so that you might know that the Lord is God; besides him there is no other."*

Deuteronomy 4:39: *"Acknowledge and take to heart this day that the Lord is God in Heaven above and on the earth below. There is no other."*

Deuteronomy 6:4-8: *"Hear, O Israel: The Lord our God, the Lord is one. Love the Lord your God with all your heart and with all your soul and with all your strength. These commandments that I give you today are to be on your hearts. Impress them on your children. Talk about them when you sit at home and when you walk along the road, when you lie down and when you get up. Tie them as symbols on your hands and bind them on your foreheads."*

Deuteronomy 13-15: *"Fear the Lord your God, serve him only and take your oaths in his name. Do not follow other gods, the gods of the peoples around you; for the Lord your God, who is among you, is a jealous God and his anger will burn against you, and he will destroy you from the face of the land."*

1 Kings 8:60: *"So that all the peoples of the earth may know that the Lord is God and that there is no other."*

Isaiah 44:8: *"Did I not proclaim this and foretell it long ago? You are my witnesses. Is there any God besides me? No, there is no other rock; I know not one."*

Isaiah 45:5: *"I am the Lord, and there is no other; apart from me there is no God."*

So, witches and Hindus can live like they are God, but I don't recommend it because after their last breath, they will find out they have not been God. And neither is the tree that their casket will be made from. At that moment they will be standing before the One and only God, Who they had a chance to freely get right with by His grace through Jesus Christ, yet, they said, "No." At that point it will be too late.

The third pillar of witchcraft is polytheism, which is the worship of multiple deities. "Poly" means "many," as in "politics," which means "many ticks" (bloodsucking creatures). Hey, that explains a lot. I have to give politicians a kick every time that word comes up. "Polytheism" is the belief in "many gods." So, they embrace animism that claims everything has a life force and "pantheism," which makes all things God, but then they take a contrary, illogical view with polytheism that breaks God down to certain individual entities that they individually worship. How does that even make sense if they think they (and everything else) is God? In fact, they even greet each other as goddesses and gods. So, why would they even worship something outside of themselves, let alone pick out specific entities to worship as though those entities are special, being above all the rest of creation that is supposedly equal to God?

Hinduism believes there are a huge number of gods and goddesses who deserve their worship and that is why they feel they can merge with other religions that also worship a multitude of gods and goddesses. Again, with Wicca witchcraft it is hard to codify all of Wicca, but mainly their polytheism is the worship of two deities, which is a dual theism. Now, the moment I say that, a coven can pop up to counter that by saying they worship a bunch more than that. But typically, Wiccan's worship two, which are the Mother goddess and the male Horned god.

Some say that the Horned god must be satan, but that is not necessarily true. I will say that we have seen satan-worship several times in this study, including the witches in that last video transcript. What was that head witch, Minca, saying? She was invoking the spirit of the devil. And as we saw with Alex Sanders in his documentary, he too was worshiping Lucifer. Wiccans will claim they have nothing to do with satan, or at least that they are not practicing satanism. Well, I will give them that, they may not be practicing satanism, but they are working with and invoking, (some openly) the entity called the devil and Lucifer. And by the way, who is the father of all lies, including the lie of witchcraft? It is satan. So, either way they can't escape who they fall under. But typically, they will say we Christians are dumb dumbs for claiming the Horned god is satan. There is an element of truth to the Horned god being a different entity. It's not necessarily satan, but Wiccans still work with satan. In this video transcript, I'm going to let witches themselves break down the differences, though this worship of two different entities is all the same demonic practice:

Title: *"the Wiccan God and Goddess"*

"Wiccans evoke deities from a variety of polytheistic religious traditions. The two most common deities are the Horned God and the Mother Goddess, who are worshiped in their balance to one another. Neither is held greater than the other, as both aspects are needed for the continuation of life. The Horned God is also called The Green Man or The Sun God, as each Wiccan practitioner relates to the masculine energy in a different way. The Mother Goddess is a three-part fertility goddess consisting of The Maiden, The Mother, and The Crone. The God and Goddess can manifest themselves in many sacred forms.

In Gardnerian circles, Gods and Goddesses are not specifically named, but rather referred to as The Lord or Lady or Mother Goddess and Horned God. However, many Wiccans forgo the generic terms and align their rituals or spell work with specific deities from various pantheons. In either case, connecting with the feminine and masculine through the representation of a deity is an essential component in Wiccan rituals as it honors each aspect of the Goddess and God's nature through the cycles of the seasons.

<u>*The Horned God*</u>*: Historically, gods with horns generally related to the primal nature of man. The Horned God represents the masculine portion of nature, the wild beast that is unencumbered by society's regulations. Residing in the forests just outside of the realm of human civilization, The Horned God lived by his instincts in a fully natural state of being. He relied solely on the forest and his own skills to provide food and shelter. Being in tune with the forest meant understanding the duality of the hunt. He is both the hunter or life taker and the hunted or life giver, which completes his cycle within the cycles of nature. The Wiccan God is also referred to as The Green Man. The Green Man is a variation on The*

Horned God, as he too lives in the forest and dwells with the animals. He is the quintessential spirit of vegetation. He is the ruler of the green flora and the growing fauna. He is the field, the forest, and the animals, all bound together in harmony. The Green Man is a God who dies and is reborn through the turning of the wheel of the year. At harvest he dies as the crop is gathered in the fields. He is buried again as the seed. He lives again as the new shoot of life that springs forth from the fields. He grows and matures through the earth, which is the womb of The Great Goddess, and the cycle continues as the harvest comes again.

The Mother Goddess: Wicca's primary emphasis is on feminine energy and power. This aspect is one of the most distinctive features in a predominantly patriarchal world. There are three aspects of the Goddess, which relate to the phases of the moon. The Goddess is believed to be so ancient that humans cannot remember all the names she has been given. Throughout time, she has lived as both the one and the many, taking on multiple forms for the people, who have worshiped her. In all her forms, she is the bringer of life. While the specific nature of the goddess can be debated, Wiccans do agree that she is comprised of three parts, The Maiden, The Mother and The Crone.

The Maiden encompasses the stage in life where women are full of promise. New beginning and youthfulness abound. Enchantment about life, innocence, and beauty surround The Maiden. She learns to become independent and she has unlimited possibilities before her. The Maiden is most often worshiped during the Spring in fertility rituals.

The Mother is an experienced lover who has gained maturity through her understanding of the world. She is often depicted as a parent but does not have to have given birth. She represents selflessly giving to others, nurturing energy, and fierce protectiveness of her creations. The Mother is associated with the domestic aspects of women through children, family, and the home. She is also strongly connected to sexuality and the moon. As the moon grows full, so does the mother with child. The mother is most often worshiped in the summer, as is the time of her pregnancy through *the winter when she gives birth. It is through this process of birth, literally and figuratively, that new life and ideas come forth into the world.*

The Crone: As the Goddess moves into old age, she becomes The Crone. The Crone has gained an immense amount of knowledge from a lifetime of learning. She has transformed and become strong through many trials and tribulations in life. The Crone is a respected elder who is able to guide others through transitions in their lives and provide wisdom and understanding to those who come after her. She represents the darker side of womanhood, the fears and destruction of life. But she is not referred to as sinister for The Crone is the last phase before the cycle begins again; the ever-turning cycle of birth, maturity, and death. The experience with the God and/or Goddess is a deeply personal endeavor. It is subjective and requires further investigation and exploration to find the path that fits for your own personal practice."

In other words: Make it up as you go and here some generalities you can buy into, as well as add anything else you would like. Relativism is basically what is going on there. Again, most Wiccans follow these two prominent deities of theirs: The Mother Goddess and the male Horned God. The Mother Goddess has a bunch of different names:

"She is invoked by a variety of names: Aphrodite, Artemis, Astaroth, Astarte, Athene, Brigit, Ceres, Cerridwen, Cybele, Diana, Demeter, Friga, Gaia, Hecate, Isis, Kali, Kore, Lilith, Luna, Persephone, Venus, and more."

If you were able to see that video, you'd have noticed a rabbit, which has to do with Astarte, the goddess we get Easter from. And you may know about the Old Testament reference to Asherah poles? That was the same female-and-male fertility worship that was meant to supposedly get the cycle of nature going for a good harvest. So, again, Wicca is nothing new.

These pagan Asherah Poles were what Israel was buying into through practices from the Canaanites with their different pagan religions which were practiced on the hills surrounding Israel. God spanked them for it and eventually the Israelites even lost their nation over those kinds of occult practices. Here is more about the Asherah Pole and it is about the same pagan goddess the Wiccans worship today:

*"An Asherah pole was a sacred tree or pole that stood near Canaanite religious locations to honor the pagan goddess Asherah, also known as Astarte. In the Bible, Asherah poles were first mentioned in **Exodus 34:13**. God had just remade the Ten Commandment tablets, and Moses had requested God graciously to forgive the Israelites for worshiping the golden calf. Verse 10 begins the covenant God made: if the Israelites obey Him, He will drive out the tribes living in Canaan. But they must cut down the Asherah poles. **Deuteronomy 7:5 and 12:3** repeat the command nearly verbatim, while **Deuteronomy 16:21** commands the Israelites not set up any wooden Asherah poles of their own."*

So, they had already gotten spanked by God because they were worshiping the golden calf shortly after God freed them from slavery in Egypt, a place flooded with witchcraft. In fact, when Moses saw what they were doing, he was mad enough that he smashed God's first set of Ten Commandments. And then, when God banished them to wander the wilderness because of that cow issue, they started right back into more witchcraft practices with things like the Asherah Poles. God let them know he was going to eventually let the Israelites get into their promised land but that they were not to practice this Asherah-type female goddess worship. What happened then?

*"Two books later, In **Judges 3:7**, 'The sons of Israel did what was evil in the sight of the LORD and forgot the LORD their God and served the Baals and the Asheroth.'"*

Today, Wicca witchcraft practices the same occult methods and beliefs that got Israel into sin, trouble and judgment from God. Wicca is the same old female-and-male-false-god worship that is all about fertility. Now, let's look more at their male Horned God:

"He too is called and invoked by many names, including Adonis, Ammon-Ra (Egyptian version,) Apollo, Baphomet, Cernunnos, Dionysius, Eros, Faunus, Hades, Horus, Nuit, Lucifer, Odin, Osiris, Pan, Thor, and Woden."

In some of our studies, we have seen pictures of the Baphomet being put up in our city, state, and federal buildings. Also, notice the Marvel superhero names mentioned toward the end of that list. Again, different witchcraft traditions emphasize the male or female part more and some even balance the importance of both. But those are the big two in Wicca.

Now, before we continue on, very quickly, I want to give you the first part of **Deuteronomy 12**, that predicted long ago how this occult stuff would even be coming into the Church, as it is today. So far, the beliefs we have seen from Wicca are based on what? It is basically, "Do whatever you want to do." But is that a good way to live? Is that something God is going to bless? No! Let's look back at the Old Testament times with passages where Israel got in trouble when they did their own thing, inviting the judgment of God.

Deuteronomy 12:1-8: *"These are the decrees and laws you must be careful to follow in the land that the Lord, the God of your ancestors, has given you to possess—as long as you live in the land. Destroy completely all the places on the high mountains, on the hills and under every spreading tree, where the nations you are dispossessing worship their gods."*

Again, a lot of that was the Asherah stuff God told them to get rid of. Here is more:

"Break down their altars, smash their sacred stones and burn their Asherah poles in the fire; cut down the idols of their gods and wipe out their names from those places. You must not worship the Lord your God in their way. But you are to seek the place the Lord your God will choose from among all your tribes to put his Name there for his dwelling. To that

place you must go; there bring your burnt offerings and sacrifices, your tithes and special gifts, what you have vowed to give and your freewill offerings, and the firstborn of your herds and flocks. There (when you do it God's way,) in the presence of the Lord your God, you and your families shall eat and shall rejoice in everything you have put your hand to (you are going to be blessed and prosper,) because the Lord your God has blessed you. You are not to do as we do here today, everyone doing as they see fit (Other translations say, 'Everyone doing what is right in his own eyes,') since you have not yet reached the resting place and the inheritance the Lord your God is giving you."

That is relativism, which is not only the premise of witchcraft, but also the mindset that our whole society operates on today. And according to God's word, is going to lead to a terrible life.

Now, to finish up this chapter, I want to give you an idea of how much the Church has been overtaken by these occult practices. Do you wonder why our society is in such an apostate condition today? It is because this relativistic mindset has now even crept into the Church. We're making the same mistake Israel did, pursuing whatever we want to do. We are not following what God says in the Bible, but, instead, even we Christians are following whatever we want to be true.

Let me share this with you: A recent survey reveals that many Christians are deeply confused about Biblical theology.

"The results show a confused collection of beliefs held by American Christians and especially evangelicals."

This isn't talking about apostate faiths in the Church. Evangelicals are supposed to be, if you will, the cream of the crop, Biblically. We are supposed to be the ones who have the best chance at remaining true to God's Word in the Bible. Again, this is a recent survey:

"High percentages of respondents again revealed clearly heretical beliefs when they were asked about the nature of God and belief, their opinions

on certain sins and the role of the Bible, 52% responded that most people are basically good."

That's from evangelicals! Hey, if you rely on yourself being good as your way to get to Heaven on your own, you are not headed there. How do you get around this?

Romans 3: *"There is no one good, no, not one."*

Folks, these are evangelicals and over half the Church claims people are basically good. That is scary! What are they trusting in? Are they even saved? Here's more:

"...51% believe that God accepts the worship of all religions... "

That is from a recent survey. Alarmingly, that percentage used to be 25% and I know because I have been quoting the statistic for years. Now, it has doubled! If you really believe God accepts worship from all religions, you are not a Christian because there's an absolute truth in the Bible that says Jesus is the only way. We just quoted it. And this is in the Church! This next part talks about the Christians believing in animism with its so-called life force in everything:

"A majority of 59% stated that the Holy Spirit is a force, not a personal being, and the most shocking of all, the survey showed that 62% of American Christians surveyed believe that 'religious belief is a matter of personal opinion and not of objective truth.'"

Then why do we even have the Bible? Think about that? This is the evangelical Church and of course the unbiblical teachings spill downhill to the rest of society.

"Only 52% of Christians identified abortion as a sin..."

That means 48% of evangelicals say abortion is perfectly fine. And we're not even talking about those kinds of false teachings in the apostate part of the Church. These are the so-called evangelicals.

"Likewise, 41% of Christians interviewed believe that the Bible's condemnation of homosexuality does not apply today."

That statistic used to be 33% so it too is going through the roof. Can I tell you why? Few in the Church will touch the subject of homosexuality, even with a ten-foot pole. Sunday schools and preachers stay away from it. On top of that, people do not read their Bible. And even if they do when they come across a passage warning against homosexuality, they discount it with a statement like, "Well, I know that's what it says but what I believe is that God is a God of love and He won't hurt them." But that is just more relativism. You might as well be practicing Hinduism or witchcraft. One guy says this:

"How much of this heretical belief is the result of poor education in Christian theology, what is taught from the pulpit with Christians not being discipled, and how much indicates the influence of external cultural factors that are slowly warping what millions of Christians across the country believe?"

Those cultural influences are creating a moral relativism and the combination of that with preachers getting away from what Jesus demanded as He left the earth, "Go and make discipled learners of all nations," is why we're in such a big slide toward false teachings.

So, we have just seen that half of the evangelical Church is living with witchcraft beliefs. They are tolerating everything, believing whatever they would like, and going against God's demand that we not just do whatever seems right in our own eyes, especially if it goes against the Bible. But this is the status of today's Church. On top of that, there is a large chunk of the Church that is all about experience and mysticism. And today we wonder why the Church is full-on merging with witchcraft. It is crazy!

Let me give you two examples from Bethel Church in Redding, California. This demonstrates how parts of the Church are actually merging with witchcraft. This first video transcript shows how they supposedly "fixed racism," and it does not include the obvious remedy, which would be preaching the Bible and having a Bible study:

Man drinking coffee and searching for Church services online through his laptop (he finds Bethel's service): *"Well, let's see what's streaming today."*

Seven people on stage at Bethel with a man in the middle speaking to a costumed woman with them: *"Apostles have authority to make decrees and declaration. So, why don't you share your vision and then we'll do the apostolic decree."*

He passes the microphone to a woman wearing a long robe and holding a tall wooden staff. She is dressed like Gandalf from *The Lord of the Rings* movie.

Wizard-dressed woman: *"Okay, so I am an artist."*

Man watching online: *"Is she dressed like a wizard?"*

Wizard-dressed woman: *"One of the movies that has really touched my heart is 'Lord of the Rings.'"*

Man watching online: *"She's for real dressed like a wizard."*

Wizard-dressed woman: *"If you know 'Lord of the Rings', everybody understands what's in my hand (the large wooden staff)."*

Man watching online: *"What is happening?"*

The wizard-dressed woman demonstrates how Gandalf lifted the staff toward the Balrog monster (on the underground stone bridge in the caverns) as Gandalf spreads his arms wide in defiance of the Balrog, just before he is about to pound the end of the stick down on the stone bridge to release his spell that holds back the Balrog.

Wizard-dressed woman: *"Just opening his arms...opening his arms."*

Man watching online: *"Is this lady drunk?"*

Wizard-dressed woman: *"And I heard myself speak, 'Why he (maybe speaking of God??) asked me to do that? Normally it would only be Scriptures.'"*

Man watching online: *"Am I drunk?"*

Wizard-dressed woman: *"But the Lord told me I needed to repent for the participation I had with the racist spirit."*

Man watching online: *"Oh, I think the Spirit has done left this...uhm, hmm."*

Wizard-dressed woman talking to the others: *"So I'm gonna ask us right now to all grab ahold of this staff in my hand."*

Man watching online: *"Please don't do what I think you're about to do."*

Wizard-dressed woman with the other six all have a hand on the large staff: *"We are going to lift the staff, and we will command the spirit, not only to leave..."*

Man watching online interrupts as he's yelling to his wife: *"Rebecca, did you put LSD in my coffee again?"*

Wizard-dressed woman: *"No more! No more! No more!"*

Man in the middle takes back the microphone: *"Well, two things: I think it's important for you to share the vision of Gandalf, putting this* *stake (staff) down because that... (the others on stage say, 'Yeah...yeah...yeah,' in agreement.)"*

Wizard-dressed woman: *"Yes...oh...oh, okay."*
Man watching online: *"Oh, I've been to PTA meetings that were less awkward than that."*

Man in the middle on stage: *"We decree and declare that racism will end. It's over in the ekklesia from this night forward."*

Man watching online chuckles and says: *"Oh, Gandalf."*

Man in the middle on stage: *"Come on let's lift it up and bang it."*

The seven people with a hand on the staff, lift it up and bang it on the floor like Gandalf did in the movie.

Man in the middle on stage: *"Hallelujah! Come on give it up praise over."*

Man watching online: *"Gandalf, whatcha doin?"*

Wizard-dressed woman tells the audience to repeat what Gandalf said in the movie when he banged the staff in front of the giant Balrog monster, as those on stage lift and slam the staff on the floor one more time: *"Repeat with us, 'Thou shall not pass!!'*

Man watching online: *"Congratulations, guys. You fixed it. All those racist groups are just running for their lives. They heard about your little staff deal, and they just said, 'You know what? We're done.'"*

How is that any different from our earlier video transcript with the head witch, Minca, and her wizard friends, who were gathered together in their ritual garb with ritual equipment and throwing out spells to attempt to effect change? This was the same thing, and they want us to believe it is a way to fix racism. Do we really do that with wizardry? And we are to believe that God gave her a vision while she watched that movie, which is full of sorcery and witchcraft? How could these people be dwelling in those kinds of false teachings? And what else did she give us as a clue to her flawed thinking? She said she normally relies on Scripture, but this was from her "experience." So, she is relying on what she felt at that time and also what she now feels is right. It is merging personal experience and the feeling gained from it to modify Biblical teaching.

As if that isn't bad enough, Bethel Church is the same entity that has been using something like a sort of Christian tarot cards which are supposedly meant to function as an outreach, as if that somehow makes it okay. They call them "Destiny Reading Cards" and set up booths that purposely resemble those used by psychics. They even call the process the same as the psychic practice of "readings." The program Bethel put together is called, "Christ Alignment" and claims to allow their parishioners to empower their own destinies instead of someone controlling them. That is obviously from the idea that no one should tell another what to do; not even God. They use these psychic booths to perform readings "about relations, jobs, and issues to help people make better decisions in the future." How about reading the Bible?! God will tell you what to do for a better life and future. Instead, they are running with a Christianized version of occult witchcraft's tarot cards. Here is that video transcript:

A beautiful woman (Ali) with an Australian accent sits at Bethel's "Christ Alignment" booth and greets Darryl, who has come to her for a "reading."

Ali: *"Hi, I'm Ali. What's your name?"*

Darryl: *"Darryl"*

Ali: *"Hi Darryl, welcome to Christ Alignment. Uhm, anyone that does a reading hears from the spirit realm, which exists outside of time and space. We are hearing from the Christ spirit. Uhm, therefore it's possible for us to hear about your past, your present, and your future. However, we don't like doing future predictions because it confines you to time, spaces,* *and events that you've got little control over or choice over; it locks you into things. So, we are hearing from a higher realm that wants to empower your destiny, not control it. So, does that make sense?"*

Darryl: *"Yup."*

Ali: *"Awesome. Uhm, so, it's our goal to empower you from this third heaven realm. Uhm, and what I have here are the destiny reading cards, and uhm, they're going to reveal to you the gifting that you've been born with. And the gifting affects your relationships and your jobs, uhm, and it will also address issues in your life, which will empower you to make better choices in the future. Now, uhm, did you come with a question or a problem that you'd like a resolution to today?"*

Darryl: *"Maybe."*

Ali: *"Yeah, well, the cards can address that problem as well. And then at the end of that, we're going to an encounter where you can get the answer for yourself."*

Darryl: *"Sounds good."*

Ali: *"Okay, great. The way that it will work is that I'll get you to place the cards in order of the most important at the top near me and then you put them down to the least important like that."*

But hey, don't bother sharing the gospel with Darryl or quote Bible verses to him. Instead, let's consult the "higher realm" with so-called Christian tarot cards. This is what is going on in the Church today with Christian practices being reduced to that in some parts of the Church. Why is that? It's because churches say they follow the Bible, but Scripture seems to only be around them for appearance, while they focus on people's individual experiences that result in unbiblical beliefs. And they emphasize whatever each person thinks the Bible should say, according to his or her desires. The Church is basically telling folks to do whatever they feel is right in their own eyes, and it helps us understand how they can get to the stage where they are full-on merging with witchcraft. It's because their premise is a witchcraft belief. It is a perfect marriage and, unfortunately, it's even infecting the Church.

"Wicca is attractive for many people who do not desire or appreciate absolute truths. In Wicca, a person is free to discover his or her own 'path.' In other words, he or she is free to invent a religious system that suits his or her desires."

Again, what does that sound like? It is **Genesis 3**, as a lifestyle. Here is what Wicca says and listen to how many times it is all about the unholy trinity of "me, myself, and I":

"If you are just beginning a study of paganism, you may need to evaluate many different traditions or paths before finding the one for which you are looking. Your chosen path in the old religion must be one that is uniquely suited to you as an individual and one that lets you speak to the Lord and Lady in your own fashion."

Here's what one guy says about that:

"In other words, you are free to invent, devise, and develop a religion that suits your personal wants and interests."

Again, what are they telling their Wiccan followers? They are suggesting that people do not need to listen to God (their Creator) and they don't have to follow the Bible, which recorded God's messages to us. Instead, they advocate Satan's way with his rebellion against God. In fact, they can actually be God and just decide right and wrong for themselves. That's not only the premise of witchcraft, but it's now being promoted in the Church. Here is more evaluation of Wicca's prescribed practices:

"Furthermore, in Wicca you may attempt to manipulate your surroundings and other individuals through spells and incantations. This combination of developing a religion that suits your personal preferences

and trying to influence others to do what you want them to do is very appealing to a lot of people (our selfish, self-centered society today.)"

And we wonder why it's so popular. They are telling people they can be in control of their own manufactured false reality. Those who go to the charismatic extreme will get an experience just like Wicca witchcraft gives people because of the merger in some core beliefs and practices of the two. But it is not from God and not blessed by God. Because of that, what is it going to lead to? Those people are in for some serious bondage.

And they will not turn around from being led further and further down that dark path until, on stage, they are doing things like acting out and Christianizing a vision that one of them had while watching Gandalf wield his wizard, witchcraft staff. Or maybe it will go so far as substituting a witness for Christ with a psychic booth where a "reader" is flipping through occult tarot cards, like that is going to help. What people need is for us to share the gospel of Jesus Christ! In doing so, instantly the power of the gospel is available to save anyone; just as it did with this girl:

Brooke Gardner: *"My brother and sister had to go and take all the guns from the house and hide them just to keep me safe. I was at a really serious stage. I planned on how I was going to do it."*

Narrator: *"Brooke Gardner was only eleven when persistent feelings of hopelessness put her on the verge of suicide. Her parents took her to a psychiatrist who prescribed medication, but it did little to alleviate her despair."*

Brooke: *"Really it just numbed me and made me...I didn't have any thoughts or feelings anymore. I kind of just walked around like a zombie."*

Narrator: *"After a year, she searched for other ways to cope with her depression."*

Brooke: *"I had started looking online about spells and about Wicca and went and bought some spell books. I started doing these spells in my room.*

I was burning lots of sage and, uhm, you know, I thought they were positive spells, and they were going to help my depression. I thought that by controlling the environment that I could control my feelings."

Narrator: *"Performing the spells also gave her a sense of power."*
Brooke: *"I just wanted to connect to something more powerful. You want to be bigger and better than a lot of the people around you. You know, everyone better stay away from me or you're gonna get it."*

Narrator: *"But one night, Brooke discovered the magic she thought was helping her, had invited an unexpected presence into her life."*

Brooke: *"I was sleeping and beside me was this dark figure and it was touching the bed...like right beside me. I do not know what it was doing or why it...it had one of its hands on me. And I woke up and I still felt something with its hand on me. At that moment, I couldn't even scream or make a noise. I was so scared that whatever this was, was still in the room. You know, after a while, it went away."*

Narrator: *"Despite her fear, Brooke continued practicing witchcraft and her condition only got worse."*

Brooke: *"I didn't feel more powerful. Actually, really more so, I felt powerless, and I felt like a failure. It didn't make me feel any better than what I had felt. It just got me deeper and deeper into depression."*

Narrator: *"Brooke lived with a debilitating depression for three years, going on and off various medications. But what remained was her need to have meaning and control in her life. And while she kept casting spells, she also started reading her father's dusty King James Bible, hoping she might find some answers there."*

Brooke: *"I read in the book of Leviticus how God is not pleased with people who practice witchcraft and practice that kind of thing. So, that's what really gripped me; really believing all my life that it was okay to do those things. So, after that, I took all my (witchcraft) books, everything* *that I had, that had to do with it, and I threw them all in the trash and just turned away from all those things. I asked Christ to come into my life. It just kind of opened my eyes to this whole other place of what I really desired and wanted inside.*

It was something I had never experienced in my life. It was (she tears up)... For once in my life, all the sin that I had in my heart, all the stuff that I've ever done, was forgiven. It was just a complete, complete change. I would look at a flower and be like, wow, like, I can't believe God created this flower. I felt a complete release and just a huge weight taken off of me. And I knew that I was right with God."

Narrator: *"She found a church and started attending. Soon, her family started going with her and one by one gave their lives to Christ."*

Brooke: *"That was just an amazing, amazing experience to see your parents, for the first time, just have a joy that I've never seen before, you know. And pretty much everybody in my family has received Christ and is serving Him today."*

And how did that happen? Was it because her Church had a skit involving *The Lord of the Rings* with a Gandalf character pounding his or her staff on stage as they yelled at that bad-old depression to go away? Is that what provided her breakthrough? No! You've got to be kidding me! Or maybe she was delivered by church folk flipping Christianized tarot cards out at her! Actually, that's not what happened either. Instead, it was probably when someone told her she could believe whatever she wanted because her truth is just fine for her and ours is good for us. Maybe it was letting her know life is all about making up our own realities, which is the way she then got free. Was that the key to pull her out of a suicidal depression?

No! God's word convicted her of her sin, including the sin of witchcraft, and then she heard the good news, the gospel of Jesus Christ. That is what got her out of bondage. And that is what every one of us Christians need to focus on today and every day.

Chapter Seventeen

The Symbols & Calendar of Wicca

As we've seen on our long journey through witchcraft, Wicca is just another name for witchcraft and its occult practices have spread all over the world since the origin of witchcraft and other occult behaviors at the Tower of Babel. The only protection from witchcraft is for Christians, and it's through the power of Jesus' authority over evil. So, if you have not been born-again, you can speak to Jesus right now and get out of demonic oppression, praise Jesus! As I did years ago.

A huge portion of this study has shown that the Bible is right again when it tells us there is nothing new. Wicca is the same old witchcraft that came out Babylon and then went to Egypt, Greece, Rome, Asia, India and the nearby island nations, Africa, Latin America and Europe. That last spawning ground is where the latest version of witchcraft, Wicca, came from. We traced the trail of Wicca's origins and how it came to America. We also looked at some generalities of what they believe, which is somewhat hard to codify because individual witches and covens are left to choose from a huge eclectic variety of possible beliefs and practices.

Like Eastern religions, the New Age movement and even our society's overall mindset in the United States today, we saw how Wicca witchcraft allows adherents to supposedly create their own reality. Why? It is because a major belief they have is that they can discern truth through individual experience, which leads to a relativistic philosophy that says:

"Whatever I believe is true to me, whatever you believe is true to you, and that is just fine. Making it up as you go."

That belief is not only popular in our politically correct culture, but it is also the underpinnings of Wicca witchcraft today. It is just the same old lie satan originated way back in **Genesis 3** when the devil approached Eve to claim she should not listen to God or do what God says. Instead, satan told her to listen to his suggestions and then she could be like God, deciding good and evil for herself. Then we saw how another core belief of Wiccan witchcraft is supposed to be tolerance. But a Southerner would say they are "Hypo-Crites" (hypocrites) with that one because they do not tolerate us Christians or even our elected President.

That brings us to another core belief of most Wiccans: Their Wiccan Rede says they can do whatever they would like as long as they harm no one. However, does that declaration from Wiccans play out in a peaceful disposition? No! That completely flies in the face of their hexes and spells aimed at harming people, including our President. And frankly, it also goes against witch practices involving the killing of animals and murder of people in their ritual sacrifices, that still goes on today. To say the least, last time I checked, those behaviors are harmful. So, there is double hypocrisy going on with that.

Then we talked about their core belief in animism, which claims that a life force exists in all things and that leads to their related belief in pantheism that says all things are God. The latter uncovers more of their hypocrisy, and even illogical thinking, because they also adhere to polytheism that is the practice of worshiping many supposedly separate gods. But how can you believe there are many gods, which implies that everything is not a god, and then claim you also believe in pantheism that claims all is God. It makes no sense.

Again, it's hard to say these beliefs are universal to Wiccans, because any coven can pop up and say they don't do this or that. That said, what it boils down to is that most of Wiccans subscribe to dual theism, which means worshiping only two main deities. Of course, it is all demonic and untrue, because God has let us know in the Bible, that there is only one God and He is God. That is not just Biblical; it's also plain logic. By definition, God is the Supreme Being who is all powerful, all knowing and everywhere present at the same time. If there was another God, then neither could be Supreme because they would have someone that can compete with them. It is illogical to say there is more than one Supreme Being because, by definition, you then would have no Supreme Being at all. The idea of more than one is ridiculous but does not keep Wiccans from worshiping both a female Mother goddess and the male Horned god.

Those beliefs are where we left off in the last chapter and now, we are going to move on to their symbolism. In the next chapter we'll talk about some of their practices.

But before we look at their symbolism, once again, let's continue to look at the Bible's warnings that tell us to never, ever, ever get involved in witchcraft and other occult practices. **Isaiah 8:11-22** talks about fearing God, who is the One and only God. He made the Heavens and earth so only He is worthy of worship. He alone is Holy and without sin. Therefore, we need to do what He tells us and not listen to people, especially witches and other occultists. Unfortunately, Israel listened to occult people in their day and, boy does God have strong words for those like Israel who make that mistake. Here is what God says:

"This is what the Lord says to me with his strong hand upon me, warning me not to follow the way of this people: 'Do not call conspiracy everything this people calls a conspiracy; do not fear what they fear, and do not dread it. The Lord Almighty is the one you are to regard as holy, he is the

one you are to fear, he is the one you are to dread. He will be a holy place; for both Israel and Judah, he will be a stone that causes people to stumble and a rock that makes them fall.'"

They are being disciplined by God because they are not following Him and doing what He says to do. Here is more of what God said to Isaiah in these first two sentences and then Isaiah adds his comments after:

'And for the people of Jerusalem he will be a trap and a snare. Many of them will stumble; they will fall and be broken, they will be snared and captured.' Bind up this testimony of warning and seal up God's instruction among my disciples. I will wait for the Lord, who is hiding his face from the descendants of Jacob. I will put my trust in Him."

Again, God is disciplining Israel for disobedience, and we'll find out what that defiance was as Isaiah continues with what he said after the Lord's warning:

"Here am I, and the children the Lord has given me. We are signs and symbols in Israel from the Lord Almighty, who dwells on Mount Zion. "

Israel was to be a sign (symbol or light) unto the Gentiles. God wanted others to be able to look at the Jewish people and see them as a symbol pointing to God and that everyone is in need of a Savior. But that is not what they were doing. Isaiah tells us what they were following instead:

"When someone tells you to consult mediums and spiritists, who whisper and mutter..."

When we think they are speaking in so-called tongues, they may actually be sitting around whispering and muttering their incantations, just as the occult has done since Babel. And they are still doing it today. Here is more from Isaiah asking why Israel would listen to those crazy people when they have God's law; he can't believe this nutty stuff they are doing:

"When someone tells you to consult mediums and spiritists, who whisper and mutter, should not a people inquire of their God? Why consult the dead (necromancy) on behalf of the living? Consult God's instruction and the testimony of warning. If anyone does not speak according to this word (God's Word,) they have no light of dawn. Distressed and hungry, they will roam through the land; when they are famished, they will become enraged and, looking upward, will curse their king and their God. Then they will look toward the earth and see only distress and darkness and fearful gloom, and they will be thrust into utter darkness."

Why was God disciplining them so hard? It was because, once again, they were not doing what God said to do. They were not following God even though our Lord will never lead us astray. There will never be a command from God that is bad for us. But instead of the reliable, tried-and-true path that comes with doing God's will, they were following the terrible advice and direction of those involved in witchcraft. And what does that lead to? It certainly led to their pain, distress, doom, darkness, and destruction.

Yet, with all that already known, because it's been written as hard-earned lessons from man's past, meaning no one else in the future of man will have to go through the similar horrible consequences for ignoring God, these same practices still happen today through Wicca witchcraft and other occult behavior. Anyone who wants to forsake God's Word by going down that occult route of listening to flawed, fallen men and woman, is going to get the same calamitous results. It's going to catch up to him or her and one day lead to pain, darkness, gloom, and destruction. And dare I say, the awful outcome will not just be for the individual. As these evil practices permeate society, similar consequences can happen for whole nations as it did to Israel when they went down the occult route. That is the rotten fruit of the occult. God's watching it all, and His judgment of sin doesn't change over time. Now, let's continue to look at more Wiccan symbolism.

This is not nearly all of them and I can't even get to all of them because they have way too many symbols to cover here. So, I'm just going to have to hit some of the big guns. I was excited to get to this part because you have probably seen some of these symbols out in society today. You may have noticed them on graffiti, bumper stickers, or tattoos.

Not knowing all the symbolism or what it means, we cannot recognize what is being promoted or who's involved with the occult. Graffiti can speak as to whether the occult is in our neighborhoods or if it goes on at night. We have no idea what it means because we do not know the symbols. So, that is what we are going to deal with in this chapter.

As we just saw in our Scripture text, the situation was sad because Israel was supposed to be a sign and symbol of God. But God had to discipline them became they became a symbol of witchcraft instead. Can you believe that? It is what those people followed at the time, which meant God had to discipline them.

When it comes to signs and symbols, that's not a foreign concept. Many belief systems codify their beliefs in symbols but, as we will see with witchcraft, they also work their symbols into their practices as part of their rituals. Sometimes they carry their symbols around in the form of talismans, good luck charms, and depictions of their gods and goddesses.

We'll talk about that in a minute with the Triple goddess. But they also wear them for supposed protection. Besides using them to perform rituals and for supposed protection, they also carry and display them because they believe the symbols give them power.

They work with symbols in amulets, jewelry, and other trinkets that have to do with energies, spells, and rituals, which are meant to repel negative energies, thoughts and intentions. So, symbols are a huge part of the occult, especially Wicca and other branches of witchcraft. Let's take a look at a few of those, starting with these two:

As you can see there, the one on the left is the goddess that is part of Wiccan duel theism with their female Mother Goddess and the male Horned God. You may have seen either or both and did not know what they were. Now you will recognize them. As you can see with the goddess, there are three aspects to it and those serve a purpose. They are the three phases of the moon with a crescent, full and then another crescent. They represent the three phases of a female goddess worshiper's life. The crescent on the left is the young maiden, the full moon is the mother in the prime of life, and then the right-side crescent is the crone, who is old but has wisdom.

Wicca's young maiden side of the goddess symbol is a crescent, or waxing moon, which symbolizes fresh starts or new beginnings. And that is because it is supposed to represent the youthful age. For us older folks, we may remember those as the days when we could keep going until 4 a.m. and then get up two hours later and head straight to work without missing a beat. Do you remember those days when you could tear it up all week long and still spring from bed each day with your body functioning correctly and zero aches or pains? For some of us that seems like it was 1922, right? But notice they don't just have that goddess symbol for a common identifying image. It also tells them when to do their rituals. During a Waxing Moon, witches do rituals for new beginnings.

The middle circle in that goddess symbol represents the Full Moon, which is a time witches like to ramp up all magick (witchcraft) because the moon is said to be pregnant with power. That is why you see occultists more active at full moons because they think that's prime time. The Waning Moon in their goddess symbol represents a time of endings.

"It is the best time to perform magick related to banishings, clearings and endings."

So, when they want to get rid of something, this waning moon is when they go out at night and perform those types of rituals. They also have what is called the New Moon.

"Many Wiccans do not perform magick on the New Moon. It is a time of rest and contemplation."

Another moon phase you have probably heard of is about their Blue Moon: "Once in a blue moon." Well, believe it or not, that has significance in the occult because it is the 13th moon of the year. Besides symbols, the occult is hugely into numbers and 13 is certainly a prominent one for them, just as the number 3 is.

"The saying 'Once in a blue moon,' means once in a great while. A blue moon is not a common occurrence. They believe it is a great moon phase for special empowerment during magickal workings."

The other symbol you see there next to the goddess is the Horned God one. It appears to have a crescent moon on the top and the full moon on the bottom. Of course, that crescent part resembles horns, and it is no shocker because the whole concept is satan-inspired.

"The 'full moon' portion of the symbol is the god's head, and the crescent moon represents the horns... The Horned God is a deity representing the wild and untamed natural world, animals and the primal nature of humankind."

Here's more about that from this video transcript:

"Like other religions, Wicca has its own symbols, which carry spiritual meanings and sacred power. You have likely seen some of them before. So, here is an opportunity to learn their meanings and origins. The Triple Moon is a symbol of the goddess that represents the Maiden, Mother and Crone. These are considered to be the three stages in a woman's life and are represented by the waxing, full, and waning moon. This symbol is also associated with feminine energy, mystery, and psychic abilities."

"The Horned God is the symbol of the masculine aspect of the divine. He is associated with nature, wilderness, sexuality, and hunting. In traditional Wicca, the Horned God and the Triple Goddess are seen as equals and opposite in gender polarity. Together, they make up the dual aspect of the Wiccan pantheon. Cernunnos, sometimes spelled Kernunnos, is a name originating from France where it was found on an ancient stone carving. The word itself means 'The Horned One.'"

The Horned god symbol also represents this guy:

We have already talked about the flute-playing Pan, who is another demonic deity that goes all the way as far back to ancient Greece.

"In ancient Greek religion and mythology, Pan is the god of the wild, shepherds and flocks, nature of mountain wilds, as well as rustic and free-form music. He has the hindquarters, legs, and horns of a goat, in the same manner as a faun or satyr."

He's also affiliated with sexual behavior because he's supposed to be a god of fertility. I'm not even going to show you some of the horrific things this entity gets into and encourages his occult followers to do, as well. Again, this demon is where we get our word, "panic." Here is more on that and also his erotic aspects:

"Disturbed in his secluded afternoon naps, Pan's angry shout inspired panic. Women who had sexual relations with several men were referred to as 'Pan girls.'"

Being associated with music, do you suppose this Pan demon could be involved with causing a sort of panic, unrest, agitated state, or anything of that nature? And hey, the music industry certainly does not encourage erotic, sexually immoral behavior, right? Wrong! They have done so for a long time and it is still going on today, unfortunately.

227

"In the late 19th century Pan became an increasingly common figure in literature and art. He appears in poetry, in novels, and children's books, and is referenced in the name of the character Peter Pan."

Once again, Disney picked an occult character and turned it into a whole series and franchise. Notice Peter Pan is playing a flute. So, Peter Pan appears to be the exact same entity as this demonic god that witch's worship, showing another fit with this occult pattern we've seen from Disney. We have got to wonder why they just keep pushing the witchcraft angle with story line after story line. Why do they go around the world digging up occult figures and then glamorizing them with cartoons?

Now, if you look back to the picture of Pan with the flute, it is that same appearance of the Baphomet, which also identifies him with satan, even though Wicca witches will claim they have nothing to do with the devil. Pan is where we get the common pictures of satan with the horns.

So, this dual theism of Wicca witchcraft with the Mother goddess and the male Horned god are the first symbols I wanted to show. Another is the Spiral.

Notice that the spiral is associated with the female aspect or Mother goddess, with the three aspects involving the triple moon phases. Here is more about the Spiral:

"Spirals have been primary goddess symbols since the late Paleolithic when they were marked on tombs. They represent the divine feminine, the movement of creation, death and rebirth."

They are talking about an ongoing cycle of life with the spiral that never ends. It is just old-fashioned reincarnation, which the Bible tells us is absolutely not true.

Hebrews 9:27: *"Just as man is destined to die once, and after that to face judgment."*

We are all going to die and stand before God and Hebrews also says Christians will have Jesus Christ there as our mediator and advocate to speak up for us. He will confess to the Father that we Christians have been forgiven. However, if you are not a Christian and you have rejected Jesus' free gift, He won't be there for you, and you're in a heap of trouble.

Only those Jesus saved will have Jesus as "mediator"! All mankind reject Jesus' free gift" Rm. 3:11(b)

Wiccans believe the spiral and Mother goddess represent the continuation of life, death, and rebirth in a supposed endless cycle. But that is not going to end well for those adherents going down that false route. They will be in for a rude awakening after taking their last breath in this life. A third symbol ties into that same life, death, and rebirth, with what's called, the Triple Crescent.

Triple Crescent

Now that you have seen it, you might be amazed at how much this symbol is actually out there in our society while we weren't realizing it, it is an occult witchcraft symbol. Notice it is also one that emphasizes the triple goddess:

"A triple crescent moon icon is another means of expressing the Triple Goddess concept. It weaves together three crescents, with one crescent facing upward and the remaining two crescents facing left and right. The icon is also a visual representation of the three aspects of the goddess: The Maiden, Mother, and Crone. The interior of the knot or space represents the Dark Goddess aspect."

Occasionally I get emails that are typically about tattoos that someone's niece, nephew, or coworker got. This relative or friend is concerned because it looks odd and they are wondering what it is that the person close to them has gotten. Often, it is young people getting tattoos of this occult stuff. A similar one to the Triple Crescent is this Triple Horn of Odin.

Hey, has there been any movies lately that glamorize the Norse gods? Yes, the *Avengers* series does, and we'll cover that in a future study.

"The Triple Horn of Odin is made up of three interlocking drinking horns and represents Odin, the father of Norse gods. In some stories, the horns represent the three draughts of the Odhroerir, a magical mead, a brew he drinks. For three nights (there's that 'three' again) Odin managed to take a drink of the magical brew Odhroerir for power and the three horns in the symbol represent these three drinks."

As I have mentioned, that symbol is portrayed in popular movies like *The Avengers* series with Sir Anthony Hopkins portraying Odin, King of Asgard. In fact, there is a scene where Odin even has some of that magical mead that he drinks. An Odin character also appears in a 2001 movie called, *American Gods*, which is said to be really dark, so I certainly don't recommend that. Now I want to show you the most prominent of Wicca witchcraft symbols, one you are probably familiar with. The Pentagram appears all over our society today with the music industry, movies, and all kinds of occult practices like Satanism. Here is the meaning and symbolism of that:

"This Wiccan Symbol is a five-pointed star. Alternative names include the 'star pentagon,' the 'pentalpha,' or the 'pentangle.' Sometimes it has a circle around it, but it is still a pentagram even without the circle. The word 'pentagram' stems from the Greek, 'pente' meaning 'five' and 'gramme' meaning 'line.' To witches, the pentagram is a symbol referencing 'high magick' in some circles."

They believe that carrying their pentagram around is going to give them extensive protection and power. This symbol goes back to the Greeks and even as far back as the Babylonians. Again, that is no surprise because it is all evil witchcraft, whether Wicca today or the origin of witchcraft back in Babylon. This is nothing new. It started way back then and is still going on today. In fact, the pentagram symbol was once a secret sign used by those involved in the Pythagoras school. For those hooked on math, Pythagoras was the mathematician who came up with the Pythagorean Theorem.

Secret signs like that have been common throughout history, including in the early Christian Church that used the fish symbol at a time they were under heavy persecution from the Roman Empire, who was killing Christians in arenas with the help of hungry lions. Christians would write that fish symbol in the dirt to secretly let people know they were Christian. Similarly, the Greeks, who were involved with the Pythagoras school would let people know they were part of it by using the pentagram.

And speaking of the early Church, another historical use of the pentagram included the Roman emperor, Constantine, who used it as his government seal and was the guy responsible for bringing paganism into the Christian Church. He made Christianity accepted and even popular but also allowed it to get flooded with a bunch of phony-baloney pagan believers. Before that time, it was not easy to be a Christian with all the persecution happening over a couple of centuries. During those times, your life was on the line as a Christian. Do you think there were a lot of fake Christians then? No! Who would pretend to be Christian and risk being thrown to the lions?

That persecution kept the Church pure until Constantine came along, claiming he had converted to Christianity. In fact, he made it the official religion of the Roman Empire. To this day there is a big debate about whether he was really Christian or just an opportunist pagan. But that combination of Christians and pagans into one religion formed the future Roman Catholic Church. And that changed from the persecution of Christians and took the heat off them, so that anyone and everyone could start attending church services.

Do we have to deal with that same false teaching in our Christian Church today? Yes, there are still a lot of phonies in our churches. Shortly after Constantine, Roman Catholicism took off with the first pope. That resulted in civilization being plunged into what is called the Dark Ages, where Roman Catholicism not only controlled the governments in that whole hemisphere of our planet, but they also controlled religion. They had a stranglehold on both until the Protestant Reformation came along to lead people away from those pagan practices and back to the Bible where the Church again followed the teachings of God over man. Again,

Constantine's official seal, and his amulet, were pentagrams. So that speaks to his true background.

Pentagrams are often worn by witches around their necks as amulets and used for occult rituals like necromancy. Here is more about the pentagram, according to witches:

"If the star has one point up, the star has positive meanings (pentacle) With two points up it maintains more sinister meanings (pentagram)."

Those are their words and not mine. Now that you know this, do you remember the exciting new logo of the Democrat Party? What version of that star do they have? Is it the one point up that is supposed to be the good version? No. They chose the two points up and one point down.

Witchcraft tells us that version has the sinister meanings. It reminds me of the catchphrase Jeff Foxworthy uses: "There's your sign."

"Today, some Wiccans still use the pentagram with a single point up (pentacle) to serve as a form of magickal protection."

"The Five-Pointed Star or Pentagram, is by far the most easily recognizable Wiccan symbol. Each point represents one of the five alchemical elements: air, water, fire, earth, and spirit. It is said that the upright pentagram symbolizes the triumph of the spirits over matter and earthly desires, while the inverted pentagram symbolizes personal gratification over spirituality. The pentagram is used to invoke or banish forces and also as a shield against psychic or physical danger. It can be used as a protection symbol or a lucky charm, but it's generally considered sacred by Wiccans and other pagans."

Notice that keyword, 'pagans.' The pentagram is huge in the occult. Also, notice how they say the five points represent what are called the five elements.

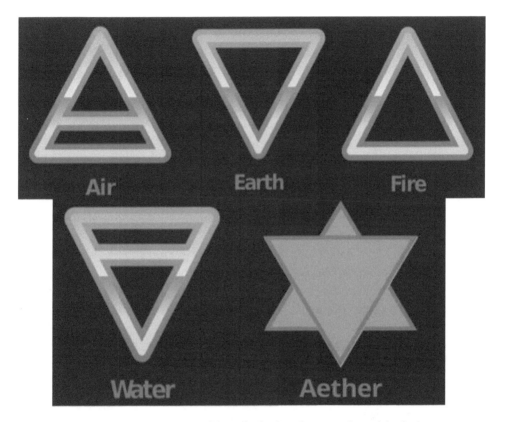

These elements are used in witch rituals to assist with their supposed dirty deeds like spells, incantations, and hexes. The elements are air, fire, water, earth, and what is called, 'aether' or 'the spirit.' Here's more on those:

"Alchemical Symbols: Greek philosopher Empedocles was the first to propose four elements: fire, earth, air, and water. He called them the four roots which make up everything else. The fifth element is known as aether, or spirit. These five elements are invoked during many magical rituals; notably when consecrating a magic circle."

So, the pentagram isn't just important to them for the shape used, or to wear as a talisman for protection. Each one of those five points represents what they call the five elements and, depending on what a witch wants to do, they steer their incantations toward the right element. This aspect of the elements is huge in the occult so let's break those five down, beginning with the first one you see there at the upper left:

"Air is one of the four classic elements and is often invoked in Wiccan and other occult rituals. Air is the element of the East, connected to the soul and the breath of life. In many magical traditions, air is associated with various spirits and elemental beings. In some belief systems, angels and devas, demons, are associated with air."

That's interesting because, Paul, mentions something about air:

Ephesians 2:1-2: *"As for you, you were dead in your transgressions and sins, in which you used to live when you followed the ways of this world and of the ruler of the kingdom of the air, the spirit who is now at work in those who are disobedient."*

Obviously, that refers to satan and his demons. It is the kind of practices the Ephesians used to follow before becoming Christians. So, witchcraft believes and practices the same as those people had with the air element aspect of their pentagram symbol. The next one we want to look at is the Wiccan idea of the earth element and its supposed ley-lines that the occult and New Age are also into:

"In the four classical elements, earth is considered the ultimate symbol of the divine feminine. In the spring, at the time of new growth and life, the earth quickens and grows full with the beginnings of each year's crop. The image of Earth as Mother is no coincidence, for millennia people have seen the earth as a source of life, a giant womb. Some people believe that lines of energy, called ley-lines run through the earth."

"The idea of ley lines as magical, mystical (occult) alignments is a fairly modern one. One school of thought believes that these lines carry positive or negative energy. It is also believed that where two or more lines converge, you have a place of great power and energy."

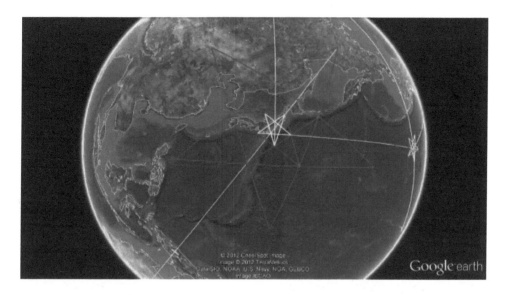

They believe a witch can go to one of these super-duper hot spots where their rituals, spells and hexes will be ramped up to turbo mode.

"It is believed that many well-known sacred sites, such as Stonehenge, Glastonbury Tor, Sedona, and Machu Picchu sit at the convergence of several lines."

Of course, those locations love this idea for the tourism it brings. However, what other horrible behavior are they inviting with it, including New Agers, witches, and other occult practitioners? The earth point on their pentagram also symbolizes Gaia (Mother Earth) worship. The Egyptian god of the land was Geb and with Wiccan tarot cards, earth is associated with the pentagram (suit of pentacles). Let's move on to the third element, which is fire:

"In the symbolism of the four classical elements, fire is a purifying, masculine energy, associated with the south, and connected to strong will and energy. Fire destroys, and yet it also can create new life."

Witchcraft believes fire helps provide transformation, growth, and change for witches and their desired outcomes. The way they perform a fire ritual often involves candles, which is why candles are prominent in the occult. They are a quick way to get a flame. Often when police visit spots where Wiccan rituals have been carried out, they will find evidence of a fire or candles. Sometimes Wiccan witches and other occultists also build large fires called, bonfires.

Witches use fire for scrying and divination, just as "Nose-Hair Damas," or Nostradamus, did. He used water with his witchcraft technique of scrying, which can also involve staring at fire. Often scryers take hallucinogens while scrying to help give them visions. That process can work with fire or water. In our study, *New Age & The Last Days Deception*, we talk about Shirley MacLaine's television series from the 1980s: *Out on a Broken Limb*. Actually, that should have been the name but the real one is, *Out on a Limb*. In it they showed a lot of her meditating to get into an altered state of consciousness by staring at a candle flame (a fire). That is a classic occult technique to produce visions and connect with spirits (demons). Bonfires are an important pagan tradition for witches on an annual day they call Beltane. We will look at their holidays and rituals but the word, "holiday," comes from "holy day" so we really need to call the pagan ones "unholy days."

Besides Halloween, Beltane is an unholy witchcraft day where it is common to have a bonfire. It is also called a "balefire" because it is often made from bales of straw or wood. It was started back with the Druids and the Celts. They would also call it a "bone" fire because they burned animal bones. Some reports say this ritual even included human bones that they would burn in their bone fires, which supposedly would ward off evil spirits. Today, witchcraft still does these bone fires, or balefires, but the name has been cleaned up a bit to make it "bonfire." They may have had a harder time getting people to stop over to burn animal or human bones. But when someone says, bonfire, that sounds like a good time and a chance to have s'mores! But you do not want to be a part of that. Bone fires were also used in rituals to supposedly purify. And as we saw earlier with some modern-day witches and Wiccans, they like to leap over their fires.

"Couples who were to be wed on May Day would leap through the flames of the bonfire to seal their vows. Coals from a bonfire would be taken home to light the fires in family hearths. This practice was thought to bring good fortune."

When you think about it, those may have been hot bones they were taking from a fire, potentially including human ones. So, it was kind of revolting. Besides their bone fires, they would also have a Maypole on May Day, which included Maypole Dances, which they still have today.

phallic pole :) !!

The Maypole dance you see there is a sort of cleaned-up version being depicted to look like colonial times. Originally though, the Celts, druids, and pagans did their Maypole dance around a tree as part of their nature-worship ritual to help them with fertility. Again, it was typically performed on May Day, which was normally May 1st, and that is still a public holiday all around the world, including here in the United States.

But it is about this ancient occult festival. Also, something interesting happened in 1889 with the choosing of May Day as the date for a celebration by an organization called, the International Workers Day of Socialists and Communists. I am sure they just chose that occult holiday randomly, right? No, they did not. I do not have time to get deeply into this but the originator of communism, Karl Marx, was involved with the occult. In fact, on his deathbed, he burned (fire) candles to Lucifer. I don't know if he was trying to purify himself of whatever sickness he had, but it obviously didn't work. And the report is that Marx screamed this at his nurse, who asked him if he had any last words:

"Go on, get out! Last words are for fools who haven't said enough!"

Then he died and is probably, unfortunately, still in hell to this day. Another prominent part of May Day celebrations are flowers and it goes back to the Floralia pagan festival in Rome (in worship of the Roman goddess, Flora), which is also where we get our word for the state of Florida, meaning "land of flowers."

The next element on their five-pointed star is water.

"In the four classical elements, water is a feminine energy and highly connected with the aspects of the Goddess. The inverted triangle itself is considered feminine and is associated with the shape of the womb. Water is connected to the West and is typically related to healing and purification."

Especially at the time of a full moon, Wiccans, other witches, and occultists use water to do their water scrying. Just like the way they use fire, water is put into in a bowl, pot, or wherever, and they stare at it to get into an altered state of consciousness so they can receive visions and communicate with demons. In fact, witches believe water can be used to meditate until you are able to communicate with water spirits. They call them undines, which are just more familiar spirits like pixies or leprechauns, which the Bible points out as the same-old demons. Again, witches say water symbolizes purification and they actually say they use it to create what they call "holy water." They typically combine it with salt and their magical occult workings to make a concoction that supposedly purifies and cleanses them for their rituals.

Do you know of any other faith that has this holy water practice, which is straight out of the occult? Roman Catholicism uses so-called holy water, and it is useless. If you have ever been doused with Catholic holy water, nothing happened except for you getting wet. But it is very interesting to see more of this pattern of behavior coming out of Roman Catholicism that also comes straight from Roman witchcraft practices. Witches and Catholicism both still use "holy" water today.

Witches also prescribe water rituals for love spells, supposedly because water is fluid, like love is a fluid emotion. They also prescribe water spells for rituals meant to carry away anything negative, because water transports things away from us. So, water is the fourth element. The last of their pentagram points that we want to talk about is the aether or spirit.

"Believing 'nature abhors a vacuum,' Aristotle, the Greek philosopher, believes Aether is what fills all invisible space. It is the Quintessence or 'The Fifth Essence.' In ancient India, Aether is Akasha."

We dealt with aether in our New Age study, as far as what is called the Akashic Records.

"The Akashic records is a compendium of all universal events, thoughts, words, emotions, and intent ever to have occurred in the past, present, or future in terms of all entities and life forms, not just human."

Theoretically, they are claiming all that information is stored on some mental plain of existence above us, which is something we can tap into through the occult and have access to all knowledge and experiences in history to supposedly help us gain wisdom and help the success of whatever rituals witches perform. Obviously, it's not true, as we dealt with it extensively in our New Age study. Here are more of their claims about those Akashic Records that can supposedly be accessed from your mind when you use occult techniques that will get you into an altered state of consciousness, allowing demons to contact you more easily.

"Only a trained occultist can distinguish between actual experience and those astral pictures created by imagination and keen desire."

It's all demonic and none of it is coming from God. So, those are the elements from all five points of their pentagram. We spent a lot of time on that because it's very involved, as you see.

The next Wiccan witchcraft symbol we want to mention is the Hexagram, which is two triangles put together.

"In putting all the element triangles together, it is like merging two pyramids: One pointing towards the earth and the other pointing toward the sky. When merging two triangles in this manner, it creates a six-pointed star called a hexagram. It also shows the merging of the Feminine and Masculine Divine."

It is also representative of a prominent occult axion that says, "As above, So below." The hexagram is also part of the Hindu belief system, as well as many others. In fact, some say this hexagram symbol proves the Jewish people are involved in the occult because it is the same shape as their Star of David.

I don't necessarily buy into that. We do see other entities who have
abused it for
occult purposes,
just as witches do
today, but that
doesn't
necessarily mean
it's what the
Jewish people
are using it for.
That said, if you
do the research
as I have, that
Star of David did
become instituted
in Israel through
Jewish
Kabbalists, who
are those Jews
involved with
Jewish

mysticism, which is about occult practices. So, there is an occult tie there,
but common sense tells us that doesn't necessarily mean the Jewish people
are following the occult. The Star of David has become the flag of Israel
that you see depicted as a blue star on a white background between two
horizontal blue stripes. Israel adopted that five months after they became a
nation in 1948 and it is called the Flag of Zion.

So, it may be used by witches and others in the past, but that
doesn't mean Israel is involved with those pagan practices, even though it
was introduced by those following Jewish Kabbalah. Maybe some Jews do
see it as an occult symbol because there is a huge variety of beliefs in
Judaism, just as other large communities of believers. As we saw in our
study called, *Judaism*, not all Jews are Orthodox. Some are even very
secular and of all places this could be true, Israel is actually one of the
most welcoming places for homosexuality on the planet. A lot of Jewish

people are secular these days, so they tend to be pro-abortion and extremely liberal in many other ways. Again, they are not all orthodox, but I don't think we can throw the baby out with the bathwater on that. Just because the country's flag is a hexagram, does not mean they are representing witchcraft with it. I don't think that will fly, even though Judaism is an eclectic group.

Here's another occult symbol:

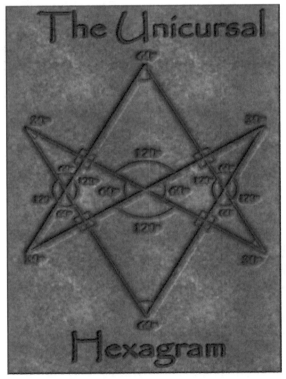

"The Unicursal Hexagram is a six-pointed star that can be traced in one continuous line rather than by two overlaid triangles. This is significant in ritual magic when invoking and vanishing hexagrams must be made. It is typically associated with the teachings of Thelema or the Golden Dawn."

We'll get to the Golden Dawn in a minute but first let's talk about Thelema, which was created by a familiar guy who comes into play again: Aleister Crowley used the unicursal hexagram and even added something you can see here in the middle of it.

The symbol is a version of the occult phrase that is number one law of Satanism: "Do what thou wilt shall be the whole of the law," which came from Aleister Crowley. And then in the middle, Crowley put what looks like maybe a clover but is actually a five-pedaled flower, which represents the pentagram. If you see that out in public, now you will know what it is.

The unicursal hexagram is also used in the secret society called, the Golden Dawn, which was active in Great Britain, as well as other parts of Europe and areas around our world.

"The Hermetic Order of the Golden Dawn, the Golden Dawn was a secret society devoted to the study and practice of the occult, metaphysics, and paranormal activities during the late 19th and

early 20th centuries. Many present-day concepts of ritual and magic, such as Wicca and Thelema, were inspired by the Golden Dawn, which became one of the largest single influences on 20th-century Western occultism."

Another familiar organization pops as the founders of this Hermetic Order of the Golden Dawn, which is full-on occult. The three founders of Golden Dawn were Freemasons and, Lord willing, we will have an in-depth study of them during our series. Long explanation short: Freemasons worship a light that ends up being Lucifer.

This next witchcraft symbol is the Witch's Knot.

It's also called, the Witch's Ladder, and symbolizes knots that witches put together during rituals for cursing and hexing people. Here is more on that:

"The Witch's Knot is a protection symbol in folk magic. It represents the knot magic practiced by witches during the Middle Ages and was used as a charm against witchcraft; usually carved on doorways, homes, and stables. It can be a powerful protection amulet, as it symbolizes the binding powers of witches and magic."

Again, it was not just for protection because witches use it also for subjecting people to spells, hexes, or curses. In practice, they take cord and recite their incantations as they tie the cord into knots. Other times they tie items like feathers or beads into the knots as prescribed by a particular ritual. Here is more about what they do with their knots:

"The whole is then hidden in the mattress of the one you are bewitching... The maker would weave into it aches and pains and other ailments intended for the victim. Sometimes feathers, bones, and other trinkets are braided into the string as symbols for a desired spell effect. Either way, special chants are spoken during the creation process to empower the talisman to do its creator's bidding. It was believed that witches of old cast a death spell over a person by tying the knots and then hiding the cord, and the only way to undo the spell was to find the secreted cord and untie each knot before it killed the person."

That brings us back to their phrase from so-called witch ethics in their Wiccan Rede:

"Do what you will so long as it harms none."

But we just read about their attempts to inflict aches, pains, ailments, and even death spells meant to kill people. What part of that am I missing here? What does it mean when you claim not to harm anyone but then in your practices you even go to the point of trying to kill people with your ritual symbols?

Another common witch symbol is Hecate's Wheel, and you'll remember she is the ancient Greek goddess of witchcraft:

"Hecate is the Greek goddess of magic, witchcraft, and crossroads. She is often depicted as a woman with three faces and she rules the underworld. The symbol shows a labyrinthic serpent, (which represents rebirth), surrounding a spiral as a symbol of the emanations of divine thought. These are channels which connect the material world with the celestial world."

As we saw earlier, Hecate is supposed to be the goddess of crossroads and the go-between from our world to the spirit world for people to tap into deities, which is all demonic. And notice she has three heads. The Hecate's Wheel symbolizes the triple goddess (maiden, mother, and crone). The maze in that symbol is supposed to represent the spiraling of the serpent. This symbol goes as far back as the first century with curse tablets that were found having Hecate's Wheel on them. Hey, did they just call those "harm-none" tablets? No, they were curse tablets.

Now, speaking of threes, we're going to look at that occult number a bit deeper with this next symbol:

The Triquetra is huge in witchcraft. Of course, "tri" means "three" and is common with triple moon symbols. Again, it is nothing new for modern-day Wicca witchcraft, which is just old-fashioned witchcraft.

"This ancient Wiccan symbol of power and protection has been around for centuries. It is a symbol appearing on 11th-century Swedish runes and Germanic coins. It also appears in Nordic and Celtic inscriptions. The triquetra represents the connection between the mind, body, and soul. It also signifies the sky, earth, and ocean waters."

Over and over again, witches use the number, three, and it's so pervasive in witchcraft that they call it the "power of three." Unfortunately, a lot of people watched a show that featured the triquetra:

Charmed (1998-2006) had three witches representing witchcraft's power of three. The idea is that one witch can be powerful but when you get three together it amplifies the witchcraft to a whole new magnitude. There is something about three that they believe will really put witchcraft into turbo mode. Sadly, the *Charmed* show was restarted again in 2018 with an emphasis on that power of three. So, they did a reboot to promote that stuff to a whole new generation. Here is more on the triquetra:

"Triquetra, also known as the Trinity Knot, has many different meanings. In Wicca, it can represent the law of threefold return, the power of the number 3, or the threefold nature of the Goddess. The Celtic Christian Church used it to represent the Holy Trinity, but other cultures use the symbol too, and each attached its own meaning to it."

Lord willing, we will have a future study on this topic of numerology (number symbolism) because the occult is hugely into numbers. You're getting a taste of it with their 3 and 13. A lot of people believe that even certain notable events, catastrophes, assassinations, and other happenings of that nature are carried out by the occult and witches on specific dates. The dirty deeds are done by the dark occult on specific dates. That is how much they are into their numbers. In fact, a mathematician named Martin Gardner, wrote a book called, *The Magic Numbers of Dr. Matrix*. He brought out some interesting numerical aspects surrounding the assassinations of two of our presidents. We will see if you think it's all just a coincidence. Here are some quotes from the book:

"Lincoln was elected president in 1860, Kennedy in 1960.

Both were assassinated on a Friday.

Lincoln was killed in Ford's Theater.

Kennedy was killed riding in a Lincoln convertible made by the Ford Motor Company.

Both were succeeded by Southern Democrats named Johnson.

Andrew Johnson was born in 1808, Lyndon Johnson in 1908.

The first name of Lincoln's private secretary was John. The last name of Kennedy's private secretary was Lincoln.

John Wilkes Booth was born in 1839. Lee Harvey Oswald was in 1939.

Booth shot Lincoln in the theater and fled to a warehouse. Oswald shot Kennedy from a warehouse and fled to a theater.

John Wilkes Booth and Lee Harvey Oswald both have fifteen letters.

The first public suggestion that Lincoln should run for president, proposed that his running mate should be a guy named, John Kennedy, (who was a Maryland politician at that time).

Shift the letters, FBI, forward six letters in the alphabet and you get LHO, the initials of Lee Harvey Oswald.

These coincidences are quite startling."

I'm not promoting numerology or things of that nature, but what I am telling you is that the occult is very into numbers to the point that they carry out their plans on certain days. Along with occult numerology, what we will look in the next chapter is the witches' calendar. With that, they do things like planning an event for the 31st and then flipping the numbers around so they begin working toward it on the 13th. It is all part of occult numerology.

And speaking of numbers, I don't want to put too much into this, but it is interesting and goes right along with what we've already seen from today's Democrat Party and their affiliation with Wicca witchcraft, as well as other occult practices. Again, I believe the Democrat Party has been completely infiltrated by the occult with aspects like the BLM movement being run by three lesbian witches and how witchcraft promotes socialism just as the Democrat Party does, as well as murdering children in the womb and older adults through euthanasia. Both those last two are practiced in witchcraft with their curses, hexes, and human sacrifice. Today's Democrat Party has core views that are anti-God, anti-Christian, and anti-Bible. Because of that, where have they turned to for their foundational "ethics?" It is the occult, which just so happens to be into numerology.

And here is what's interesting with this 2020 election: The Democrat nominee for president, Joe Biden, has been out there promoting people to text the campaign at 30330. With what I'm about to show you, the mathematical odds of them picking this exact number are exponentially astronomical. Why in the world, of all the possible combinations of numbers on the planet, did they come up with 30330?

Try this: The Democrat Party is running Biden for president here in 2020. So, put 2020 in your calculator and divide that by the number for the Mark of the Beast, (the Antichrist), or "666." What pops up? It's 30330. Now, is that by chance?

Again, I'm not going to say that carries the weight of, "Thus saith the Lord," but it is interesting, especially when you know that 3's are prominent in occult numerology. Why didn't they make it something easy like 12345? I mean, if Biden has an issue with memory, as he may very well have, why not make it much simpler with something like, 11111. I find that interesting.

Speaking of 3's, we'll continue that theme with their Triskelion symbol:

We just finished dividing 2020 by the number that the Bible warns about, 666, and the occult has an opposite view of that number. The Bible lets us know it is the number of the Beast, or Antichrist, and we don't want any part of it. But the occult actually likes the Antichrist. They want to be a part of the Antichrist's so-called kingdom. Well, some say that Triskelion is representative of three 6's because it is straight out of witchcraft.

"A Triskelion has three spirals, all which interlock. It signifies the ocean waters, earth, and space or the cosmos. This symbol also aligns with the Triple Goddess/Goddess symbolism."

"The Triskelion or triskele is a symbol used primarily by groups with a Celtic cultural orientation, which may have its origins in an ancient solar symbol. It can represent a variety of triplicities, such as the three realms of body, mind, and spirit, the Threefold Law."

So, 3's are very important in the occult, including the Triskelion, which is an ancient symbol that even appears in Buddhist writings. Another version is the Three Hares Triskelion that features three rabbits with interlocking ears.

Another important number in occult numerology is 13. In fact, that number has been associated with evil to the point where millions of people are so terrified of 13 that it's hard to find a hotel with a 13th floor, airlines sometimes omit row 13, and many other areas of our society shy away from it, like the numbers for the Formula One cars skipping from 12 to 14. If they have 20 cars, they are numbered 1 through 21 with no 13th.

Many cults and religions have sacred numbers, including Freemasonry, which is an organization that is all about the occult. Another occult symbol is the Septogram, which has seven ("sept") points in a continuous unbroken line. Here is that with the pagans describing more familiar spirits (types of demons):

"Neopagans view the septogram as a symbol representing the [fairies] and elves; It is therefore called the 'Fairy Star' or 'Elven Star.

The septogram is a symbol worn by practitioners of 'Blue Star Wicca': they refer to the symbol as the 'septegram.' Each of the points aligns with the first seven planets discovered and used in ancient astrology. Each point of the star aligns with the seven days of the week.

The heptagram is also a reference to the Islamic Quran's first seven verses."

That last point tells you a bit about the Muslim faith's background. Here is another occult symbol called, The Wheel of the Year, which has four intersecting lines that create eight spokes. This symbol tells witches when, on the calendar, to perform their rituals:

"The Wheel of the Year: This symbol represents the cycle of seasons, which serve as a calendar for Wiccans. The seasons are divided by eight holidays called sabbats.

These are celebrations that honor the particular qualities of each time of the year and the relationship of followers with the divinity."

Again, we'll look at the Wiccan witches occult calendar in the next chapter. It follows the phases of the year, step by step, and the Wheel of the Year symbolizes that. Now, I want to deal with this final symbol that will also bring up what was going on with Adolf Hitler and the Nazi Party:

Wheel of the Year

"The Solar Cross represents not only the sun but also the cyclical nature of the four seasons and the four classical elements."

"The Solar Cross has many different representations, and it's probably the oldest religious symbol in the world, appearing in Asian, American, European, and Indian religious art. Consisting of an equilateral cross inside a circle, it represents the solar calendar; each arm being one of the solstices and equinoxes."

One of witchcraft's Solar Cross representations is something we all know well but didn't realize it was from occult witches: It was not by chance that Hitler chose his Swastika, or Solar Cross. This symbol goes way back in the occult to Hinduism and other areas of the world that have been covered in witchcraft. Hitler chose the swastika as his symbol because it is from the occult and the German Nazis wore their swastikas everywhere. Now, I'm not going to say it would have turned everyone away, but if the Germans and others would have known that the swastika was about Nazis confessing that they were all about the occult, do you think it might have deterred many from supporting that movement?

Like then, our great disadvantage around the world today, is that most people do not know about the occult. They have never been taught about it and certainly don't know the symbolism. The occult will tell you what they're up to, so you only need to pay attention and understand the symbolism. But if you do not get equipped with what to look for, they can broadcast their numbers and symbols widely to the public and it just goes in one ear and out the other. Studies, like this one on witchcraft are valuable to help people realize the secret societies and other occult organizations that constantly project the fact that they are right in our midst and doing dirty deeds through their numbers and symbols.

It was the same with Hitler. From his beginnings, when Hitler chose the swastika as his symbol, he was announcing that he was all about the occult. I will give you some of that proof from non-Christian (secularist) authors, who wrote what witnesses said at the Nuremberg (Nazi) trials; those who'd been around Hitler. This is what they said about the man who was an evolutionist and heavy into the occult:

"Any close look at the life of Hitler will reveal the potentiality of such a man being a type of the Antichrist."

In fact, he's probably the greatest model for the Antichrist that we've ever seen in history.

"Hitler not only hated God and Jesus Christ, but he hated the Jews and attempted to wipe them from the earth in a satanic plot to eliminate them before God could redeem them and give them a kingdom as he has promised in the Bible. Hitler was not just demonic, but if ever there was a man possessed, not just by demons or a demon, but by satan himself, it had to be Hitler."

If only Germans would have realized what Hitler was about, he might have been stopped right from the start when he flat-out told the world that he was all about serious dark occult magic. Here is more of what the authors wrote (with my comments interspersed so I won't put quotes around it, but this is mostly excerpts from their book):
It is impossible to understand Hitler's political plans, beliefs, and convictions without an understanding of his magical relationship with the occult. Hitler was fascinated with mysticism and immersed in it. (He saw his own rise as a result of spiritual forces that were pushing him in that direction.)

The explanation of Hitler's deeds was powered by a mystical satanic covenant. Hitler and the Nazi society were a secret occult society. (That's why he chose the swastika symbol.) Hitler's whole Third Reich was wedded to the black occult. One of the greatest Nazi generals was a well-

known man named, Karl Haushofer, who was, for many years, a member of the secret society of the Golden Dawn.

It's an age-old black magic occult society. Kaushofer inspired Hitler to write Mein Kampf.

Haushofer had visited Tibet, China, and India (where the swastika appears.) He adopted Buddhist beliefs and was initiated into secret Buddhist black magic societies, of which suicide was the only way of escape (which is how many of the Nazis ended up killing themselves, because that's what the occult does.)

It was said that Haushofer had amazing psychic powers and was the black magician that controlled Hitler. Even Rudolf Hess said that Haushofer had the power as the magician between Hitler and his demonic legions. It was as if Hitler was a medium and Haushofer was the magician.

The swastika was no German sign. The swastika was a magical symbol in China and Europe, a symbol of the black occult. In fact, in 1925, a group of Tibetan monks moved to Berlin and these Tibetan monks were members of a black order, swearing allegiance to the power of darkness.

From that time on, funds were made available by the Nazis to finance expeditions into Mongolia and Tibet to dig deeper into the black occult. And when Germany fell, several hundred in the (Nazi) Secret Service (SS) were Himalaya Orientals that had no ID but were found in the SS uniforms. (So, these black occult guys were woven into the Nazi ranks.)

The whole Third Reich was infested with monks from the black occult. Rosenberg wrote that they were the last of the black monks, who helped Hitler's dark, menacing movement.

In March of 1946, Haushofer killed his wife and then himself before a Buddhist altar. His son, who survived, said that he knew his father was the magician behind Hitler. In fact, the seven founders of Nazism were all deep into the occult.

One cannot help but think of him, Hitler, as a medium. When he spoke, it was not his natural voice. He was possessed by demonic forces that he was a temporary vehicle for. When he got up in crowds to speak, the voice they heard was not his voice. It was an unearthly voice, not at all like the voice that he used in conversation.

So, Hitler was a man possessed by satan and one person describes how Hitler spent his last days:

"A person close to Hitler told me that he woke up in the night, screaming and in convulsions. He calls for help and appears to be half paralyzed. He is seized with a panic (remember Pan) that makes him tremble until the bed shakes.

He utters confused and unintelligible sounds, gasping, as if at the point of suffocation. Hitler was standing up in his room, swaying and looking all around as if he were lost.

'It's he, it's he,' he groaned; 'he's come for me!' His lips were white; he was sweating profusely. Suddenly, he uttered a string of meaningless figures, then words and scraps of sentences. It was terrifying.

Then suddenly he screamed: 'There! There! Over in the corner! He is there!' All the time stamping with his feet and shouting."

The authors say Hitler was a man totally possessed by satan, attempting to take over the whole world, blaspheming God, and attempting to wipe out the Jews. That is a preview of the Antichrist!

And the same type of person is coming to the planet again. In fact, he may be alive and well today, living somewhere on our globe. And my guess is that the rising Antichrist is involved with the same occult practices Hitler was. Like Hitler, he is going to be possessed by satan and may be already. It is not going to be good.

But again, in order for that to happen, in order for people to go along with a satanic, occult figure called the Antichrist, the planet once again has to be permeated with witchcraft and the acceptance of it, which is what's happening right now. It is a setup for the Antichrist to dupe billions, wreaking his havoc in the coming last days before Christ's Return. That final last-days version of Hitler will be going after the Jews again.

As **Zechariah** and **Revelation 12** tell us, that Antichrist is going to annihilate two-thirds of the Jewish people. Another Holocaust is coming in the Seven Year Tribulation. It's crazy. As you read this, history is being repeated with this rise of Wicca witchcraft setting the stage for the Antichrist.

And that's why people need to be warned about the Wiccan beliefs, symbols and even their numbers. They are telling you what they're doing, so you'll see witchcraft and the occult people in your community if you pay attention to what you find from the remains of their rituals, the numbers and symbols that they spray paint, the tattoos that they wear, and what they imprint on their shirts. They're letting you know they're out there and they're getting more and more bold.

And just as Isaiah warned in our opening text, those people that go down that route are being snookered. We do not need to be scared. Instead, we need to love them enough to help. God has not given us a spirit of fear, but one of power, love, and a sound mind. We need to love them enough to tell them about Jesus so they can be set free.

I wonder what would happen if someone would have witnessed to Hitler. Could God have saved him? You better say, yes! If you don't, you don't understand the power of the Cross of Christ. He can save anyone. And that is what we need to let people know, because every day there are folks being snookered to get involved with witchcraft. People need to be confronted in love and ask what a pastor asked this guy about how that is working out for him and whether he'd like to try Jesus instead:

Narrator: *"Stephen Beatty was a self-professed warlock. As a Wiccan, he cast spells and had several dark demonic encounters. His trek to the dark side began in 2001 when his girlfriend had a miscarriage."*

Stephen: *"When it didn't work out and the baby was stillborn, I was completely crushed. I had no idea where to go, where to turn. I couldn't think. All I could think about was how badly and how much I wanted this child."*

Narrator: *"Stephen blamed God for his baby's death. Partly due to the miscarriage, his relationship with his girlfriend ended. Stephen was totally broken. He turned to drinking and drugs to mask the anger in his soul."*

Stephen: *"I started getting into cocaine and prescription drugs, painkillers, antidepressants, and stuff like that."*

Narrator: *"Stephen said he felt like an outcast until he entered the world of Goth. That is where he met and married Dottie, who had two girls from a previous marriage."*

Stephen: *"They didn't care what I was doing. They didn't care what I looked like and they didn't care how I acted. I remember wearing 2 to 3-inch spikes around my neck, 3 to 4 inch-spikes on my wrist."*

Narrator: *"Stephen, Dottie, and their goth friends also participated in intricate role-playing games."*

Stephen: *"They had different roles like vampires, werewolves, a mage, which was a witch. They had what they called, 'dark angels.'"*

Narrator: *"And that opened the door to something even darker: the occult."*

Stephen: *"At first I didn't want anything to do with it, but the more I hung out and the more I was there, I think I started searching for some kind of* *religious stability because I needed a set of beliefs to live by. And I didn't want to change my life. So, Wicca kind of fit the bill at the time.*"

Narrator: "*The Wiccan rituals and spells opened him up to what he calls demonic encounters. One day at his home, Stephen and some friends noticed an object, a knife moving on its own.*"

Stephen: "*It started spinning and nobody was touching it. And one of my friends looked at me, he said, 'Did you see that?' And I said, 'Yes.' And everybody that was in the house left.*"

Narrator: "*Months later he had an encounter he would never forget.*"

Stephen: "*In the dead center of my room, there was a dark figure just kind of sittin' cross-legged. It was just sitting there looking at me and levitating off the floor. It gives you chills, and it was really scary.*"

Narrator: "*Stephen was terrified when he saw the power of satan. He knew his life needed to change. Then one day, while attending his stepdaughter's soccer practice, he met another dad, a pastor who invited him to church.*"

Stephen: "*I said, 'I'm gonna tell you why I don't go to church. I said, I'm a witch. I believe in Wicca. And he just looks me, and he says, 'Well, how's that working out for you?' And I said, 'Not too good.'*"

Narrator: "*The pastor gave him a Bible and Stephen began reading. And then on Easter Sunday, he went to church to see his stepdaughter sing in the choir. That was the day his life totally changed.*"

Stephen: "*It was just the music, the songs, and just the message. It was just the way the story of Christ was laid out, that it really, it really made me understand that I needed Christ in my life and that I was a sinner.*"

Narrator: "*Stephen began to pray.*"

Stephen: *"I told God that I knew that I was wrong in the way that I lived. That everything about my life was wrong, and I needed forgiveness and I just wanted Jesus. I just wanted Christ in my heart and in my life. It was an overnight change. I had already given up almost everything from my past. I was still drinking but it was, like, overnight. I didn't want to drink anymore. My language cleared up. Just the way that I carried myself; it was an overnight change."*

He was a guy who was completely lost and steeped in the occult. But, inside and out, what was it that completely changed him overnight? It was Jesus Christ, and He's why we have some good news to share that is called the gospel. The good news is that Jesus Christ can save and forgive anyone; no matter what they've done. And we have the privilege to tell others that joyful message!

Chapter Eighteen

The Practices of Wicca
Part 1

For a quick recap, Wicca means witchcraft and we have already seen the types and the locations of it all over the world. We also know that protection from it only comes through one magical name, and I do not mean that in witchcraft sense. Its "Jesus!" He is always the one to look to for protection. We looked at the history of witchcraft and how the latest version, Wicca witchcraft, came from Europe to America and is now the most prominent form of witchcraft, that is influencing our society in a massive way. We talked about the Wiccan beliefs that mostly revolve around their dual theism with a feminine Mother goddess and male Horned god.

Then we looked at their reliance on symbols and numbers. Why do we need to know about those aspects? Well, if we don't understand the symbol and number ties to witchcraft, we can't get the secret coded messages witches are communicating and promoting to us and our children. Some of their symbols are the god and goddess crescents, spirals, 3's, and the pentagram with its five points that represent each of the five elements they use in their rituals: air, fire, water, earth, and aether (or spirit). We also saw their hexagram, unicursal hexagram, and witch's knot. The latter is what they use to curse, hex, and put people to death. We know that abusive nature makes them hypocrites since they have a professed, but unfollowed, belief that they can do whatever they'd like as long as it harms no one. They live their lives however they would like, with no regard to their Creator's wishes. But how is attempting to kill someone with a death spell not harming them? Throughout this study we have seen total hypocrisy from practitioners of witchcraft.

We also saw Hecate's Wheel, which is a symbol representing the Greek goddess of witchcraft. Other witchcraft symbols that incorporate their "power of three" are the Triquetra and Triskelion. The latter shows how they have many symbols that resemble three 6's. We also saw the seven-pointed Septogram and then the Wheel of the Year, which we are going to get into with greater detail in this chapter. We finished up with the Solar Cross that is better known as the Nazi's Swastika. The horrible reality is that Hitler was an evolutionist and that is why he was after the Jewish people, who he had as the lowest form of human on his evolutionary scale. In fact, he felt they were close to pure ape. That idea was supported by his and his Nazi Party's extensive involvement in occult witchcraft. Had Germans understood the symbolism of the swastika to know about Hitler's black-occult-magic ties, (that he was broadcasting with that Nazi swastika tattooed all over his military), I'm not going to say it would have fixed everything, but the people may not have followed him so easily. That is the importance of knowing the symbols of the occult and witchcraft. The occult constantly tells us what they are doing, but it will go in one ear and out the other if we aren't paying attention or understanding their symbols and numbers.

In these next couple chapters, I want to break down Wiccan witchcraft's practices.

The final chapter after these next two on practices will be about the present-day promotion of witchcraft. Besides the numerous examples we have seen with Disney's glorification of occultism and witchcraft through their movies and cartoons, where is all this promotion of witchcraft coming from? We will talk more about that later.

Before we get into the practices of witchcraft, once again, let's turn to the Scriptures with **1 Samuel 28** to see why the practices of witchcraft are something we never want to get involved with. The context in **Samuel** has to do with King Saul and the Witch of Endor. This Bible passage is one of those that records a warning of something we must not do. This is about terrible, no-no-land practices that are an example through Saul's experience that let us know his type of mistake has serious consequences for anyone else attempting something similar. Saul did not just bump into and ask the advice of the average pagan on the street or the grocery store. He was not even just seeking a pagan, knocking on their door, and sharing lunch with him or her. Saul purposely went to get aid from a witch, hoping she would use her evil witchcraft for his purposes. Today people act like seeking those sorts of services from occultist witches is no big deal. But in God's mind, still today, consulting a witch can end up with consequences like Saul's fate after specifically having a witch perform divination for him. Let's take a look at where it started with Saul putting his trust in something other than God. This was unlike King David who trusted God and, in doing so, found the ability to stand up to and even slay Goliath:

1 Samuel 28:5-19: *"When Saul saw the Philistine army, he was afraid; terror filled his heart. He inquired of the Lord, but the Lord did not answer him by dreams or Urim or prophets."*

Why would the Lord not answer Saul? Well, before this time Saul had been constantly disobeying God. So, God shut him off, after which Saul then makes an even bigger mistake. If we had been there to council King Saul, we probably would have said something like, "Dude, two wrongs don't make a right. You have already rebelled, not doing what God commanded you, and now you're going to seek help from witches. Come on!" Here is more, with Saul actually thinking God can't see through his clever disguise or in the dark of night; like God wouldn't be able to drive after sundown. And before we laugh at Saul too much, maybe we should remind ourselves of times when we might have done some sinning late at night, when we're all alone, acting like God can't see it, right?

"Saul then said to his attendants, 'Find me a woman who is a medium, so I may go and inquire of her.' 'There is one in Endor,' they said. So, Saul disguised himself, putting on other clothes, and at night he and two men went to the woman. 'Consult a spirit for me,' he said, 'and bring up for me the one I name.'"

Saul is asking the witch, who does not yet know this is King Saul, to perform divination; to act as a medium and attempt to bring up a certain person's dead spirit for him.

"But the woman said to him, 'Surely you know what Saul has done, He has cut off the mediums and spiritists from the land. Why have you set a trap for my life to bring about my death?'"

Here Saul goes from bad and really bad to worse: First he didn't listen to the Lord, then he sought the services of a witch, and now he's actually going to pledge an oath to the witch, by the Lord (a triple no-no):

"Saul swore to her by the Lord, 'As surely as the Lord lives, you will not be punished for this.' Then the woman asked, 'Whom shall I bring up for you?' 'Bring up Samuel,' he said."

Samuel, the prophet, had been the one Saul had always gone to, having Samuel inquire of the Lord. But the Lord would not give an answer to Samuel for Saul and then Samuel died.

"When the woman saw Samuel, she cried out at the top of her voice and said to Saul, 'Why have you deceived me? You are Saul!' The king said to her, 'Don't be afraid. What do you see?' The woman said, 'I see a spirit coming up out of the ground.' 'What does he look like?' he asked. 'An old man wearing a robe is coming up,' she said. Then Saul knew it was Samuel, and he bowed down and prostrated himself with his face to the ground. Samuel said to Saul, 'Why have you disturbed me by bringing me

up?' 'I am in great distress,' Saul said. 'The Philistines are fighting against me, and God has turned away from me. He no longer answers me, either by prophets or by dreams. So, I have called on you to tell me what to do.' Samuel said, '(Dude...dude. That's a Crone translation.) Why do you consult me? Now that I'm dead and the Lord has turned away from you and become your enemy. The Lord has done what he predicted through me. The Lord has torn the kingdom out of your hands and given it to one of your neighbors, to David. (Here comes Saul's punishment.) Because you did not obey the Lord or carry out his fierce wrath against the Amalekites, the Lord has done this to you today. The Lord will hand over both Israel and you to the Philistines, and tomorrow you and your sons will be with me. The Lord will also hand over the army of Israel to the Philistines.'"

In other words: Dude, you are going to die because you rebelled, made it worse by consulting witches who work with satan, and then actually performed necromancy and divination. That's it! You just signed your death warrant, so you've got twenty-four hours left to live. And by the way, I can see at night, as well as through disguises, as you will understand when you get to heaven and face me tomorrow.

Of course, Saul lost the battle the next day, resulting in him, and his son's dying, because he had the audacity to turn to witchcraft's practice of divination. Wiccan witches still use it today to communicate with the dead for advice and supposed predictions of the future. God condemns that practice, so Saul and people like him (even today) are severely punished for it. In fact, Saul got a death sentence for it. That was the last straw with God.

But here is a side question about that passage that we need to tackle before getting into the practice of divination: Was that really Samuel? There is a debate among theologians in the Church: Some say it was just a familiar spirit (demon), while others believe it was Samuel. I kind of lean more towards the latter because I do not think the context tells us any different. But you are probably thinking rightly that the problem with that idea is how Scripture makes it clear that a person dies and goes straight to Heaven, praise God! Or hell. Either way, we do not come back, which you will be glad about when you get to Heaven and cannot get kicked out. Unfortunately, when a person goes to hell, he or she must stay there also. There is no crossing over or coming back. Now, that said, how then could Samuel have come back? Many who have studied this would say Samuel's incident was a special occurrence that happened only one time in the Bible. It certainly is not the norm but, since God is the Author and Creator of all life, He certainly has the ability to have Samuel do something like that for Him. This one special time, God may have used a dead person, Samuel, to come back to the earth in order to rebuke Saul and eventually have that incident recorded in the Bible as a warning for future generations. I think that is what we see in the passage.

With that said, it does not mean witches or anyone in the occult, who are involved in necromancy and acting as a medium (communicating with the dead), are seeing and communicating with a real person. God may have done that one time because He has the power to do whatever He chooses, but neither witches, you, nor I can do that. I don't doubt that witches may hear and see some entity that presents itself as someone like your Aunt Vera, Abraham Lincoln, or your old buddy, Fred, but is that entity really who it's representing itself to be? No! That is what we have seen in many, many studies over the last several years. It's a demon, or what the Bible calls, a familiar spirit, and it is impersonating a famous person or your loved one.

I want to clarify that because divination is the theme for this chapter, and it is a major practice of Wicca where they literally think they're speaking to the dead to gain supposedly friendly advice and predictions of the future. As crazy as that is, at least none in the Church are involved with mediums and necromancy, right? Hey, we've been studying Scripture throughout these books on witchcraft, so we certainly know by now that the Bible has many warnings against it in both the Old and New Testaments. So, people in the Church today, who profess to live by the Scriptures, would never get involved with that stuff, right? Unfortunately, witchcraft is getting so pervasive in our society today that even the Church has fallen into apostasy through it. In fact, before we get started on a larger conversation about divination, I have to share this tragic news with you about witchcraft being ushered into the Church:

We have Churches today that are actually hiring mediums to work on staff, helping to lead the Church. That is flat-out nuts! I must show you some of this 2020 article, so you can be sure I'm not making it up:

*"The New Testament describes the various roles needed to build up the church, including apostles, prophets, evangelists, pastors, teachers, and elders (**Ephesians 4.**) Scripture also describes the gifts of the spirit that God gives to these servants, his people, so they can minister effectively. Psychic mediums do not appear on the list of church offices, nor do psychic readings, based on communion with the dead, appear in the list of the Spirit's gifts. (However, one Church now wants to change this.) The headline reads: 'Psychic Medium, at a church near you.' (You've got to be kidding me!) According to the article, Vision Church of Atlanta has added Dr. Lakara Foster, a star of the YouTube series, 'The Gift' (supposed gift of mediumship,) and a graduate of The Interdenominational Theological Center in Atlanta."*

Crone translation: That school is not a Bible college. It is probably one of those online courses that earns a certificate. But, apparently, that makes her a doctor? Probably not. Here she says she wants to heal people, as if that makes the witchcraft okay; not to mention she is talking about bringing occult practices into the Church:

"Foster says she wants to 'heal people, give voice to the spirits, and help us reframe church and psychic mediumship.' She made the case in her doctoral thesis: 'One of the reasons I pursued my doctorate on this topic is because I really wanted to understand my gift from the intersections of Afrocentrism and Christianity, and why the church believes this gift shouldn't be considered a spiritual gift among those listed in the Bible.'"

That's because the Bible talks about it but certainly not as a spiritual gift! Over and over throughout the Old and New Testament,

Scripture lists it as an occult practice God condemns. This is crazy! Unfortunately, she continues:

"Being a medium allows me to communicate with our loved ones who are departed. For me, it was very important that I was able to merge the two: my love for God and my psychic abilities."

That is just witchcraft's relativism invading the Church. Notice how she makes it up as she goes with whatever she feels is right. She allows herself to choose her own reality, picking true and false ideas by whatever she likes and rejecting those truths she does not. Then she just merges her false reality with God's intentions for His Church, rejecting anything God prescribes that does not agree with her. It's telling that Foster patterns herself after a prominent occult figure we learned about in our study, *New Age & The Last Days Deception*:

"Foster says she came to believe she had special skills long ago, but says she kept them under wraps. Foster follows in the footsteps of Edgar Cayce, the so-called 'sleeping prophet' who combined mediumship with being a Disciple of Christ Sunday school teacher."

How could someone like that be invited into the leadership of a Church and even teach children in a Sunday School class? It's because people do not do their homework. And it leads them to take any warm body. Listen to the audacity of this woman, who is going to be in a heap of trouble with God:

"One of her goals is to re-write the Bible to include psychic mediumship as one of the spiritual gifts."

Now, listen to this, which answers the question of how a supposed Christian and so-called Church could get together, not following the Bible but promoting witchcraft instead:

"She says her unique calling became clearer to her after God told her to do her YouTube series, 'The Gift.'"

There it is! And what community in the Church claims dreams and visions from "God" as their whole basis of operation? Of course, it's the charismatics. Instead of the Bible, they go down the route of listening to those who claim they have had an experience where they felt God (Or was it a demon?) gave them a message through a dream or vision.

Even in the Church, that is how truth gets merged with flat-out occult lies. That is what we see in the article about this woman who is supposed to be a doctor, but she is not. She is also called a pastor, even though Scripture shows no record of female pastors. But these falsities make sense when you consider the source is the charismatic community that also relies on their own personal supposed messages from God rather than God's true Word in the Bible. Here is more from Foster:

"Honestly, I was reluctant at first because I felt very vulnerable and thought I would get a lot of push-back and negative feedback being a minister and a medium. I thought people would not understand but I knew I still had to do it. I knew I had been called to do it."

And listen to the audacity here:

"When I asked God, 'Why this gift? Why not singing?' God said, 'I promised my people eternal life, how will my people know that I've kept my promise if you don't demonstrate your gift?'"

Can I tell you something? That was not God's voice. You might have heard something but that was not God. And if you want to hear from God, read the Bible! Hey, maybe you want to audibly hear from him. That's okay too, just read your Bible out loud! But I want to give you that article because it is a perfect example of how far off our teachings have gotten, even in parts of the Church. Supposed Christians are shunning Bible study and replacing it with their experiences of spirits (demons) or just feelings telling them what to believe and do. It is all from emotional experience and many don't care or don't know that it's unbiblical, even as part of the Church.

Division Church of Atlanta does not only have the problem of hiring a medium. They also have a gay pastor. Unsurprisingly, they are part of the United Progressive Pentecostal Fellowship of Churches. Pentecostals also have a history of abandoning the Bible for the same reasons. The article goes on to rightly point this out:

*"The Bible, in **Leviticus** and **Deuteronomy** and elsewhere, strongly condemn spiritism, mediums, the occult, and psychics. Saul died after consulting a medium."*

Yet, here is a so-called Church that is actually hiring one. Are we living in the last days or what? Here's more about this supposedly Christian medium:

"Foster appeals to people's understandable hunger to hear from lost loved ones." But John's advice remains essential.

1 John 4:1*: "Dear friends, do not believe every spirit, but test the spirits to see whether they are from God, because many false prophets have gone out into the world."*

Along those lines, one of the unfortunate Church trends today, is having a grief class involving a psychic medium for the left-behind spouse of older folks who have died. Maybe it's because these church leaders are not in the Bible enough to think of using it to encourage those folks with God's word, but the idea with the medium is to supposedly allow these older people in the Church to talk to their dead spouse. Of course, it is not their loved one but is a demon they are being connected to. And this misguided remedy for those folks' deep grief has the tragic outcome of getting them into anti-biblical occult practices to go along with their heartbreak.

Now, let's dive into the details of today's Wiccan divination that is the same old witchcraft practice going back thousands of years. And in our time, it is getting so popular that, unfortunately, divination is even being merged into the apostate part of the Church.

With divination, there are different modes and methods that are used, which involves certain tools and rituals. So, let's take a look at some of those aspects that help witches do their dirty deeds:

"The art of witchcraft is enhanced by the way of magical tools, just like any religion since the dawn of time. Each tool has a specific purpose during a ritual. Some tools have more than one purpose and can be supplemented for another if need be. Each of these tools enables the follower to channel their energy, intent, or focus more clearly for their own magical working.

The athame is a small double-bladed knife. There are often magical symbols carved into the hilt. The athame is used to direct magical power. It has many magical uses, including casting a circle, charging objects with energy, and as a symbol of the god during the Great Rite. The athame stands for the element of fire. The athame is for cutting on the ethereal or spiritual plane. A bell is a ritual tool used for invocation and banishment that represents the Goddess. It is used to invoke the Goddess, as well as drive away negativity from a circle. It can be used to signal the beginning of a rite and/or to disperse the energy after the spell work is complete.

The Boline is a white-handled knife, often having a curved blade. It is used in rituals for physically cutting objects in the earthly plane. It can be used for cutting ritual cords, cutting herbs, or inscribing candles. It is the practical, utilitarian knife used during a ritual.

A Cauldron is a large metal pot, often made of cast iron that has three legs. The three legs are symbolic of the three aspects of the Goddess, and the large bowl is symbolic of the womb. A cauldron has many uses in rituals, including indoor or outdoor ceremonial fires, scrying, holding ingredients necessary for the ritual, or burning items during a ritual.

A Chalice is a cup that is intended to hold a drink for ritual purposes. It can be made from any material, and it often holds wine, water, or other libations preferred by the individual or coven. It is the symbolic representation of the womb as it holds and contains the life-giving force.

Together with the athame it is used to represent sexual union during the Great Rites. The five-pointed star represents the element of Earth. It is often made of copper, but can be constructed from clay, metal, or paper. Some Wiccans cast the circle by rolling it around the edges of the sacred space. The Pentacle (drawn inside the circle) is a tool that is used to summon certain energies or spirits. Normally, it is the centerpiece of an altar where it holds various objects, such as moon cakes, salt, amulets, or charms.

The wand is a thin, straight stick that is held in the hand. It is generally made from a sacred wood such as willow, birch, hazel, oak, or elder. It is generally one to one and a half feet long. Often it is carved or decorated with personal items such as crystals and gems."

So, that's a breakdown of the main tools witches use, including for divination. Notice that the cauldron is not only for boiling items during spells, working with their concoctions and potions, they also used it for scrying. We will look more at that next. Again, scrying is the use of water in a cauldron, chalice, or any body of water that can be stared at. We will also talk about how that pentagram can have a moon cake offering on it. But first, let's get more into their divination methods as it is facilitated by scrying.

One person said, if you spend any time either online or watching television, you've seen all kinds of opportunities for psychic services that advertise communication with the dead. It is all over the place. Wicca has had a long history of that practice, just as most of the rest of witchcraft and much of the occult have done since way back in the Babylonian days. They use it for personal or group activities. What they try to do with these sorts of practices is to gain knowledge about the future, often for personal advice. They think they are communicating with the world of dead people's spirits or tapping into some sort of astral plane where they can get knowledge that just floats around out there. It is a common practice with Wicca and pretty much all the occult, including the New Agers.

Getting more into the scrying aspect of divination, scrying can be done in a couple of ways. You can stare at a crystal ball or any sort of reflective like water in a cauldron. Again, water anywhere can be a reflective surface. As I mentioned, water scrying was the method used by Nose-Hair Damus (Nostradamus). He also incorporated hallucinogenic drugs as he stared into water. He used drug-aided scrying, a witchcraft technique that we are told to rely on from Nostradamus, and those like him, for predictions of the future. That is the recommendation for seeing our future rather than the very specific (tried and always true) Bible prophecy. Scrying can also be done with a mirror, which is another prominent tool of the occult. As we have already mentioned, staring at a fire or flame is another way to perform scrying.

They stare at a reflective surface because that can put a person into a deep meditative state, which is also called an "altered state of consciousness." You don't want to get involved in that but what they do, as they get into an altered state of mind, is set an intent about what they wish to have revealed to them. Then the images relating to their intent can appear within the reflective surface used, whether crystal ball, fire, bowl of water, or whatever. They also believe this method can be followed to discover a past life. Of course, that is another big mistake because we humans have not had past lives. We only get one life to live, and that's not just the title of a soap opera; it is Biblical truth recorded for us by God.

Hebrews 9:27: *"It is appointed for people to die once and after that to face judgment."*

Those scrying to get into an altered state of consciousness are looking for guidance and sometimes receive supposed images of the future in shapes and colorful hues. With scrying in movies, you will typically see a crystal ball where there is smoke or mist with different colors and shapes appearing in it. But what do those mean? Often no one knows so it is left up to the scryer to decide. So again, the witch can just make it up as he or she goes.

Scrying is one method of performing divination, of which there are many such techniques, but we'll only deal with a couple other main ones, including "Rune Casting."

In another study after witchcraft that will deal with an assortment of miscellaneous occult practices, we'll get into Druidism and more deeply into their runes than just how they are used for divination. Runes have actually been around since the second century as an alphabet for Germanic and Nordic cultures. Here's more on that:

"Runic alphabets were used to write various Germanic languages before the adoption of the Latin alphabet. Ancient tribes use them to name places and things, attract luck and fortune, provide protection, and magically divine (divination) the course of future events. Because runes were carved into stone or wood, they were formed with straight lines only. While these symbols have various origins and meanings, Wiccans attach their own personal significance to them, and all can be used as symbols of power and protection in your craft."

Runes are an ancient runic alphabet with all figures drawn through use of straight lines because they were often carved on stone. If you have ever tried writing on rock with a knife or other pointed object, you probably understand it is not fun to try carving curves and circles. But what witches do is take a bag or handful of small pieces that have a different letter from the rune alphabet on each, shake it up, and then roll them out like dice to supposedly see their future, give them some sort of information, or impart wisdom. They think the spirits are going to make those pieces show rune surfaces that come out in an order which will reveal some message. This method is similar to what we read about in African witchcraft where they do the same method but using bones that they shake up and roll out in front of them to supposedly get messages.

While doing a term paper on Babylon in Bible College, one aspect I learned about involved their witchcraft practice of using animal innards. They would cut an animal open and however the guts fell out, that would supposedly tell them something, just like the rolling out of a handful of bones or runes. They believed that too could depict the future, give special knowledge, and tell some ruler when the best opportunity would be to attack their enemy. It's all crazy but witches practice it, along with this next method of divination, which is probably one of the more popular ones:

We dealt with Tarot Cards in our study of the New Age movement. It is probably one of the most well-known divination tools and used by Wiccans, other witches, and occultists, as well as New Agers. Tarot cards have been around since about the 1400's with 78 cards split into two categories called the major arcana and minor arcana. Like the rune alphabet, each card stands for something, so the witch shuffles the deck and turns cards up, normally one at a time, to reveal a supposed message. And by the way, tarot cards are a common gateway practice that first gets people involved with witchcraft and Wicca today. These cards are being promoted all over the internet in places like online video-streaming platforms. A lot of these video transcripts I've been sharing with you come straight from the witches' online channels. From their own mouths, I want you to get the admissions of what they believe and do. As Christians, you and I come together as a Church on Sundays to worship Jesus Christ, fellowship, and be encouraged through God's word. Witches are encouraged to get together on Sundays to practice divination through tarot cards to find out how their upcoming week is going to go. Here is more on that with this video transcript promoting a tarot card activity to be performed at Sunday gatherings they call the "7-Card Week Ahead Spread":

"This is a 7-Card Week Ahead Spread to help you get insight on the flow of energy that you'll experience in the coming week. A perfect spread for a Sunday afternoon or evening, the main goal here is to determine what kind of energies will be dominant around you in the next seven days. You will need a standard Tarot deck (but you may use an Oracle deck instead), a pen, and paper. Find a printable Tarot guide, for this spread, below the video. Place the deck on your altar or table and set the mood for this ritual by diffusing essential oils such as cinnamon or lemon or burn some incense. You can also light a yellow candle for mental clarity and

decorate your space with a gemstone, such as Amber, Carnelian, or Tiger's Eye."

Wait a second; do we know any religious practice that is also hugely into incense, candles, and bell ringing? Yes, and it rhymes with Roman Catholicism. Isn't it interesting that they share those same pagan witchcraft practices that have nothing to do with studying the Bible?

What was another key word we just saw in that video transcript? It was "essential" oils. Hey, isn't that a prominent trend today, even in the Church? Christians are talking about and networking with essential oils that are somehow supposed to heal our bodies and some weird stuff that goes with it. Folks, you better do your homework on that practice if you are involved in essential oils. I'm not saying certain substances don't have properties to help, but witchcraft uses the same tool of essential oils, so we better look into it. As Christians, we also should not forget that our greatest opportunity for healing is always through prayer.

So, those were methods of divination and now I want to give you witchcraft's suggestions for how to approach divination:

"When you're involved in divination, keep it positive. Don't try to conjure up a demon or some low vibrational entity."

Well, duh. But if you conjure up anything, it is going to be a demon so that is why God condemns the practice and tells us we should not get involved with it. Here is more from the witches and it includes a slap at Christians:

"Contrary to what religions like Christianity teach, divination is not inherently evil. It's an excellent way to get in touch with your higher consciousness in the spirit realm."

No, it's the perfect vehicle for knowingly or unknowingly finding yourself involved with demonic activity. You do not want to mess with that! But that has given you a quick look at the witchcraft practice of divination. The second of their practices we want to cover is the hub (pun intended) of Wiccan activities:

The Wiccan Calendar is also called the Wheel of the Year. Wicca is considered a non-organized "religion" and, though it's an eclectic practice with different witches and covens holding more strongly to some practices more than others, the Wiccan Calendar is pretty much a centerpiece for their "religion." It is made up of eight ritual holidays that they call Sabbats. These rituals provide regular occasions for them to get together, as well as informing them of when to perform certain rituals throughout the year. These rituals can be observed as an individual or in a witch coven. It is all based on a cyclical calendar that is their driving force or the heart of Wicca. Again, most Wiccans use it and you're going to see that Roman Catholicism has actually Catholicized rituals from this occult calendar to form their own observance of specific holidays they came up with like Christmas, or Christ Mass, Easter and Halloween. The last one parallels the first major ritual holiday of the pagan year, as outlined on the Wiccan Calendar (October 31st each year). Here is more, about that in this video transcript:

"Wiccans honor both the lunar and solar cycles of nature through various rituals and celebrations called Sabbats (Sun rite) and Esbats (Moon rite). The changing of seasons, as the sun travels across the sky and the earth turns upon its axis, are marked through various celebrations and traditions called Sabbats. The solar cycle is broken into eight Sabbats and is collectively referred to as the Wheel of the Year. The Wheel of the Year represents, not just the marking and passing of time, but the never-ending cycle of nature's fertility. There are two equinoxes, two solstices, and four minor points that fall in between each of these in the Wheel of the Year.

Sabbats are celebrations that bring the community together to recognize the change in seasons. Many followers believe that these eight holy days connect them to Mother Earth and her bounty. Samhain (Halloween, October 31st) is the beginning of the pagan year, often referred to as the Day of the Dead, or the Witches New Year. Samhain, pronounced, (sa' win) translates to 'summer's end' (Old Irish, 'samain'). It's at the time when the sunlight begins to recede, and the darkness grows. During this Sabbat, Wiccans celebrate and honor the dead as the veil between the worlds is the thinnest. When the veil between the everyday world and the netherworld thins, communication between the living and the departed becomes easier through various forms of divination. Samhain is a time to remember and honor the ancestors.

Yule (Winter Solstice, December 21st) is celebrated on the darkest day of the year, as it is the winter solstice; the amount of daylight is shortest during the day. Yule celebrates the coming of the light as the daylight begins to slowly lengthen. The cycle of nature begins with the birth of the Sun God during this celebration. Yule logs were gathered from the land or given as a gift to burn in the home. In more modern times, a piece of wood is often used with three holes for candles, and they are lit to symbolize the God, Goddess and season. Mistletoe and holly are hung in the home for good fortune and to encourage a hardy crop for the following year. "

When the first stirrings of spring are in the air, it is time to celebrate Imbolc (Candlemass, February 2nd). The womb of Mother Earth and her fertility are revealed during a holiday that literally translates to, 'in the belly.' The light is becoming stronger and new life is beginning to spring forth from the earth herself. During this turn at the Wheel of the Year, the Maiden shines as the Crone recedes and the Sun God reaches puberty.

As the sun passes over the celestial equator, the Goddess Ostara (Spring Equinox, March 21st) is honored. The word 'easter' is related to the Goddess Ostara. She is the Anglo-Saxon Goddess that represents the dawn. Fertility is in full swing during this celebration, complete with eggs, rabbits, seeds, and flowers. During Ostara, night and day are in perfect equilibrium, as are the Goddess and God. As the days become longer and warmer, the earth fills with energy and life, as it is time for hopes to transform into action. The Goddess and the Sun God have begun to grow and mature.

Beltone (May Eve, April 30th) is the beginning of summer, and once again is a celebration focused on fertility. Balor, also known as, Bel, the God of light and fire, was a Celtic deity that helped to ensure the fertility of the earth. Fires were lit on hilltops in his honor to celebrate the return of life. Wiccans celebrate the mating of the Sun God and fertile Earth Goddess on this day and rejoice in the pregnancy of the Goddess. The love between men and women is honored during this sacred bond of love. Dancing and singing around a maypole are a common way to celebrate Beltone.

Litha (Midsummer, June 21st) has the longest amount of light of any day of the year. As it is a celebration of the zenith of the sun, it is essentially the opposite of Yule's darkness. On this day, light and life are abundant, as the Sun God has reached his maximum strength and potential. The Goddess is heavy with pregnancy as the earth is heavy with the ripening crops. While Litha is the celebration of the God and Goddess at the pinnacle of their life, it is also a time of sadness as it ushers in the decline of the sun. This decline is linked to weakness and death as the Wheel of the Year once again begins to turn towards winter.

Translated as 'Loaf Mass,' Lammas (Lughnasadh, August 1st), is the time of the first harvest. As the corn is ripe in the field, Lammas marks the start of autumn. Lughnasadh derived from the Celtic Sun God, Lugh (a youthful warrior hero in Irish mythology), who was associated with the sun. Wiccans believe that, at this time, the Sun God's power begins to wane. But while the Sun God begins his decline, the abundance of the Goddess is in full swing. She has provided a vast bounty of crops for the harvest. The central focus of this festival is to reap the rewards of all that has been sown.

Mabon (Autumn Equinox, September 21st): Once again, the day and night (light and dark) are in perfect balance with one another. During the Autumn Equinox, Wiccans give thanks to the harvest and begin to store the crops that were harvested at Lammas. The darkness is coming, and the Sun God and Earth Goddess have significantly aged. The second harvest allows followers to take a moment and breathe deeply, releasing the rush and hustle of everyday life. This relaxation allows for time to reflect back on hard work and enjoy the fruits of our labor that have made this harvest possible. After Mabon, the Wheel of the Year once again turns to Samhain (Halloween)."

A couple of items may have caught your attention, as far as they relate to our Christian holidays. You'll notice December 21st is their Wiccan ritual day of Yule, which is around our time of Christmas with its similar "Yule Logs." They also mentioned similar traditions involving wreaths and mistletoe. We do not have time to get into all that here, but just know that Catholicism was the religion that took the pagan Yule ritual and merged it with Catholicism's Christ Mass holiday. Notice it wasn't Christians who did that. Catholicism is not Christianity, so it wasn't done by Christians. This merger with paganism's rituals was done by the Roman Catholic Church, which is no friend of Christianity.

Catholicism also latched onto the pagan witchcraft ritual day of "Ostara" and turned it into "Easter." Some familiar parts of Easter that come from Ostara's fertility aspect, are rabbits and eggs. Catholicism combined that witchcraft ritual day with Christ's resurrection day and called it Easter. As long as I've been a pastor at Sunrise, that is why we do not celebrate Easter, the Catholic pagan ritual day. Instead, we honor what Jesus did for us by celebrating "Resurrection Day." I am not trying to be legalistic, but bunnies have nothing to do with Jesus rising from the dead and everything to do with the Wiccan witchcraft calendar.

Now, does that mean I am against celebrating Christmas in December at the same time as Catholicism's Christmas with its incorporated aspects of the witch's Yule ritual? Biblically, we know Christ's birth was most likely not in winter because that is not when the shepherds tend sheep in the hills. It was probably more of a springtime event. So, I get it that the date is wrong, and Catholicism was merging with another pagan ritual day, but I'm not against celebrating the birth of Christ and doing it every year. That said, if we're going to celebrate Christmas, which is supposed to be about the birth of Jesus, then make it about that and not what the world's turned it into, including much of the occult activity that honors the pagan Yule ritual on the witchcraft calendar.

Likewise, if we are going to celebrate Resurrection Day at the time of the pagan and Catholic Easter, Ostara, then let's celebrate Resurrection Day instead of witchcraft's Ostara. Celebrating Jesus rising from the dead is exciting to me but we Christians need to keep it Biblical if we're going to have those celebrations along with the rest of today's society. Let's not kid ourselves like King Saul who thought he could pull off occult witchcraft activity, as long as he did so in the dark with a disguise, thinking those would fool God. We do not want to ever merge Christianity with paganism because, as we have seen, God does not put up with that.

In this chapter, we're also going to see that Catholicism is the one responsible for popularizing Halloween, which is the pagan ritual day of Samhain (sa' win). But how did they change the name from Samhain to Halloween since they are such different names? We will get to that but just know it was another Catholic act of co-opting a pagan ritual day and then popularizing it.

Witches believe their divination and other practices work spiritually best by coordinating them with their calendar or Wheel of the Year. Those dates also give witches many reasons throughout the year to get together for fellowship. It sounds enjoyable, but they need to know that upon their last breath in this life, if they did not repent of their sins and turn to Jesus Christ for forgiveness, each and every one of them will, unfortunately, go straight to hell. They must exit that demonic calendar and quickly get to the cross of Christ so they can be saved by accepting Christ's free gift of salvation and life after death in Heaven instead of hell with satan and the demons who want them on the witch's Wheel of the Year so they won't seek Jesus.

Here's more about the focus of their Sabbats, which usually starts with the formal ritual that involves god and goddess worship:

"The formal ritual is usually followed by a feast of some kind. These proceedings may be simple or elaborate and may involve just a solitary practitioner, a coven, or an informal Wiccan circle. Some covens and circles, as well as other Pagan groups, even hold their Sabbat rituals in

public so that interested members of the community might come and observe and learn. Others maintain a tradition of strict secrecy and celebrate in private."

Evangelizing their witchcraft practices in public is getting much easier for them today. If they can come out to openly pray against our President and even have the news pick it up and positively report on it, that's got to embolden them to do more public rituals. Still, many continue to perform their witchcraft secretly or privately. And sometimes the secrecy is because of their ritual killings, or "sacrifices," that involve animals and can even be done to people, as we have seen throughout their history and it hasn't gone away today. They are not going to do that in the open because society would find out who they really are and what they are capable of. Here are the witches making their practice sound like a helpful form of environmentalism, which is another smokescreen movement:

"Observing the Wiccan Wheel of the Year can be a profoundly spiritually rewarding practice. Having a Sabbat to celebrate every six weeks means we stay more in tune with nature and are more consciously aware of the turning of the seasons. In fact, many Wiccans refer to their participation in Sabbat rituals as 'Turning the Wheel,' as an acknowledgment of their co-creative relationship with nature. Of course, every day provides opportunities to commune with the Goddess and the God. But it is nice to always have another Witchy occasion to look forward to, just a few weeks away!"

That's a good overview of the Wiccan Wheel of the Year and now I want to finish out this calendar discussion with Roman Catholicism's practice of Halloween.

How did the pagan witch's first Sabbat celebration of the year, Samhain, end up being the Catholic celebration of Halloween? We can thank the Catholic Church and their previous popes for that. Let me demonstrate that:

"Halloween is a time to celebrate the spooky, the scary, and the frightening. A reason for kids to don masks and demand candy from neighbors, and an excuse for some adults to dress in outlandish, sexy, or terrifying guises that would not be socially acceptable the rest of the year. Whether an innocent day of fun or a night full of fear, Halloween is for the darker side. Before Halloween, the pagans had Samhain. The pagan holiday from the old world, like the ghosts of Halloween, did not die, but lives on and rises again and again even in our most modern traditions. Samhain pronounced sa-ween, comes from Irish Gaelic for 'summer's end' and was the Celtic people of the British Isles' New Year's Eve. It marked the last day of their year and summer, and the beginning of their year and winter."

Just as our calendar starts on January 1st, the Celts begin on October 31st with the Samhain celebration at the end of summer. And here is why that particular day is best for celebrating all their ghosts, ghouls, spirits, and demons:

"To the Celts, this lent the evening to being a liminal period or a time of transition. The veil between worlds became thinned and more easily crossed. Spirits and demons could come to our world and roam freely. People would leave offerings of fruit and wine outside their door to keep these spirits from bringing the family and livestock misfortune. With the doorway between dimensions at its widest point, the dead could also freely move to our realm. Families would set an extra place for dead relatives, and special fires would be lit to guide these risen souls safely. But it wasn't just the realm of the dead that could utilize this blurring of the borders, but the living, too. Holy men and women would use Samhain to divine the future, speak to the dead, and spy on the living using mirrors."

So, that description fits our Scripture about King Saul seeking divination. The occult believes Samhain is the best time of year to practice divination. But how did Samhain become Halloween? Here is that:

"As Catholicism took hold of Europe, the church stomped out what it could and absorbed what it couldn't. The folk practices of Samhain would

not be extinguished, so they merely masked them. Pope Boniface declared the 1st of November 'All Saints Evening.'"

All Saints Evening tells us something interesting about Roman Catholicism because they have a prominent and completely unbiblical practice of praying to their dead saints. First, it makes no sense scripturally because the Bible says every born-again Christian is a saint. The word, "saint" is "hagios" in the Greek, meaning "Holy one." We Christians are made Holy in Jesus Christ. So, Catholicism has taken that Biblical term and used it to encourage Catholics to pray to dead people, which is divination. Praying to or attempting to communicate with the dead is the same divination that got Saul a death sentence from God. Still, Catholicism took their practice of divination, doubled down when they merged it with witchcraft's Samhain, and then just relabeled it as, "All Saints Evening."

"This became a Catholic holy day to celebrate all the dead saints and their works. Another term for a saint was a 'hallow,' a word used commonly in religion when something is deified. The night became known as 'All Hallows Evening.' The term, over time, contracted to Allhallowe'en, until finally Halloween."

Roman Catholicism incorporated their version of divination with witchcraft's Samhain ritual because they could not get rid of the pagan practice. That co-opting of other faiths is a common practice for Catholicism, as we saw with witchcraft in Africa. Remember how the Catholic Church facility was built right next to the snake worshiping place so locals could go honor the snake right after Catholic Mass. Catholic leadership didn't care about their people worshiping the snake, as long as they made it to the Catholic Mass. Here is more:

"Catholicism also incorporated a lot of the pagan beliefs that the spirits walked the earth at this time."

Because the Samhain season is said to be the thinnest veil of the year between us who are living and the dead spirits, those spirits can supposedly traverse more easily between the spirit world and ours. So, Catholics decided that would also be the easiest time to perform their practice of communicating with dead saints (divination). In that way, another pagan holiday was Catholicized.

"In parts of England, it was believed that the souls in purgatory would come to earth on this day, so family members would light fires to help guide them home."

Of course, the Catholic concept of "purgatory" is not at all Biblical. For Catholics, purgatory means a place to purge after death. It is a mythical place you'll never find in the Bible unless you have the Roman Catholic version that includes the Apocrypha, which is full of false teachings. Catholicism claims we go to purgatory right after death and it is a place of suffering in flames of torment. They say we need to be purged for our sins for what could be a million years, depending on how many prayers we said in life and how much we attended Catholic Mass, as well as the amount of money we handed the church and priests, so they would promise to pray their super-duper prayers on our behalf. That type of church sanctioned activities supposedly shaves off time in purgatory and then maybe we might make it to heaven. It is a completely false teaching.

Catholic purgatory works with All Hallow's Eve because that is a time when those in purgatory can supposedly come to earth because the veil between us, and the spirit world, is thinnest. Catholic families would light fires to help guide them home. Here is more from Catholicism that comes from pagan witchcraft and remember that Catholicism also incorporated witchcraft's Maypole that we talked about earlier:

"In other parts of the British Isles, bonfires (bone fires) were lit to help guide the spirits and became social events for the community. Children would dress in disguise to ward off the roaming spirits, possibly so they would not be mistaken as one of the purgatory-dwelling dead, and Catholic spirits themselves. This tradition, known as mumming, gave root to guising. These costumed children would go to houses to collect the offerings meant for the wandering ghosts."

The practice of Halloween is observed all over Britain and America. Let's break down how Catholicism meshed this important pagan witchcraft ritual with Catholicism's idea of praying to dead saints or divination. Of course, a prominent aspect of that are the costumes.

The Celts believed the dead could walk, so they had the ability to pop out anywhere around our planet when the veil between the spirit world and our reality was thinnest on October 31st. And they believed those spirits could be communicated with to divine a person's future and gain other knowledge.

"The Celts were highly superstitious and thought these evil spirits could damage crops, possess the living, and spread incurable sickness. That is why the Celtic pagans dressed up in scary costumes and animal hides while hovering in fear around bone fires. Some of the Celts wore ghoulish costumes so that wandering spirits would mistake them for one of their own and leave them alone. Others offered sweets to the spirits to appease them."

Does that sound familiar? It's where we got our candy-giving tradition (trick-or-treat), including the Catholic version.

Halloween masks were also used to hide those wanting to anonymously attend pagan festivals and others practicing Animism and Shamanism, which is still being followed today with practitioners wearing animal masks and hides because they believe their costume rituals will allow them to take on the animal's personality and power. As far as the sweets, you'll remember that one of witchcraft's rituals involves offering moon cakes. That also parallels Catholicism's trick or treating where they turned All Souls Day with the witchcraft moon cakes into the Catholic version where followers were encouraged to go around offering "soul cakes" for the spirits of the dead that were supposedly visiting earth from their time in purgatory. Isn't that nuts?!

"The American Halloween tradition of trick-or-treating probably dates back to the early Catholic All Souls Day parades in England. During the

festivities, poor citizens would beg for food and families would give them pastries called 'soul cakes' (sweets) in return for their promise to pray for the family's dead relatives."

It was important to pray for dead relatives because of Catholicism's practice of praying for their dead loved ones in purgatory so that time could supposedly be shaved off their sentence. And Catholics still do this today. When I was pastor in western New York, I learned that it is a heavily Catholic area and that realization hit me like a ton of bricks because I had no clue I was stepping into that scenario. Still to that day, at Catholic funerals, envelopes are given out with a prayer card that encouraged attendees to put money in an envelope and give it to the priest so that he will pray one of his super-duper priest prayers for your loved one to really start their purgatory time off with an immediate reduced sentence. And because people don't know their Bible, it is a great way to bring in some serious cash for the Catholic Church. They still do this practice today. Even way back in Catholic Church times, the same method of getting donations was employed through Catholic soul cakes, which were given with the idea that the recipient would promise to pray for the giver's dead relatives, thus shortening the loved one's time in the fictitious place Catholicism calls purgatory. Here is more about the Catholicizing of pagan rituals:

"The distribution of soul cakes was encouraged by Catholicism as a way to replace the ancient pagan practice of leaving food and wine for roaming spirits. The practice, which was referred to as "going a-souling," was eventually taken up by children who would visit the houses in their neighborhood and be given (sweets like soul cakes,) ale, food and money (So that the kids would pray for the giver's dead relatives.)"

"Author Scott P. Richert, content manager for Sunday Visitor, the largest Catholic publishing company, writes that the purpose of All Souls Day is to pray people out of purgatory by prayer, alms-giving, and the Mass, (which is completely unbiblical.)"

"On Halloween, to keep ghosts away from their houses, people would place bowls of food outside their homes to appease the ghosts and prevent them from attempting to enter."

Again, that had become a Catholicized pagan practice, just like the familiar "Jack-o-lantern" that started with the pagans and got adopted by Catholicism even though it is completely unbiblical but definitely fitting the pattern we've been seeing from them:

"Pumpkins and Jack-o-lanterns were also part of Celtic lore. A tale was told that a drunken farmer named Stingy Jack was so wicked that when he died, he restlessly wandered between heaven and hell, unable to enter either one. As he roamed the darkness, he hollowed out a turnip and placed a burning coal inside to light his way."

Here's how Catholicism turned that pagan practice into a Catholic one:

"In medieval Britain, Catholic 'supplicants' moved from door to door asking for food in return for a prayer for the dead and they would carry hollowed-out turnip lanterns, whose candle connoted a soul trapped in purgatory."

The Catholics initially showed up at the houses on Halloween with a pagan Jack-o-lantern made from turnips, just like the pagans were using. The candles flames burning inside were meant to represent the souls of dead loved ones. Catholic kids would show up at neighbor Joe's house, point to that soul flame in the Jack-o-lantern, and ask Joe if he wanted his loved one to get a shorter sentence in purgatory. If so, Joe had better come up with a soul cake or something else sweet. That is absolutely crazy but it's the history of more Catholicizing paganism witchcraft. Now, how did the turnip become a pumpkin?

"During the 1800's in North America, pumpkins replaced turnips because they were plentiful as well as easy to hollow out and carve. The beliefs behind this custom, the immortality of the soul, purgatory, and prayers for the dead, are not based on the Bible."

Again, whenever someone prays to a dead person or tries to communicate with them, he or she is performing occult-witchcraft divination, which the Bible tells us not to have any part of. We are NOT to do that!

"Pagan Celts carved 'Jack-o-lanterns' to guide lost souls home on the eve of Samhain."

Another Celtic practice used for divination was bobbing for apples.

"The Celts believed that bobbing for apples, or some fruit, used to be considered a form of divination. Bobbing for apples was a practice where people would dunk their heads in a vat of water and try to bite into floating fruit in a quest to figure out (divine) their future spouse. Ladies would mark an apple or a piece of fruit and toss it into the tub of water. The thinking was they'd be destined to whoever pulled it out of the water."

The man who pulled out an apple or piece of fruit with a particular woman's mark on it, was destined to marry her. Of course, it sounds like goofy child's play, but it was a pagan form of divination with them attempting to figure out the future from outside of God's Word in the Bible. The practice not only goes back to the Celts, but also Roman days, which we know were full of witchcraft.

"In ancient Rome, cider was drawn and the Romans bobbed for apples, which was part of a divination that supposedly helped a person discover their future marriage partner."

Now, let's get into some other ways Samhain was Catholicized into Halloween, the important start to the witch's calendar year. Again, it's the day that pagan witches believe to be a time of the thinnest veil between our world and that of the spirits, so the spirits are more able to travel between the two worlds at that time. And I'm telling you, still to this day the time of the Catholic Halloween, as well as the witch's Samhain, is looked at as the best time to perform divination. The Bible warns us to never participate in divination, but the occult and Catholicism teach it. Let me give you some other practices that have revolved around Halloween with people encouraged to do exactly what Saul did in attempting to contact dead people's spirits. Besides bobbing for apples, here are some other techniques used to divine future spouses:

"In 18th-century Ireland, a matchmaking cook might bury a ring in a woman's mashed potatoes on Halloween night, hoping to bring true love to the diner who found it."

If you are someone living back then, you might have stared into a big old pot of mashed potatoes, that someone threw a hunk of metal in to, and, one way or another, that ring would be found. Unfortunately, it might be at the same moment you lose a tooth. But hey, apparently the good news is, by next Halloween you are going to get married. So, that is another of their pagan forms of divination and here are a couple more:

"In Scotland, fortune-tellers recommended that an eligible young woman name a hazelnut for each of her suitors and then toss the nuts into the fireplace. The nut that burned to ashes rather than popping or exploding, the story went, represented the girl's future husband. Another tale had it that if a young woman ate a sugary concoction made out of walnuts, hazelnuts and nutmeg before bed on Halloween night she would dream about her future husband."

"Halloween traditions often involve fruit centerpieces, apples, and nuts. Three of the sacred fruits of the Celts were acorns, apples, and nuts, especially the hazelnut, considered a god and the acorn, sacred from its association to the oak. Fruits and nuts also seem to be related to the Roman harvest feast of Pomona, apparently the goddess of fruit."

The oak tree has been a prominent part of pagan worship for a long time. Now I want to give you a few more old-school forms of divination that have been used here in America during Halloween, including this first one where you can imagine a young woman peeling away on apples to divine her future husband:

"Young women tossed apple-peels over their shoulders, hoping that the peels would fall on the floor in the shape of their future husband's initials; tried to learn about their futures by peering at egg yolks floating in a bowl of water."

But why would they put that egg in water? It's because of the witchcraft practice of scrying with a reflective surface to perform divination. They would do this on the pagan Samhain and the Catholicized Halloween version of it because they believe that is the best time to do divination with the spirit (demon) world. Now, take a look at that center picture depicting another witchcraft way of divining a future husband:

"Young women stood in front of mirrors in darkened rooms, holding candles and looking over their shoulders for their husband's faces."

"Other rituals were more competitive. At some Halloween parties, the first guest to find a burr on a chestnut-hunt would be the first to marry. At others, the first successful apple-bobber would be the first down the aisle. Of course, whether we are asking for romantic advice or trying to avoid seven years of bad luck, each one of these Halloween superstitions relies on the goodwill of the very same "spirits" whose presence the early Celts felt so keenly."

Here is another oxymoron for you: Their divination rituals relied on the "good will" of "demon" spirits. Do you think demons wish us well? No, of course not! Let me give you one more form of divination:

"There are also reports of fortune-cookie like favors being given out during earlier times. People wrote messages on pieces of paper in milk, and the notes were then folded and placed into walnut shells. The shells would be heated over a fire, causing the milk to brown just enough for the message to mystically appear on the paper for the recipient."

Have you ever done that with lemon juice? You write some on paper using lemon juice, which you can't see until you put it over a flame and then suddenly the juice turns brown, revealing what you wrote. Hey, maybe that was just Kansas where we had nothing else to do.

You can see the pattern of Catholicism merging with paganism's witchcraft to make something that is not Christian. We don't have time to get into the Catholicizing of the pagan Ostara ritual celebration that became the Catholic holiday of Easter, or the pagan ritual day of Yule that Catholicism turned into Christ Mass, or Christmas. How did these pagan witchcraft-related rituals gain such widespread popularity throughout our entire society today? How did those rituals get inflicted upon and merged into the Church? And how is it that even the Church today is now merging so comfortably with witchcraft and the occult, so much so that they are hiring witches for their staff? It's because people are not studying the Bible. Instead, they are getting outside the Bible to rely on their individual experiences that claim feelings like, "God told me..." Even those in the Church these days would rather turn to witchcraft-divination practices to supposedly discern their future, find advice, or gain some secret knowledge, rather than turn to God's Word.

But all those pursuing false beliefs and practices like these should think about how God condemned witchcraft with examples like that strong judgment against King Saul for participating in occult divination. God is consistent in what He supports and condemns. So, how do you think He's going to judge those practicing witchcraft today? You don't want any part of that! And I think the reason so many, even in the Church, do not know to stay away from the occult, is because the Church is failing to teach about it. But even as long as we've been exposing witchcraft in this study online, we just had another individual, who claims to be Christian, that is rebuking us for studying this material. It was said that we should not study satan. He or she said we should be studying God instead.

But every bit of our witchcraft study has been equipping us against the practice, giving us an understanding of those involved, and showing us how to witness to witches. And all that has been from God's Word in the Bible. Satan, the occult, and witchcraft are real! They come with horrible consequences. Since God loves us, He wrote a lot about those evil practices to warn us about what not to get involved with. Knowing that, how can anyone say not to study those aspects the Bible teaches? In fact, those with a mindset to ignore this evil should wonder where that intention is coming from to keep them in the dark about what they are claiming we should not study. Where do you think the seeds of those thoughts are emanating from? It is not from God. We not only need to study these horrible practices to help us avoid them, but also so that we can warn those involved to get out. And the good news is, even if you have gone down that route, no matter how long, you can get out of it and be rescued through Jesus Christ. Just like this young woman named Liberty, it doesn't even matter how bad it got:

Liberty: *"I shouldn't have been born. My own mother didn't want me. There must have been something wrong with me because nobody wanted me, you know. Nobody wanted to raise me, love me, take care of me, let me be their daughter."*

Narrator: *"Liberty grew up with deep feelings of rejection after her mother left her and her brother on their father's doorstep."*

Liberty: *"She wanted to party. She wanted to do her thing, and she couldn't do that with two little babies. And so, you know, she just decided to give us up."*

Narrator: *"After several turbulent years with her father, Liberty moved back in with her mom, who introduced her to drugs and alcohol. At a young age, her mother also exposed her to the occult."*

Liberty: *"She always had a large bookshelf that was full of witchcraft books with spells, chants, ways to curse people. She had tarot cards, a Ouija board, all that. That was normal in my mom's household."*

Narrator: *"When Liberty was fourteen, she had an argument with her mother's abusive boyfriend and found herself rejected again."*

Liberty: *"I came home, got off the bus and there was a box of stuff sitting outside. There was a note that my mom had left that said, 'He's in, you're out. You have to find somewhere else to live.' This is my reality. My mom doesn't love me. She never wanted me. She doesn't care."*

Narrator: *"She found acceptance in the party scene and had relationships with men who gave her a place to stay and supplied her with drugs."*

Liberty: *"I did whatever I had to do to survive. I was alone. I was lost. The crystal meth and the drinking was very heavy. I mean, it was a daily thing. It wasn't just like, let's go party on a Friday night. I mean, it was every single day drinking and drugs, drinking and drugs. Staying up for days."*

Narrator: *"She also began experiencing strange phenomenon and some unsettling symptoms."*

Liberty: *"I was hearing voices. I was seeing things. I would get up in the night, and I would feel like something was speaking to me and was coming after me. I had sores; little open sores around my body."*

Narrator: *"A friend's parents set up a meeting with their pastor. Liberty reluctantly agreed to see him."*

Liberty: *"I had no belief in God or spiritual beings or anything like that. And he basically just said all these are the symptoms of a demonic attack on you and the only way to deal with it is rebuke satan in the name of Jesus Christ."*

Narrator: *"Days later, she had a terrifying encounter."*

Liberty: *"These dark images began to just cover the walls, and they were closing in on me like they were coming after me. I did what the pastor said, and I rebuked them in the name of Jesus Christ of Nazareth. And* then the fear was gone and everything I was feeling was gone. It was literally just gone. The demons, everything, just disappeared."

Narrator: *"Liberty says she learned there was power in the name of Jesus but knew little else about him."*

Liberty: *"I just felt like I needed this Jesus that could make demons flee. I don't have to wait to go to church and be called to the altar. I can just sit right here in my living room and accept Christ, you know."*

Narrator: *"She surrendered her life to Christ, then fell into a deep sleep. When she awoke, she was in a struggle for her life."*

Liberty: *"Something was holding me down and just not letting me up, not letting me speak. It was a feeling like a hand was over my mouth. I just begin to say, 'Jesus.' I was just trying to get the words out, and I said, 'Jesus.' It was a very muffled, 'Jesus,' and I felt like it was at the top of my lungs and the thing that was covering my mouth was slowly leaving; like letting go. The last thing I yelled was, 'I rebuke you in the name of Jesus.' And at that moment, whatever was holding me down removed itself and then I heard this really loud scream like an evil, loud, wretched squeal. It sounded as if it was leaving. It could no longer reside because Jesus was now the Lord of my life."*

Narrator: *"Liberty knew she was free. She began to throw away anything that connected her to the darkness she once accepted as normal."*

Liberty: *"I knew that the Lord was basically, in that one moment, cleaning up my whole life. He was just like, 'It's all going. You're letting it all go. I'm taking it all away from you. You're being set free.' I finally was me. I was never me before. Who's Liberty? You know, who's this girl, that was born with no purpose, no value, no reason to live? He took everything out of me and healed me of all the horrible things that the world basically dished out on me. My life is changed forever because of that day. This is what I've been waiting for my entire life. And this is what it feels like to know a love that you never got; you never received before. I was born for* *a purpose, and it's to serve Jesus Christ and to do His work. He's the only one that can set you free."*

And that includes freedom for those who have gotten involved in the occult. What I love about her testimony is that it's what happened to me. I was all by myself and it was just such amazing bare bones faith, calling upon the name of Jesus Christ, asking Him to forgive me, and BAM! Instantly, (literally), the demons were gone!

That's why we need to understand this, folks; because there are people out there all around us who may be involved in these things. We may not even know they are, but they're infected with and surrounded by demons. They live in torment. The good news is we can tell them about Jesus because He can set them free.

The next chapter will be a continuation of witchcraft practices and then we'll finish out this second book with an understanding of those promoting it.

Chapter Nineteen

The Practices of Wicca
Part 2

For a quick recap because that is what we do as a teaching tool, we've seen that the definition of Wicca is "witchcraft," which spread all over the world from its origin in the occult practices spawned at the Tower of Babel, a couple hundred years after Noah's worldwide flood. We have mentioned that the only protection from witchcraft is calling on the name of Jesus and relying on Him. We talked about the history of Wicca that came out of the European witchcraft. That wasn't the only place, America got witchcraft but it's the culture that contributed the most. We also looked at the beliefs and symbols of Wicca witchcraft, as well as what we started in the last chapter, their practices.

Witchcraft practices cannot all be covered here, but so far, we've narrowed them down to the main ones like divination, which is contacting spirits or dead people, that turn out to be just lying demons. Witches have different techniques for divination that include scrying, rune casting, tarot cards, all of which are being popularized today. After that we talked about the Wiccan Calendar, or Wheel of the Year, that witches use to determine when to perform their ritual practices.

Their calendar year begins on October 31st with Halloween, which witches call Samhain (pronounced Sa' win, or Sa' when). Not so surprising, Catholicism merged with occult witchcraft practices from the pagan calendar by Catholicizing those pagan ritual dates to create Halloween, Easter and Christmas. Catholic Halloween is all about divination being performed while, at the same time, the Wiccan witchcraft calendar shows their belief that the veil is supposedly thinnest between the living and dead spirits (demons) at that time. So, the spirits are supposedly more able to traverse between the two realities, making communication with humans easier. That is what it's all about for witches, pagans, and Catholics. On Samhain, witches and other occultists communicate with the dead so Catholicism came along to claim the same date and just rename their Catholic term, Halloween. Similar to witch practices at Samhain, Catholic Halloween, on the same date, they set up the practice of having Catholics pray to the dead as part of their already established worship of the saints. Supposedly in an effort to help dead loved ones get less time in purgatory.

Catholicism successfully merged witchcraft practices into their religion to make Samhain into Halloween with the result that our society has to deal with that pagan ritual day being popularized. It is all from Catholicism wanting to encourage people to practice divination (praying to dead saints), which God specifically forbids, as we saw with King Saul and every one of his sons dying for it. The witch's Samhain was Catholicized in many ways like Halloween costumes, the trick or treat aspect, Jack-o'-lanterns, bobbing for apples and many different acts of divination. It all worked together because Catholicism is just as into divination as the pagan witches. When Catholics are told to pray to a dead person for favor or whatever else, that is flat-out divination and the exact same practice as witchcraft's divination. Catholicism has just gotten away with it for a long time because no Christians want to talk about it.

Now, I want to continue with the practices of Wicca witchcraft:

However, and once again, before we get to more practices let's see another of the numerous Bible passages that tell us witchcraft, (whether ancient, Wiccan, or even Catholicized through paganism), is not something we should ever get involved with. This time we'll look at **Micah 5**, which is about the coming Millennial Kingdom of Jesus Christ. During that time, He will rule and reign on earth for a thousand years. And of all the sins and evil behavior the Bible could mention here, what do you suppose He specifically calls out as something that will be eliminated when He sets up His kingdom? It rhymes with witchcraft. Let's take a look at another of the many, many passages from the Bible that tell us not to mess with the occult because God condemns that behavior. Here in **Micah,** it is speaking about the Day of the Lord, when Jesus comes back at His Second Coming, in the last days, to set up His kingdom. (This is after the Rapture of the Church and will be the most horrible time ever to be visited upon the earth, the time of the Seven Year Tribulation):

Micah 5:10-15: *" 'In that day,' declares the Lord, 'I will destroy your horses from among you and demolish your chariots. I will destroy the cities of your land and tear down all your strongholds.' "*

The Lord is saying He will destroy all the things these people think are going to give them victory, including those man-made structures that have helped cause them to grow arrogant and rebellious against God. Here He lets them know they are not going to be practicing any more occult evils like witchcraft:

"I will destroy your witchcraft and you will no longer cast spells. I will destroy your carved images..."

Those witches will have no more carved figurines they can worship. Is there also a huge religion on this planet that will also lose the carved figurines (idols) they worship? Yes, it rhymes with Catholicism, and we will see a lot more of that thread in this chapter. Here the Lord continues condemning the witchcraft tools, like amulet stones, that they use to gain secret power, supercharge their good luck and all the other baloney:

"I will destroy your carved images and your sacred stones from among you; you will no longer bow down to the work of your hands. I will uproot from among you your Asherah poles when I demolish your cities."

In this chapter, we will see more of that female-deity worship talked about in the Old Testament.

"I will take vengeance in anger and wrath upon the nations that have not obeyed me."

My Crone translation for that is this: Jesus will come back and clean house on this whole planet, including those left over from Israel. His wrath will be poured out and the planet's slate will be wiped clean because His reign is about His kingdom of righteousness. Jesus is going to be the ruler of the earth, so the government will be on His shoulders, as Isaiah talks about. Do you think he is going to allow unrighteousness to flourish like we see today? No, that is why it's called His Millennial Kingdom, as well as a Christian's great hope and comfort. We look forward to it for it will be a time of peace with nature and Jesus getting rid of all unrighteous baloney like rebelliousness and wickedness, including the occult and all the satanic practices of today that will be gone. He is not going to allow that stuff and we Christians get to be part of His kingdom. But of all things for Him to call out, He is clearly saying He will not allow witchcraft, sorcery, spells, or any other occult behavior. Those practices are not just condemned by God, but Jesus won't be allowing them to exist when He takes charge, literally and physically ruling and reigning this entire planet from Jerusalem.

Now, we have seen nineteen different warnings from God and still haven't exhausted all the passages throughout the Old and New Testaments where God deals with the occult and its witchcraft. Despite those messages from God being all over the Bible, churches will not touch the issue with a ten-foot pole. For us Christians, that is actually a sign we're near the time of fulfillment of our great hope, which is the Millennial Kingdom with Jesus ruling; a time with no more of this evil and wickedness like witches praying against our people and government.

The Scripture tells us it is a time when Satan himself will be bound for the entire thousand years. That is awesome and surely something to look forward to. But it means we are in that time prior, when churches turn a blind eye to the rise of witchcraft. They will not preach God's Word about Bible prophecy, God's wrath, sin, hell, and judgment. That includes a lack of warning about the occult. And while ignoring Bible prophecy, they leave out any teachings on Christ's Millennial Kingdom. Yet, we wonder why people look so hopeless these days. Christians have the brightest future on the planet, but our teachers won't engage with anything involving this dark realm of the occult and witchcraft. Because of that, those who stumble into witchcraft do not have much hope of being rescued by those in the church. Here is something about that:

Male news anchor: *"CBN News has reported witches have been increasing their political involvement since the president was first elected back in 2016. Now, this comes as witchcraft is on the rise in America. Investigative journalist Billy Hallowell delves into the strange phenomena of supernatural activity. He tells CBN News' the Prayer Link, that it's a subject the church cannot ignore and must be equipped to handle."*

Journalist interviewing Billy Hallowell: *"Why do you think the world and the church sometimes tends to avoid or even ignore the topic of demons and spiritual warfare?"*

Billy Hallowell: *"Yeah, I can't think of a topic that is spoken about more in Scripture, especially in the New Testament, and talked about less in churches. Now, I don't want to say that's every church because lots of churches do a wonderful job dealing with this and talking about it. But I think we know overall that this is a topic that is avoided. And we did a survey, for our book 'Playing With Fire', where we went out and talked to church leaders. These were volunteers and pastors. And we asked them, 'Do you believe that demons exist?' Of course, the vast majority said yes. 'Do you believe that demons are impacting culture?' The vast majority said absolutely.*

And then we asked the question, 'Are pastors in churches talking enough about this?' Seventy-eight percent said no. And so, it was a really fascinating moment to, again, look at this issue and say we are not speaking about it. And I know there are lots of stories I encountered, in writing 'Playing With Fire', of people who have gone for help. They've gone to their church, and they've said, 'I have something going on. I can't explain it.' And they are not given any assistance or help. And so that is a troubling piece of the puzzle. I feel like every pastor should be equipped to deal with this so that people aren't dancing around, going to other denominations and going to other places; because, realistically, outside of the charismatic world the only place people really know where to go would be the Catholic Church."

Wow, and that won't help people! When we really think about what he just said, it's very sad because the Protestant Evangelical Church won't touch this witchcraft occult problem even though it is really happening. Unfortunately, their family and friends encounter the demonic realm either knowingly or unknowingly, getting involved with the occult on a daily basis. It needs to be dealt with. But if their options are to either go to the charismatics or Catholics, they and the entire society are in real trouble! As we saw in our *Charismatic Chaos* study, the charismatics have merged with witchcraft so going to them will not help. And a Catholic priest may result in one of those scenes from *The Exorcist*. And we saw, the Catholic Church merged with witchcraft long before the charismatics. The disservice we Protestants are doing for society is extremely hard to understand since the Bible warns us that this ignorance of the issue would be present in our day. Folks need help and the Protestants are turning them away to be gathered up by those who have merged with the same witchcraft that is causing the problem.

So, what we as a ministry are going to do about it, is what the Bible, over and over, tells us to do. We are to study the entire Bible whether we like some of it or not! And dark occult practices are high on God's list of those subjects we need to deal with! We are going to keep looking at the practices of Wicca witchcraft, and this chapter will deal with their rituals.

We already talked about Wiccan spells, potions, divination, and their calendar of ritual times of the year. Those ritual dates are when they get together as a group or even perform them solitarily, and their goal with a ritual is to what a witch wants in life. It is about themselves and attaining what he or she desires from a spirit (demon). Here is a look at what witches say they do when they get together for these rituals:

"Wiccan rituals can take many different forms, with no two events being exactly alike. Some may be highly structured and elaborate. This is often the case with coven rituals..."

They admit the public isn't told about a lot of their coven rituals because they are secret. Now, why do you think they would keep their rituals secret until a person is initiated into the group? It's because some of those dirty deeds are not just the killing of animals, they also include the murder of adults and children. Among their secrets are those sorts of blood sacrifices. We have seen that with plenty of witchcraft practitioners all over the world and throughout history. That idea should not come as a shock to us now, because we know it is still going on around the planet today. Some areas have had enough of it that at least they are talking about it. Here in the United States where we have the same thing happening in secret, we won't deal with it at all. We're not going to know everything they do in their rituals, but we can look at some generalities with what goes on:

"Other rituals, particularly those practiced by solitary and eclectic Wiccans, may be fairly simple by comparison and may even be made up on the spot (because it's based on relativism.) The content of any given Wiccan ritual will depend on the occasion. For example, Esbats, or Full Moon celebrations, are focused solely on the Goddess, while Sabbats honor the co-creative relationship between the Goddess and the god."

Some of the tools they use during their rituals are candles, herbs, holy oils, and holy water. Another term used with rituals involves the "Law of Attraction." Most people don't know what that term means and especially where it came from because they've never learned about witchcraft and the rest of the occult. The Law of Attraction is a ritual the occult and Wicca witchcraft use to try getting what they want or hexing and cursing those who do something they don't like. Again, their sketchy actions versus their pledge of no harm through the Wiccan Rede, point to exposing the bankruptcy of their so-called ethics. It shines a demonic light on their hypocrisy. And when they do not get everything they want through the attempts at the Law of Attraction, they may blame someone for that shortfall and that person becomes their next target they'll attempt to harm. And folks, the Law of Attraction is all over the internet, as well as even in the church now, brought to use through the Word of Faith false preachers, who are part of the charismatics.

Again, the Law of Attraction is a Wiccan ritual being promoted through the Word of Faith movement. I don't want to retell a year of our *Charismatic Chaos* study here but in that we showed how their practices in the Church are merging with witchcraft and the rest of the occult. This false teaching says people can perform the Law of Attraction ritual to get what they want. Just do what the Word of Faith preachers prescribe, like give money to those false preachers through the offering, buy their books or trinkets, usually along with performing some technique they prescribe, like repeating a Christianized Hindu-type mantra. For this the false preachers promise those donors will get material desires they have, like stacks of money that will buy them fancy cars and beautiful homes. Folks, that is flat out occult stuff that witches do. It is an actual witch ritual. In fact, the Word of Faith preachers even call it the Law of Attraction as if that is some Christian way to live. It's nuts! But people do not catch the scam, because few in society teach the dangers of the occult and almost none in the church will ever teach on occult witchcraft. And these Word of Faith guys in the church aren't even hiding their occult terms.

Now, let's talk about more witch rituals but, again, it's sometimes hard to codify for all witches since their overall philosophy is to pick and choose whatever occult aspects they'd like in their eclectic and relativistic practice. That said, I will give you the general process followed in witch rituals; the steps witches go through to try getting what they want. The first thing they will typically perform is what's called a purification ritual.

With this ritual, they purify the people who are there, the celebrants, and the place where it's being done. Sometimes they will perform a ritual bath or "Smudging Ceremony." During the latter they burn herbs, such as sage, rosemary, and lavender. The whole idea is for those burning herbs to supposedly cleanse a person or people and the space where they are doing the ritual. Who else is really into their incense at services?

Does Roman Catholicism do that because the Bible tells us to swing a pot of incense when we pray? Is that the way to really connect with God? No! That would be teaching from a book of blasphemy or whatever you want to call it. Hey, do you think it is by chance that they perform that pagan witchcraft ritual? Why are they so hung up on that? Well, it seems to fit the same old pattern from them that we are going to see in a huge way with this chapter! Besides coming up with Halloween as they have merged with the witch's Samhain ritual, a lot of Catholic practices are pagan rituals. Another parallel is the Wiccan and Catholic altars.

After purification, the Wiccan celebrants will build and equip an altar which has the Mother goddess and the male Horned god. Of course, they have their important candles and certain other accouterments. Typically, they will have somewhat hidden altars out in nature at places that are more forested or deserted. Often the forest rangers, police, and hikers will find these places and those first two have had some training about it, but hikers do not usually know what they are looking at is a ritual area. It may just look like someone had a campfire with leftover bones in it. Those folks stumbling upon something like that might want to be careful that the witches do not come back to the altar while they are still there.

Wiccans also often set up altars in their homes, showing their figurines that also depict a female goddess and the male horned god. They decorate it depending on the ritual dates on the Wiccan calendar. For example, with the autumn equinox they will bring out fall colors while Samhain (Halloween) might have different even darker shades. But no matter the ritual time of year, they always include their tools and symbols on the altar.

Hey, who else has their followers build altars in their homes and out in public; altars that include candles and figurine idols for worshiping a female deity? Catholicism does, but I'm sure that's just another coincidence, right? Why are Catholics told to do that? Why would Catholic leadership tell their people to build an altar that is equipped with a figurine that is supposedly the Biblical Mary, turning her into a female goddess that is literally worshiped and sought after for guidance and supplication? It's interesting how that matches exactly with ritual practices witches perform. And we have a long way to go as we list these similarities.

Another practice of the witches during their rituals is what they call "casting a circle." By this point, they've already found the spot for their ritual in a home or nature. They've supposedly cleansed and purified the place and celebrants, they've built the altar, and now they must cast (draw) the circle, which is supposed to represent the two different worlds of our reality and the supernatural. Witches will put the altar in the middle of the circle, so they are taught to be sure their circle is made big enough for that.

"The circle may be marked with sea salt, a long cord, several stones, herbs, and candles."

Now, because these rituals are all about getting what the witch wants, the next step is to start the invocation where he or she will attempt to contact a spirit, which is really a demon, that is supposedly a dead person. This is how he or she hopes to gain or acquire what they are looking for.

"Once the circle is cast, the invocations begin. The order here can vary, but typically the god and goddess are invited to join the ritual, and then the four Elements—Earth, Air, Fire, and Water—are invoked, as these are the raw materials that make up all of existence. (In many traditions, a fifth

Element—Akasha or Spirit [or aether]—is also called in.) In
other traditions, this step is known as Calling the Quarters, and the four
directions (North, East, South, and West) are addressed, either instead of
or in addition to the Elements."

They may end up connecting with a spirit, but it will not be the Spirit of God. After all the setup of the ritual, the heart of it begins with a witch stating his or her intent. This is a statement about why they are performing this ritual. The intent could be just to celebrate a witchcraft Esbat or Sabbat. Using their word, it can also be about 'petitioning' (praying to) the gods and goddesses (demon spirits) to aid the witch to gain favor, protection, luck, healing, or anything else they want.

Hey, does any other organization teach their followers to pray to entities for things like favor, healing, and protection?

As we saw in our study, *Roman Catholicism and the Last Days Deception*, Catholics are even taught to bury little figurine idols of a certain saint that is supposed to help them sell their homes faster. I wish I was, but I'm not making that up! Folks, when Catholics pray to dead people, like dead saints and Mary, what is that practice called? It is divination and God says it's an abomination. Completely contrary to the Word of God, just like witches, Catholics are taught to pray to dead people's spirits (demons) to supposedly help them get what they want. But Scripture tells us not to. And besides, that practice is only going to connect them with lying demons instead of approaching God for whatever they want. And the Creator knows what is good for us to have. But divination is an abomination to Him while Catholicism teaches it daily as a Catholic practice. Now, let's get back to the witchcraft ritual:

"Prayers might be offered, whether they are personal or on behalf of
others. In fact, it is common in some traditions to use ritual space intended
for the benefit of an entire community, or even all of humanity."

Also, at this time, witches typically do their spell work (cast spells).

Again, those spells are more ways to try whipping up what they intend to acquire or make happen like attempts to inflict harm on someone that did something they didn't like. It is the evil intention of, "I'm going to get you!" From that point we move on to what they call the main body of the ritual. A witch has already prayed to the deities (demons) or made his or her requests to the spirits (demons). Here is what the main ritual involves:

"After the intent is stated, the main body of the ritual may consist of various activities. The focal point may be the performance of a ritual drama—such as reenacting scenes from ancient myths or poems—or other liturgical material, depending on the tradition of Wicca the group is following. Solitary Wiccans might also read from ancient mystical texts or compose their own poetry for the occasion. Chanting, singing, dancing and/or other ritual gestures may be part of the proceedings..."

They are adding all those aspects as a way to sort of make sure the deal gets done. Another prominent part of the ritual that they do at this time, as well as even earlier during cleansing and even all throughout, is the use of bells. Witchcraft is very into bells, which are a tool that can be bought, like all the other occult tools and materials, on the internet. They are big believers in bells and Wiccan bells show their pentagram slapped right on them.

"A Ritual bell is used in opening and closing your ceremony or ritual, clearing energies and bringing focus. Use your bell to clear energy before, during and after a spell or ritual. Also, your bell can be used in rituals for magic and healing as you call upon gods, goddesses, deities, as well as elemental powers and energies."

Do we know any religious organization that has an affinity for bells? Catholicism does. Is that because Scripture tells us to ring some bells when we need something from God? Do we need bells when communicating with God because the Bible tells us that is His method or He's deaf? Yes, and I think the passage explaining that is either in Scripture's book of Hezekiah 3, or Second Opinion 2. So, take a look at those if you'd like. Of course, I'm messing with you because there are no such books. But how many of us new believers fell for one of those. Maybe that is just a new seminary student thing and it was only me. But anyway, of all the tools Catholicism could add to their rituals, (besides the many other pagan practices we have seen), they are very into bells. Anyone else seeing a pattern? In our study on Catholicism, we saw that the popes' and priests' hat is an almost perfect replica of the Babylonian Dagon Fish god's head gear. So, where did Catholicism come up with their 'fish mouth looking hat'? And then it seems like most of their other ritual practices have nothing to do with the Bible.

We Christians see these Catholic practices and wonder what is up with them swinging pots of incense, ringing bells, or praying to saints and a female deity, as well as building altars to them in Catholic homes. That is blasphemous. We are not to pray to dead people—period! We pray to God! Why did "Roman" Catholicism merge with the pagan calendar ritual of Samhain and even add in the false teaching of prayers to dead people; the same practice of witches that is called divination, and which God calls an abomination? It goes right along with Catholicism's prayers on behalf of dead people, who are supposedly in purgatory. That is a lie from the pit of hell. Everything they do seems to be Catholicized paganistic witchcraft. I wonder why. Maybe it's because their foundational beliefs and practices come from the pagan religion. Let me give you one more example with another practice by both Wiccans and Catholics:

Some of those cakes the Wiccans make are circular with a solar cross or shaped like a crescent moon.

"In many traditions, a ceremony known as "cakes and ale" (or "cakes and wine") is an important part of Wiccan rituals. Food and drink are offered and symbolically shared with the god and goddess, typically at the end of the body of the ritual (although some traditions begin with it)."

After all the rest that we have seen from witches that parallels Catholic practices, witches top it off with treats and alcohol for their demons as a way to say thanks and maybe help seal the deal.

Unsurprisingly, Catholicism has their followers act similarly in one more example of this pattern:

Every time there is something like that supposed Mary looking stain on a concrete wall or a demonically animated apparition that gives lying messages, Catholics claim those are communications from Mary so they put offerings in front of it. It's no different than people going to a Chinese restaurant, rubbing Buddha's belly, and putting money in the cup in front of it. Those are offerings and the act of honoring Buddha, which is a practice and a religion from the East where they're still doing witchcraft to this day. And Catholics are taught to do the same. They offer candles, flowers, and money, as well as trying to touch the supposed Mary stain to hopefully gain some sort of favor in life. How is that any different than the aspects we have seen with Wiccan rituals? It is the same mentality of giving food and offering to a so-called goddess that is going to supposedly give divine favor in return.

Now, if you still think the similarity that I'm pointing out is not valid, let me give you a couple of examples. Still to this day, when a supposed apparition of Mary shows up, here is what Catholics do:

Reporter: *"Some people believe this is just a carving in a tree. Others believe that it's a miracle. It's a small carving in a tree, measuring about six inches in length, but now hundreds of people are coming by just to take a glimpse of the carving; a carving they believe is of the Virgin Mary."*

Reporter interviews a local: *"Why do you believe?"*

Interpreter for Elba, who is being interviewed by the reporter: *"She says that she feels it in her heart. She feels it inside, that it is the Virgin of Guadalupe, Mary."*

Reporter: *"Elba was the first to spot the carving Tuesday afternoon on her way to the store here on busy Bergenline Avenue in West New York, New Jersey. By nightfall, word began to spread, and the faithful began to gather, so much so that police had to put up barricades and station*

*several officers here. The site has become a sort of tourist attraction with
pictures of the carving now being sold here."*

Reporter asks a young man named Gianni about his experience: *"The
spiritual energy in that one carving of her, it's amazing."*

Reporter: *"Gianni and his mother Lillian are among the many also
praying here. People here believe this carving resembles the Roman
Catholic icon known as Our Lady of Guadalupe. Many in the crowd tell
FOX 5 that they believe the carving also holds mystical powers."*

Another woman tells the reporter about her experience: *"Right now
I'm having a lot of sensation or feelings and a lot of energies flowing
through my body and when I touched her, it's like my fingers felt numb."*

Switching to a second news report: *"Believers are flocking to this Baton
Rouge neighborhood to see a statue of Mother Mary with their own eyes."*

One man who came to see the Mary statue: *"The faith of all the people
who are coming here is at stake."*

Reporter: *"You see, everyone here believes the statue is bleeding. Hai
Nguyen is the owner. His daughter translated for us and says he was
doing lawn work when the unexpected happened."*

Hai's daughter: *"He looked up and he saw blood flowing down."*

Reporter: *"Blood was dripping from the side of Mary's face and the word
spread quickly."*

Hai's daughter: *"He don't know how to explain it. He says he just knew
that maybe the God send a message through Mary."*

Reporter: *"One faithful says he has seen these manifestations before."*

Switching to a third news report: *"A possible miracle right in their living room; a family in northern Israel bought a statue of the Virgin Mary last year. Now, they say the statue appears to be crying. Osama Corri, his wife, and children are Greek Orthodox. Some Muslim neighbors have seen the tears, as well. It started when Amir Corri recently noticed the statue was seemingly covered with oil. She says it even spoke to her telling her not to be afraid. Word of this has quickly spread. Some 2000 people of all faiths have come to see the statue in just the last week."*

That is just nuts, and it is only the foul tip of that demonic iceberg. Folks let's be honest. If a statue were to speak with us, how many of us would run out of the room, screaming like a little girl? Most all of us would except for the Catholics and Wiccans. If you'd have seen the video of all that, you too would notice they put the Mary statue into a glass case, and it has to be hot with all those people coming through. So, it's likely just condensation, which is God's doing and not Mary's. By the way, when Mr. Nguyen describes that red stuff flowing down Mary's face, one local guy commented that there is a tomato patch in the area where birds eat and fly around relieving themselves on the neighborhood.

This kind of supposed Mary incident still goes on today all over the Catholic world. And the frequency of these incidents is increasing. With each one, people are falling for it more and more every day. Here's my Crone theory on that: The solution to those false teachings of Catholicism should not be all on the church's shoulders, but at least they could quit ignoring it. The church does not talk about the occult, including the false practices of Catholicism. When was the last time you heard Christians and churches warn about these false teachings of Catholicism, including actual Mary worship? We don't hear it from the Christian Church so, along with witchcraft, it's allowed to run rampant on a massive scale. And just like the promotion of witchcraft that we will cover in the next chapter, who does the media march out to answer Christian questions that come up day to day? It is not a Christian at all. Instead, they speed dial a Catholic priest, a non-Christian, to promote them as having the correct answers to Christian questions.

And all this is going on while the average non-believer is out there looking for something to believe in and follow for their spiritual life. As they do so with no warnings against the occult and Catholicism, unfortunately, those are the arms people are often falling into these days. Let's take a look at some of these supposed Mary visions that are happening around the world:

Narrator: *"Around the world, reports of supernatural events are drawing millions to apparition sites where the Virgin Mary is said to be appearing. Thousands of visionaries from every conceivable background describe a beautiful young woman, glowing in radiant splendor.*

Teenage girl watching a Marian apparition: *"Her hair is going up. Yeah, she's beautiful. She's real big. She's just standing there."*

Narrator: *"Millions flock to apparition sites hoping to encounter the Blessed Virgin Mary. Consider that fifteen to twenty million Marian followers visit a single shrine in Guadalupe, Mexico, every single year. An estimated thirty million pilgrims have visited Medjugorje since the apparitions of the Blessed Virgin Mary began in 1981. Besides the six visionaries who regularly receive messages from the Virgin, thousands of pilgrims claim to see signs and wonders, experience healing, and hear the voice of Mary at Medjugorje."*

Medjugorje children "visionaries" are shown reciting while staring at an actual apparition.

Narrator: *"She appears as a living, breathing, three-dimensional lady enveloped in exquisite light. Seers, when describing her, admit that the Queen of Heaven transcends human description."*

Of all the titles to give this apparition, it's interesting that Catholicism picked the "Queen of Heaven." We'll talk more about that in a minute but if you've seen some of these apparitions on video, you know this entity often appears wrapped in light. Does that help prove that it must be Mary? No! Let's look at:

2 Corinthians 11:13: *"For such people are false apostles* (fake brothers,) *deceitful workers, masquerading as apostles of Christ. And no wonder, for Satan himself masquerades as an angel of light."*

We hear people claim miracles like, "Hey, you can't say what happened to me wasn't from God. When I was sitting in the bathroom finishing off my chili cheeseburger, this vision of an angel appeared in the mirror and I cried big old elephant tears. A great light came into the room, so it had to be from God!" No, there is zero guarantee of that being the case just because you saw a bright light.

"And no wonder, for Satan himself masquerades as an angel of light. It is not surprising, then, if his servants also masquerade as servants of righteousness. Their end will be what their actions deserve."

You don't want to be there with those servant entities or servant people when they get what is coming to them from God. So, those lights around Mary certainly do not prove she is the biblical Mary, let alone the fact that the Bible says the enemy can appear as an angel of light. In fact, next we are going to talk about the proof that those Catholic apparitions are not Mary. The phrase they call that entity is the Queen of Heaven, which is the exact same false female deity worship that God rebuked Israel for. Roman Catholicism has Catholicized female deity worship to grab one more practice from witchcraft that also worships their female goddess entity that goes back to Ishtar in Babylon.

Again, these occult witchcraft practices originated at the Tower of Babel with their female deity, Ishtar, who become Salene, the Greek goddess of the moon in Grecian witchcraft. Then along came the Romans with Diana, their goddess patroness of the moon, followed by Roman Catholicism also having their Queen of Heaven that they converted from the persona of the Biblical Mary. Just like witchcraft, Catholics are taught to worship this supposed female deity.

One of the false teachings that Catholicism calls the "immaculate conception" is their claim that the Biblical Mary was sinless. But that phrase only means she gave birth to Jesus while still a virgin. It does not mean Mary was born to live a life without sin. That's a false teaching of Catholicism, among many, many others. Let's take a look at what God says:

Jeremiah 7:16-20: *"So do not pray for this people nor offer any plea or petition for them; do not plead with me, for I will not listen to you. Do you not see what they are doing in the towns of Judah and in the streets of Jerusalem?"*

He is talking about people like we saw earlier who find a knot in a tree or stain on a concrete wall that they think looks like Mary.

"The children gather wood, the fathers light the fire, and the women knead the dough and make cakes to offer to the Queen of Heaven."

What are we talking about here with these apparitions? Just like the Queen of Heaven entity God pointed out as evil, Catholicism is even admitting the entity they tell their people to worship is the Queen of Heaven. We are to have nothing to do with the Queen of Heaven because God rebukes that.

"'They pour out drink offerings to other gods to arouse My anger. But am I the one they are provoking?' declares the Lord. 'Are they not rather harming themselves, to their own shame?' Therefore, this is what the Sovereign Lord says: 'My anger and my wrath will be poured out on this place—on man and beast, on the trees of the field and on the crops of your land—and it will burn and not be quenched.'"

To put it mildly, God does not at all like this Queen of Heaven worship, so what is going on with Catholicism on that issue? Besides so many of the other concerning practices and beliefs they have which perfectly match the same from witchcraft, even the very term they use for the feminine deity they worship is the same name God warns about in the Bible. Where are the Christians, let alone the Catholics, pointing this passage in the Bible out? And then when we read the context about this entity, or demon, is this something anyone should be involved with? And, is it also to be avoided at all costs just because any worship of any idol is demonic? But when people do not heed that warning in the Bible and do communicate with entities where people hear or see the supernatural, it's a demonic familiar spirit and neither a dead nor live person.

We know this Catholic apparition is not Mary from the Bible because of one simple fact: She's dead! She's really dead and has been so for a long time. Jesus' mother Mary was a Christian, which means she is in Heaven right now. And in reading the gospel of **Luke**, we know that Mary sinned because she even admitted that she needed a Savior, just like the rest of us.

"And Mary said: 'My soul glorifies the Lord, and my spirit rejoices in God my Savior...'"

I'm sure Mary was a great godly woman and what a fantastic ministry God chose her for, carrying and giving birth to Jesus Christ the Messiah, who is our Lord and Savior. That is fantastic! I'm not downplaying her, but she's not God and we don't worship her. She is dead. And what happens when Christians die? In **2 Corinthians 5:8**, we are told this: *"To be absent from the body is to be present with the Lord."* Mary went straight to be with Jesus in Heaven, who is at the right hand of the Father.

These apparition entities may claim to be Mary and even come shrouded in light, but it is not Mary because it can't be. The Bible is very clear that every Christian, upon death, goes directly to Heaven. And everyone who dies without Christ goes straight to hell. Either way, no one is coming back from those places. None of these people who claim to be witches communicating with spirits or Catholics connecting with saints, Mary, or whoever, are getting in touch with an actual person or spirit of a person, whether dead or alive. I agree that people can have a supernatural experience where they hear or see something, but that is not the real person. The Bible is very clear about this. Here are a couple more passages on that where Jesus is speaking about the tormented rich man in Hades calling out to Abraham:

Luke 16:24-26: *"So the rich man called to him, 'Father Abraham, have pity on me and send Lazarus to dip the tip of his finger in water and cool my tongue, because I am in agony in this fire.' But Abraham replied, 'Son, remember that in your lifetime you received your good things, while Lazarus received bad things, but now he is comforted here, and you are in agony. And besides all this, between us and you a great chasm has been set in place, so that those who want to go from here to you cannot, nor can anyone cross over from there to us.'"*

Back before Jesus rose again from the grave, Sheol was a compartment in the earth where one half of it was Abraham's bosom (paradise), which is where the righteous people who died had been sent. The other half was and is still hell, the place of the unrighteous. The latter is still there but after Jesus rose from the grave, the righteous side (Abraham's bosom) went up to be with Jesus in Heaven at the right hand of the Father. After the resurrection, that is why we Christians today become immediately present with the Lord when we are finally absent from the body at death.

But back before Jesus, when it was still the two separate compartments of Sheol (the place of the departed dead, the grave, or Hades in the Greek), there was no crossing back and forth between the two areas of Sheol. A person died and went to the hell part of it and they are stuck there, while the others went to paradise, which was an awesome place to be stuck. And now when Christians die, they go even further away to Heaven where they are also not coming back from. If we want to get even more clear on this, we can read:

Job 7:9-10, Job 10:20-21, and Job 16:22: *"As a cloud vanishes and is gone, so one who goes down to the grave does not return. He will never come to his house again; his place will know him no more."*

"Are not my few days almost over? Turn away from me so I can have a moment's joy before I go to the place of no return, to the land of gloom and utter darkness..."

"Only a few years will pass before I take the path of no return."

Would you agree that God bluntly tells us our death will be immediately followed by either Heaven or hell and we will not return? It's a common truth in the Scriptures and there is only one occurrence that is outside of it because that is our Creator's prerogative. The Bible dictates certain eternal truths and spiritual matters. Many believe Scripture tells us that God, the Author and Finisher of life, chose to allow God's prophet Samuel to come up from Sheol temporarily to rebuke Saul for resorting to witchcraft and announce Saul's judgment from God for that wicked act. Samuel let Saul know that judgment would be for him to die the next day, along with his sons.

Every other biblical occurrence of a person dying in the Bible was one where they went to Heaven or hell and has not returned. That tells us what is going on with these Catholic apparitions. Again, I do not doubt those people are seeing something that probably even looks like Mary or what they think Mary should look like. But what they are dealing with is a familiar demon spirit that God warned about long ago. We are never to get involved in divination, which is the attempt to speak to spirits of any kind, including all dead people like Mary and the Catholic saints. That practice is a demonic abomination against God, and the lying demons are going to dupe people anyway.

Deuteronomy 18:9-14: *"When you enter the land the Lord your God is giving you, do not learn to imitate the detestable ways of the nations there. Let no one be found among you who sacrifices their son or daughter in the fire, who practices divination* (trying to communicate with the dead) *or sorcery, interprets omens, engages in witchcraft, or casts spells, or who is a medium or spiritist or who consults the dead. Anyone who does these things is detestable to the Lord; because of these same detestable practices the Lord your God will drive out those nations before you. You* *must be blameless before the Lord your God. The nations you will dispossess listen to those who practice sorcery or divination. But as for you, the Lord your God has not permitted you to do so."*

Should we be involved with those practices our Creator finds detestable? Other than knowing that she was a Christian sister who is now with the Lord, should we give even an ounce of thought to a supposed image of dead Mary, even if we might think we can see her in the bark of a tree, a Mary statue that is bleeding tomato paste from side of its head, or an actual vision of something we think is Mary? The answer is no and that includes whether or not she is surrounded by light. Mary is dead! A familiar spirit posing as her is a demonic deception.

Besides, what is the motivation to this communication with demon familiar spirits? It is to have a supernatural experience and get something that you want, which is both the charismatic and Catholic mentality. Both will say they felt the spirit (demon) speak to them. They claim to hear a voice and get a tingling in the fingers. But I don't care if you tingled. If you are standing in a puddle of water at the time, you might want to check for a short in the electrical cords nearby. The Bible dictates how we live and believe, not your experience or feelings like the practices of Catholics and charismatics, who have merged with witchcraft. It is all that same mentality. They go against Scripture to let their feelings and other experiences rule their lives. No, I was not there when anyone had a vision or felt the strong emotion that they did, but he or she better listen to God over any of that.

Now, let me give you a bit more of these demon apparitions that are said to be, but certainly are not, Mary. This video transcript shows how they receive these visions of the supposed Mary by getting into an altered state of consciousness, after which the entity suddenly appears:

Catholic priest: *"Recent appearances of Mary have been reported in nearly every habitable nation. Are these events legitimate? Is God sending us a message? However you answer, one thing is certain: The apparitions of the Blessed Virgin Mary draw millions to every corner of the globe."*

Shown are tens of thousands of followers coming to see and worship the apparitions of the supposed Virgin Mary.

Catholic narrator: *"Many followers believe the Blessed Mother is present."*

Catholic woman: *"Currently, she is appearing all over the world, hundreds of times. There are many visionaries. Nancy Fowler is one of the links, and the time is running out and Our lady said that she is stopping in everywhere."*

Catholic man: *"I definitely believe something is going on."*

Catholic narrator: *"And for all those who believe, they may now have the proof they need to convince others. Two scientists from Columbia came to the farm yesterday to study Nancy Fowler and they say she is definitely seeing something when she goes into trances."*

Columbia scientist: *"It has a brain activity that looks and seems to be like a coma, but she is awake and fully responsive."*

Even the secular experts attest to the fact that these people are getting visions during trances (an altered state of consciousness, or coma-like state). Who else does that? Those organizations are the New Age movement, Eastern religions, witchcraft, and most of the rest of the cults and occult. That is the classic way to communicate with the spirits (demons). But in that transcript, you see how their Queen of Heaven worship is ripe all around our planet? Besides witches, millions do the same witch practice while no one puts the two together because people aren't taught about witchcraft.

I want to give you a few more examples of these apparitions that conclusively show they are not the biblical Mary. What we've already discussed should suffice, on top of the fact that the Bible is very clear about that, these can't be Mary because she's dead and in Heaven. But what do demons do? They are liars and deceivers, just like satan who

Jesus told us is the father of lies **(John 8:44).** Demons are followers of satan, so they cannot help lying. They may start out with a truth, but their nature is such that they just cannot help themselves from lying. If people listen to a demon long enough, a lie is going to pop out. So, when these so-called visions of Mary entities talk to people, is it likely to be the truth? No, it is probably all lies because that is what demons do. Now, let's examine some of those apparitions and their messages as we simulate a little television gameshow. Here is the first one:

Catholic narrator: *"The following represents common messages from the apparition of Mary."*

Message from Our Lady of Medjugorje (Bosnia/Herzegovina Mary apparition): *"Dear children, today I invite you to ask yourself why I am with you this long. I am the mediatrix (mediator) between you and God.'"*

Wrong Answer - Uh, no, you are not! Jesus is! The Bible says this...

Is Mary the mediatrix (mediator) between us and God? That entity is either not reading the Bible or it is a different version. Here is what the Bible says:

1 Timothy 2:5: *"For there is one God and one mediator between God and men, the man Christ Jesus."*

It is NOT MARY!

But that's not all. Here's another lying message...

Message from the Lady of All Nations (Netherlands Mary apparition): *"The world is degenerating, so much so that it was necessary for the Father and the Son to send me into the world among all the peoples in order to be their advocate and to save them."*

That's strike two! One more whammy and you'll exit this gameshow early! Only Jesus is our advocate! What Bible are they reading? None at all.

1 John 2:1: *"If anyone sins, we have an Advocate with the Father, Jesus Christ the righteous."*

It is NOT MARY! Mary and demons cannot help but lie.

But that's still not all. Here is yet another lying message...

Message from Our Lady of Medjugorje (Bosnia/Herzegovina Mary apparition): *"If I call upon you to open yourselves completely to me, so that through each of you I may be enabled to convert and save the world."*

What?! Mary will convert and save the world?

I'm sorry...but that's the wrong answer. Uh, no you won't! Only Jesus can do that! Here's what the Bible says...

John 3:16: *"For God so loved the world that He* (did NOT GIVE MARY) *gave His one and only Son* (Jesus,) *that whoever believes in Him shall not perish but have eternal life."*

They are called lying demons for a reason.

But that's still not all. Here's yet another lying message...

Message from Our Lady of Akita (Japan Mary apparition):
"I alone am able still to save you from the calamities which approach. Those who place their confidence in me will be saved."

What?! So, Mary will save us from the planetary calamities to come?

That's four strikes. I don't know if you can get that many and still be on our gameshow. There is only one way to escape God's wrath to come during the Seven Year Tribulation when He brings judgment on our planet through calamities. It is through Jesus Christ.

1 Thessalonians 5:9: *"For God did not appoint us to suffer wrath but to receive salvation through our Lord Jesus Christ."*

It is NOT MARY! Jesus is the One Who rescues us from God's wrath.

But that's still not all. Let's take a look at just one more...

Message from Our Lady of San Nicolas (Argentina Mary apparition): *"My daughter, in this time I am the ark for all your brethren. I am the ark of peace. I am the ark of salvation; the ark where my children must enter if they wish to live in the Kingdom of God."*

We started this chapter reading about the coming kingdom of Jesus, His Millennial Kingdom. But the Catholic apparition says the way we make it to that kingdom is through Mary.

Sorry, wrong answer. Uh, no, Jesus is the only way to the Kingdom of God!

Excuse me?! Jesus is the way to the kingdom.

John 14:06: *"Jesus answered, 'I am the way and the truth and the life. No one comes to the father except through Me.'"*

It CANNOT be Mary! When we put all this evidence together, there is no way those Catholic apparitions could be the Mary from the Bible. But the reason people are falling for it is because Catholics have been encouraged to get involved with divination through praying to dead people like Mary and the saints. And what they are connecting with cannot be any of those dead people.

From these apparitions, Catholics are looking to get (supplicating for) inspiration, protection, favor, and other gains for their lives. It is no different than witchcraft rituals used by witches to get things from spirit entities that are really demons, just like these apparitions. And it blows me away that they call it the exact same Queen of Heaven that the Bible warns about as being a false female deity demon that God rebuked sharply in the Old Testament. At that time, Israel had the audacity to do the exact same thing with the same entity, which is all the same witchcraft.

As witchcraft practices flourish and Catholicism performs the same Catholicized pagan witchcraft, both are getting away with it because few, even in the Christian Church, will even talk about it. People are being encouraged to continue down these deceptive routes like Catholicism's witchcraft practices while witchcraft overall continues to rise. And Christians refusing to talk about it is a huge aspect of the problem even though witchcraft is warned about all through the Bible. Here's what one guy says about that:

News anchor: *"Thousands of witches gathered last week to cast a spell on President Trump, which they say was to prevent him from harming the country. Well, with Halloween coming up this week, should we take witches seriously? Author and radio host Dr. Michael Brown says that we should. He says the rapid rise of witchcraft in America is real and frightening. "*

Dr. Michael Brown: *"I see the same demonic powers that operated of old, operating again today. And to me there's a clear line between radical extreme feminism, between the shout-your-abortion movement, between the seduction of America through Internet porn, the rise of witchcraft and the fascination with sorcery. It is all of the same spirit, the same demonic forces operating. And last week, the New York Times had an article asking, 'When did everyone become a witch?' It said we had reached 'peak witch.' So, this is real. We don't focus on satan, we focus on the Lord. But the Bible tells us we're not ignorant of satan's devices. And as I was doing research for 'Jezebel's War With America', I was stunned to learn that among millennials there are more witches than Presbyterians. We cannot ignore what's happening spiritually."*

News anchor: *"That is crazy. Well, you found out, as you mentioned in your research, that witchcraft is on the rise while Christianity is on the decline. Those are sad statistics."*

Dr. Brown: *"Yeah, even if you look at the fascination with sorcery, the most read books in America today, six or seven out of the ten most read books in America today, are Harry Potter books. There is a massive increase in tarot cards that people are talking about. And with witches, they have been gathering regularly to hex the patriarchy or to bind President Trump. But you are talking about people gathering together, appealing to other spiritual powers, and they are militantly against the Bible. They are militantly against Christian values. This is something that is really happening. And what you often see...we have the rise of what we call the 'nones,' the religious nones: people with no religious affiliation. As people turn more and more away from God, it's not, as Chesterton said, that they believe nothing, but they believe everything. They begin to engage in all types of alternative spiritual realities and things that they're seeking after. So, the window is wide open now for deception to come flooding in. You even have people professing to be Christian witches. The spiritual warfare is real. We need to be equipped. We need to take on the spirit of Jezebel. It's a real thing."*

And yet what is the trend in the Christian Church? We do not talk about it. Just tell the people that come to our services how to be financially successful and continue to build up their self-esteem. Because they need to really get more understanding about how life is all about them. And as pastors, if we don't cater our services to them, they might leave and take their money.

That said, I've actually been very encouraged by this study of witchcraft that has really opened my eyes, especially when we went through the world history of witchcraft. It is amazing to see how long it has been infecting every single continent on the planet since Babylon rose after the flood of Noah's day. All that opened my eyes to the realization that we are doing the right thing by delving into these subjects much of the church won't touch. What we are doing is extremely needed.

In studying Bible prophecy here in this age of apostasy in the church (that God prophesied would be coming in these last days), it's a hard pill to swallow that we are living that church apostasy live right now today. And I used to think our problem in the church was mostly from pastors not wanting to touch Bible prophecy. That is a huge issue with a third of the Bible being deleted by the leaders of the church. But this study has helped me to understand that the issue is way beyond that. In fact, I think we can add other areas of the Bible that are not being preached today, even besides that third.

Of the two-thirds remaining after stripping God's Word of its prophecy, today preachers don't want to talk about subjects like hell, sin, and wrath. Along those lines they also don't want to mention those subject's spiritual warfare with its devil and demons that might scare people. So, witchcraft and other occult practices are out, as well as anything of that nature. So, they are basically left with the table of weights and measures. From that, the sermon of the day can then be about encouraging the Church with important weights and measures that are really our sign from God that will help us be a financially successful Christian.

Do you see how they can be led to whip out a dumb sermon like that because it's all they have left? Do you see what is happening?! Folks, this study has opened my eyes to the fact that our situation in the church is worse than what I ever thought. I thought it was just one-third of Bible being kicked to the curb. But what is really going on is them skipping 99% of God's Word. That is how bad it is! And then in that church community, when a particular group does teach the whole Bible like we are supposed to, then we are the bad church and the bad pastor. We are one of "those" churches, those wackos. Don't we understand that people don't want to come to services to hear rebuke and correction (from God)?

Oh, the days we live in. The church isn't getting it, beginning with those who pick the pastors and attend church services that aren't necessarily Christians. Maybe because many are not, they don't hunger for God's Word anyway. Contrary to that mindset, when I got saved, I couldn't wait to get in the Bible. I was excited to find one and start reading it instantly. The Spirit of God drives a Christian to God's Word. If you want to have nothing to do with Scripture, that's not a good sign! But as pastors, we need to preach all of God's Word no matter what is going on in the church, even here in these days of apostasy. There is a great and growing need to reach people out there who are getting involved in this occult baloney, even through Catholicized versions of witchcraft practices. Some people just flat out rebel against God like satan has, and go the way of witchcraft. And it is not working out well for them. They need to know there is a way out of that dark-arts mess! As this girl learned, the only way out is through Jesus Christ:

Jessica Galbreth: *"I think it's very, very likely that there was some kind of demonic possession going on here. I almost felt like there was a cloud of darkness around me."*

Narrator: *"For years, Jessica Galbreth was known worldwide as a fantasy artist. Her specialties were vampires, winged fairies, and haunting gothic goddesses.*

Jessica: *"I would try to give them a look like, you know, they were gazing at you with bad intent. They had power and secret knowledge, all is wrapped up with the occult."*

Narrator: *"It was a power that Jessica discovered when she was a child."*

Jessica: *"I think I always had a strong sense that there was a supernatural world. So, it kind of progressed from liking the pretty unicorns to buying a tarot deck and bringing it home and doing readings for my friends and getting a Ouija board. We would ask for someone to come talk to us; inviting anyone, whoever's out there to come talk to us. Things would happen all the time, unexplainable things, terrifying things."*

Narrator: *"She saw radios scream on, out of nowhere, as well as flying picture frames, broken glass, and complete power outages."*

Jessica: *"The spirits that you think might be ghosts are not. They are demons. You're inviting them in. So, the demons thought, 'Let's mess with these girls. Let's terrify them.'"*

Narrator: *"Jessica stopped using Ouija boards in high school but kept seeking the supernatural."*

Jessica: *"I was looking for knowledge and power and secrets that I thought maybe other people didn't know. I would say that people thought I was a witch."*

Narrator: *"More than anything, Jessica was curious about death. I would read any kind of book I could get my hands on in the New Age about near-death experiences or the paranormal. My greatest fear was that there was either nothing after death and you're just annihilated, or worse, that there was a hell and that I was going there."*

Narrator: *"Jessica majored in art in college and began creating images that reflected her obsession with death. She married Josh and they had two kids."*

Jessica: *"I was very empty inside. Josh and I both were really financially driven, and we would set these goals for ourselves and once we would reach them, we would be dissatisfied again."*

Narrator: *"As her artwork got darker, she began noticing that her daughter Julia was having abnormal fears. The images from Jessica's paintings were becoming real to Julia."*

Julia: *"I was afraid of my parents or me dying. I used to have nightmares about this troll guy giving me poison and then driving me away in this brown jeep."*

Narrator: *"Jessica and Josh took Julia to a therapist, but the fear and the nightmares continued. Not long after this, the couple sent their son Joe to a preschool that happened to be Christian. The father of one of Joe's* *classmates befriended Josh and began questioning the couple about their beliefs. Jessica's mother and stepfather were Christians, and Jessica had already decided that she didn't want anything to do with Jesus."*

Jessica: *"I felt that perhaps God was just a set of rules; a judgmental, scary, authoritarian figure. But I felt like He was removed, and we were just kind of off on our own here and there was no satan. It was just all our imagination. I was very prideful at this point, and I didn't need to be saved from anything. I had fallen for that deception that it was trying to hold women down; it was a male dominated religion. And he was able to show me in the Bible how that's not the case at all."*

Narrator: *"As Jessica and Josh read the Bible, everything they had believed, and not believed, changed."*

Jessica: *"I read the gospel of John first and I remember looking at Josh saying, 'Wow, I think this is it. This is the truth.' And my heart softened, and I believed that Jesus was who He said He was. He was God and the Bible is the Word of God. I just remember Dan looking at us and he just said point blank, 'Well, have you guys accepted Jesus as your Lord and Savior?' We both blurted out, 'Yes!' And we meant it. I remember Dan saying, 'Well, then your eternity is settled. Isn't that something?'"*

Narrator: *"When Jessica got home, she had to face the reality of the evil characters she'd created and introduced to others."*

Jessica: *"All these dark images; I'm watching them come out of the printer and I'm thinking about everything and I just felt utter despair."*

Narrator: *"Jessica called her mom."*

Jessica: *"I said, 'Mom, I just accepted Jesus as my Lord and Savior. But I don't know what to do. I don't feel like He can forgive me.' She said, 'For your art?' I said, 'Yeah.' She said, 'Because it's kind of satanic?' That just really hit me like, 'Yes, it's the truth.' Something told me, 'Go open the shade.' There wasn't a voice that I heard. It was just in my heart, and I* *crawled over with tears coming down my face, lifted the shade, and there was a huge rainbow just straight up over the field. I just felt like God walked right in that room with me and said, 'I forgive you. It's okay.' I haven't looked back since."*

Narrator: *"Jessica and Josh literally dumped all of the dark artwork they had in their house. Jessica removed herself from everything to do with the occult. The couple started going to church and studying the Bible."*

Jessica: *"It's like a veil lifts when you see it and all the power or intrigue that you thought was with the occult is nothing compared to the light of God and His supernatural power. I want everyone to know that God forgives anything, and His grace is big enough for all of us. All you have to do is ask."*

How did she find that out? Some Christian who knew the truth of God's Word loved her enough to reach out and speak up. The man did not ignore their trouble. Instead, he told her and her husband the truth that set them free. And now she wants to tell others, just like the rest of us need to. I don't know what other churches are doing but we need to teach what we've learned and learn more so we can teach more. We need to be discipled in all of God's Word, whether it is Him explaining Heaven or hell, sin versus forgiveness, wrath and mercy, or the occult and satan. Christians need all of Scripture! When we get equipped with the truth, God can use us to make a huge difference in the lives and eternal destinations of those acting like they have it all together. You may not even know what they're involved in, but they all need Jesus Christ. Amen?

Now, looking at that account of Jessica's witchcraft experience before getting saved, what was she doing to "draw" people into the occult? She used art, and its part of the reason we're finishing this study with a look at the promotion of Wicca witchcraft. What we will see in the last chapter of this study is how the promotion of Wicca witchcraft is on steroids and they are getting results to match because the vast majority of the church refuses to talk about it. Witches are out and proud all over the place, taking advantage of every communication recruiting angle available these days. They are gaining major ground. They use art like Jessica did, major culture impacting cartoons from Disney and others, video streaming channels, and all the latest social media like TikTok that was supposed to be banned in the U.S. but it's still going. What's up with that? But witches are capitalizing on every marketing tool available to promote their successful proliferation of witchcraft. At the same time, the churches are playing games and remaining as quiet as a mouse.

Chapter Twenty

The Promotion of Wicca

What do we know so far about the big picture with witchcraft? The definition of Wicca is witchcraft, which is a practice that started at the same time as other occult behavior that originated during the building of the Tower of Babel. God condemned it and confused the language as judgment for it. Since that time which was a couple hundred years after God's worldwide flood judgment, witchcraft and other occult practices have spread like sewage pipes of evil behavior distributing filth all over the world. The only protection from witchcraft comes through belief and trust in Jesus' work on the cross. We saw that European witchcraft is what gave rise to most of those occult practices America must deal with today through the rise of Wicca witchcraft. In the last few chapters, we've been cataloging Wicca's beliefs, symbols, and practices.

Because God loves people, throughout the Old and New Testaments, He clearly condemns the practices of Wicca witchcraft. His warnings are all over the Bible about not getting involved with the occult because it is all demonic so it will lead us astray. Like God, we need to love people enough to speak out about it. If you saw that someone was about to be hit by a car, would you tell them? Or would you not want to lower their self-esteem by pointing out their issue? Would you not get involved and just smile and wave at them? Of course, not! You would say something, right? Well, God loves people and understands the damage that happens to them if they get involved with witchcraft. In fact, those going down that route are fooling around in the middle of a busy freeway. They are playing with fire and are headed toward eternal flames. It is all demonic and if we love people as Jesus does, it's just as crucial for us to speak up as if they are sleeping in a burning building.

Over the last couple chapters, we found out about Wiccan practices like all different forms of divination. We saw how the Wiccan calendar or Wheel of the Year, dictates the witchcraft rituals throughout their calendar year, which starts with Samhain (Halloween). In the last chapter, we took a look at their rituals, including how they get together as part of their belief in the law of attraction. They do the rituals so they can get what they want. It's the same belief and practice we see from the Word of Faith false preachers in the charismatic part of the Church. And it is straight out of witchcraft. That is why we spent the better part of a year studying the charismatics and the resulting warning against it, in our study called *Charismatic Chaos*.

As we learned, a Wiccan's first step during their rituals is purification with things like incense and their smudging prayers. Hey, who else does that? It's no shocker that Catholicism uses incense too. Also, like Roman Catholicism, the next witchcraft-ritual step is to build an altar at home or outside. It seems this sort of similarity between paganism and Catholic practices keeps showing up. Another part of witch rituals is to draw a circle, get in it, and start an invocation, asking the supposed deities (demons), like the "Goddess," for whatever the witch wants. Who else is taught to pray to dead people for stuff? Catholics are told to ask dead saints for what Catholics want.

Next with their rituals, witches start performing their spells and ringing those bells. Does any other religion's practice include bells as part of their Sunday rituals? Catholicism does. That whole pattern is interesting. Witches finish their rituals with offering of cakes and ale to their deities for granting witches what they want. Catholicism does the same with offerings to the "Virgin Mary," who they call the Queen of Heaven. That name for the pagan's goddess is the same one mentioned in the Old Testament's Jeremiah. Catholicism has used the person of Jesus' mother Mary and turned the idea of her into the pagan goddess they worship. So, it's no wonder that their rituals are also carbon copies of occult practices and we know that Catholicism even organized their calendar around the pagan year with ritual holidays like Halloween (the pagan Samhain), Easter (the pagan Ostara), and Christ Mass (the pagan Yule).

Here's my point from all that: Catholicism, witchcraft, and the rest of the occult get away with these practices because Christians are silent about it and most people don't know anything about the numerous warnings God gave against the occult and its witchcraft. God speaks about it over, and over, and over throughout the entire Bible. However, the Church is paying no attention so practitioners of these evil deeds and behaviors just keep getting away with it. And that is part of the reason that these are the days God talked about as being the last days, where we would see a major rise of witchcraft.

Let's take a look at that one more Bible passage about that. This one comes from **Revelation 9** and it concerns what will happen during the Seven Year Tribulation. This is going to tell us how bad society is going to be during God's Trumpet Judgments against the stiff-necked people of earth. **Revelation** tells us this wrath from God will begin with the Seal Judgments, then the Trumpet Judgments, and finally the Bowl Judgments toward the end.

Revelation 9:20: *"The rest of mankind who were not killed by these plagues still did not repent of the work of their hands; they did not stop worshiping demons."*

Wait, that says we will have a society where people will worship demons instead of their Creator!

"They did not stop worshiping demons, and idols of gold, silver, bronze, stone and wood..."

Isn't that exactly what we've seen with witches worshiping figurines, just like Catholicism does?

"They did not stop worshiping demons, and idols of gold, silver, bronze, stone and wood, idols that cannot see or hear or walk. Nor did they repent of their murders."

Hey, if you're going to worship demons, what do demons do? They are liars and murders like their father the devil. Because of that, witchcraft and other occult practices are not just sacrificing herbs to their demons and satan. They sacrifice animals, as well as people.

"Nor did they repent of their murders, their magic arts, their sexual immorality or their thefts."

In the Greek, Revelation's word for the magic arts is "pharmakeia," which is where we get our English word, "pharmacy." So, it certainly implies drug usage and, of course, that is something we see going through the roof. Drugs are important in the occult as a turbocharged way to get witches and other occultists, as well as New Agers, into an altered state of consciousness so they can commune with demons. **Revelation** is specifically talking about the dark arts fostered by drug usage. Some translations of the magic arts, or pharmakeia, will have it as sorcery or witchcraft because that's drug use with the dark arts.

But God tells us what to expect in the last-days society leading up to the Seven Year Tribulation. It will get so bad that we will see a massive global increase in witchcraft and other occult sorcery. Has this study given us signs of that? Yes! Like mine, I am sure your mind has been opened to just how pervasive this evil has gotten all over our planet today. It blew my mind learning about the history of witchcraft growing worldwide since the Tower of Babel. But these days, it has gotten so bad that we are literally fulfilling **Revelation 9's** description of the last days leading up to the Seven Year Tribulation.

I think two things have been happening with our world today: First, we have seen a massive promotion of Wicca witchcraft. When we were growing up, if you wanted to learn something about the dark arts, there was no Internet. They didn't promote it like they do now on television and in much of our media. People would have to go into a dark back alley to contact some seedy character in a dingy bookstore. That was the average occultist hangout back in the day. Or someone might introduce you to their secret stash of occult material kept hidden at their house. But not anymore. It is everywhere. It is being promoted on a scale that just blows me away! We are going to talk about that here, but that's only half of the reason it is increasing on a massive scale.

The other is because those in the Church today are keeping their mouths shut! That's allowing Wicca to rise with almost no hindrance. And those ignoring the issue, whether churches, pastors, or whoever, are fulfilling another prophecy that God said would come upon us in the last days. That Biblical prophetic warning from God is in **2 Timothy 4**. Again, besides the huge worldwide promotion of witchcraft these days, the Christian Church is absent from the battle against these practices. Both of those have contributed to the rise that is talked about by God for these last days. Instead of equipping us on this crucial issue that God repeatedly warned us about, churches are busy playing funny reindeer games for their audience, keeping the show going. Churches have people attending but since they're not teaching from God's Word, they have to give the congregation something. So, what are they teaching instead? Well, God called this out 2000 years ago with Paul's excellent instructions for young Pastor Timothy.

2 Timothy 4:1-5: *"In the presence of God and of Christ Jesus, who will judge the living and the dead, and in view of his appearing and his kingdom, I give you this charge: Preach the word."*

Is Paul telling Timothy to pick and choose from God's Word and preach whatever he'd like from the Bible? Did he tell Timothy to skip around in it? Did he say to leave out the third that covers Bible prophecy? Besides chopping out prophecy, churches today have also stopped talking about sin, hell and repentance. So, that takes a bunch of passages away too. Pretty soon all that's left is the Biblical table of weights and measures. Is that what Paul is suggesting for young Timothy to preach about? No! He said to preach the Word, which means all of it. And we are not to preach only those parts that people are going to like! Paul continues:

"Preach the word; be prepared in season and out of season; correct, rebuke and encourage..."

Whoa! Aren't we just supposed to preach pleasantries because it's nice to encourage others? No! According to that last sentence, it looks like two-thirds of the time should be correcting and rebuking. The people should be squirming in their seats as they are corrected and rebuked by God's Word in the Bible. If you are at a church where you never felt corrected or rebuked, someone is not teaching the Bible. Think about that. In quoting from the Bible, if all you ever get is encouraged, someone is skipping by two-thirds of the Scripture and that is not a faithful preacher, teacher, Sunday school helper, or whoever it is.

"Correct, rebuke and encourage, with great patience and careful instruction. For the time will come when people will not put up with sound doctrine. Instead, to suit their own desires, they will gather around them a great number of teachers to say what their itching ears want to hear."

Notice that the problem is not just the hireling shepherds who don't give a rip about their congregations; the ones that won't preach the Word. Even before them, who is taking the initiative to put that shepherd up in front so he can sell out? The church is. There are two reasons this problem has festered to the point of a massive issue in the Church. Besides fluff preachers doing their thing, first it is the churches that will only hire that type of guy. So, even if a pastor is faithful to preach the whole Word in season and out, the people of the church do not want him! They will not hire him and if they do hire someone who later gets corrected, rebuked, and convicted by God to start preaching the whole Word, they will fire him! I have stories of that. But a preacher who is not giving God's Word still has to keep the show going so what does he do? Here is what Paul said would happen in our day and what he told Timothy to do as a preacher of God's entire Word:

"They will turn their ears away from the truth and turn aside to myths. But (Timothy,) keep your head in all situations, endure hardship, do the work of an evangelist, discharge all the duties of your ministry."

Pastors are to preach the Word and share the gospel. Notice that it is not one or the other. A pastor is not to make excuses, saying he doesn't have the gift for either one or the other. We are to preach the Word and evangelize. Those are not mutually exclusive tasks. Pastors do not pick one and then exclude the other. And the reason a pastor preaches the Word is so the Church (the saints) can also be equipped to evangelize.

Now, let's break that passage down: "Itching," comes from the Greek word, "Knetho," which means "to desire only that which is pleasant." The Greek word, "muthos," means "stories made up." Putting those together we get "pleasant stories that have been fabricated." And **Revelation** tells us that is how we'll know we're living in the last days. It's when we begin seeing a rise of the occult with its witchcraft and sorcery. And another sign is when "Church" services give people only pleasant stories that have been made up. Today, I would guess, that describes about 95% of the so-called American Church. Unfortunately, in a very negative way, today's Church is fulfilling this Bible prophecy.

And here's my whole point in bringing that up: The occult is getting away with what they've been able to accomplish on a massive scale and Catholicism keeps performing pagan witchcraft rituals with no one calling them on it. This is because 95% of today's churches are not preaching God's Word even though God warned them that this was coming in the last days. We are living His prophecy, live today, with the occult thriving because pastors are not feeding their people the Word of God.

But again, the problem is not just fluff preachers. The people hiring them are the ones who only want to hear pleasant and invented stories. In other words, they want just feel-good, fluffy talk from the pulpit, and I want to give you an example of that so you can see how far it's gone. The people take the initiative. And these days they are craving pleasantries instead of God's Word. According to 95% percent of today's Church (my estimate), we here at Sunrise Bible Church have it all wrong when we teach all the Bible. Yet, pastors warn that we better not talk about sin because people will stop coming to our church services and paying attention to our messages online. They say our funds to do ministry will plunge and soon we'll go belly up. They say we cannot do that because it's no longer the way to "do" church.

Well, first of all, we Christians don't do church. We are "The Church." This is not a business, we do not just spit out money-making products, and each individual person is not someone to throw on our pile of people like another notch on a pastor's belt. This Christian life is not about money; it is about God's truth, eternal lives are on the line, and getting people equipped to make a difference in our society for Christ. The truth is what sets people free.

But that 95% of today's prophetically anticipated, last-days church, tells us that this is all just a game that we're not playing right. We have it all wrong with our Bible Church being focused on the Bible. We don't need the convicting Word of God anymore. And it is because we are higher minded these days. What the world supposedly needs now are daily nightstand or bathroom messages to play while getting ready for work. What we really have to have in our life is Pastor Joel Osteen's Inspirational Cube. When I first saw what I'm going to give you with this video transcript, I honestly thought it was just a parody. But it's an actual commercial that advertises a product being sold right now. Here's that shameful sales pitch:

Narrator of the commercial: *"In today's uncertain times, life can feel overwhelming and leave you struggling for answers. But you can overcome life's challenges; wake up every morning, inspired, and looking forward to each day. Introducing the Inspiration Cube: The easy-to-use portable audio system filled with life-changing messages of hope, guidance, and strength from Joel Osteen, one of the world's most inspiring spiritual leaders."*

Joel Osteen: *"You may feel, today, like you're trapped. That is not how your story ends. Some dreams are waking up! Hope is waking up! Abundance is waking up!"*

Narrator: *"With the simple push of a button, remove those negative thoughts with a new message to inspire your day. "*

Osteen: *"God is saying to you, you have struggled long enough. Unexpected blessings are coming your way."*

Narrator: *"Over 400 of Joel's greatest inspirations ever assembled, all on this easy to use audio-listening cube."*

A man gives his testimonial for the product: *"It's all positive. It's not negative. Our lives have changed completely."*

Narrator: *"Start each day with just a touch and sit back for a powerful message of hope, guidance, and inspiration."*

Osteen: *"The forces that are for you are greater than the forces that are against you."*

Another testimonial for the cube: *"It makes you really energized. God is in control of your life and, boy, have I seen blessings. He put the hope in my heart."*

Narrator: *"Refuse the negative thoughts that prevent you from reaching your goals and take back control."*

Osteen: *"You can't think negative thoughts and live a positive life. If you'll get your mind going in the right direction, your life will go in the right direction."*

Third product testimonial: *"It was almost like a friend was speaking to me. I'm at peace. My victory is already accounted for."*

Narrator's wrap up: *"The Inspiration Cube: filled with the best of the best from Joel Osteen for the ultimate collection of the most powerful daily inspirations ever assembled."*

Last time I checked; the Bible is the most powerful daily inspiration ever assembled! But that gives us an idea of how bad it has become. What really got me about that is how the King of Fluff is encouraging people to turn to an electronic cube of pleasantries (knetho) instead of the Bible. That **2 Timothy** passage exactly parallels what we see going on right now!

But again, my point in bringing all this up is to show how 2000 years ago, **Revelation 9** predicted exactly what we see today with the rise of Wicca, witchcraft, and the rest of the occult. The Bible warned that the occult would be bursting out on a global basis like we could never imagine and that it would take us down the dark road toward the Seven Year Tribulation; the worst time in the history of mankind. It will be so bad that people are going to actually worship demons over God and even continue that while God's wrath is being poured out on this planet.

And why is it happening? Two reasons: Today's church is keeping its mouth shut about the occult and not teaching the whole Bible. Instead, they are encouraging their followers to pass around the inspiration cube. On top of that, society's around the world are seeing the promotion of witchcraft and other occult practices on a massive scale.

The promotion of witchcraft is pervasive in our lives today and the church seems completely unprepared to deal with it. Those two factors are why the number of people participating in occult practices is exploding!

Most of the entire church community is keeping their mouths shut while the world is going nuts promoting the occult! And those promoters know exactly what they are doing, so I want to expose how they are encouraging everyone to get involved with witchcraft and other occult practices. First, let's recap some of the ways we've seen that these horrible destructive practices are being promoted. One way is through feminism that is a smokescreen to get our ladies involved with witchcraft. Another of today's promoters is at least one of our two huge political machines, the Democrat Party, which has been infested with witchcraft and the occult. Examples of witchcraft in the Democrat Party can be seen clearly with recent efforts within the party that include the BLM movement led by witches and a practicing witch running for their presidential nomination in 2020.

Another pervasive promotion of witchcraft in our society today is something we talked about briefly, but I haven't shown you much proof yet. That is the Environmental movement which is just another smokescreen to get people involved with Mother-goddess worship that comes straight out of pagan witchcraft. Instead of the true Father God in Heaven, they worship His creation, the earth. They worship "Mother Earth" and tell us we all need to save her. We must listen to "the voice of the earth."

But that directive from witches and other pagans is the same violation of God's Word that we see with those people talked about in **Romans 1:18**, where God's wrath was being poured out from Heaven because people had the audacity to worship created things instead of their Creator, Who is to be praised forever. Last time I checked, the earth is a created thing and God is its Creator, so it is just crazy what these environmentalists are trying to get away with in their promotion of the occult. Here are some examples of how the environmental movement is really a smokescreen to get people into earth worship of the "Mother Goddess":

Reporter: *"Mr. Coburn, why should we care about Earth Day or Mother Earth?"*

Actor, James Coburn: *"Well, Mother Earth is your mother. She's the Mother Goddess. She's the one that we should be praising, rather than raping. (Pointing at a large gathering of people outdoors.) I mean, all these people here today are here for one reason; because they are concerned about what's happening; what mankind is doing to the earth. I mean, the negative emotion we carry around, a lot of us, is another contributor here. What we must do is be true to ourselves. If we are true to ourselves and true to Mother Earth, Mother Earth is going to be bountiful; she's going to give us everything we need. She has for a long time. We have lost our way. The pagans used to know how to do it. And the Indians; some of them still remember how to do it. The earth is a living organism. We're killing the one we love the most and she loves us. We've got to praise our Mother Goddess."*

Switch to news anchor, Tom Brokaw: *"And back in this country, there is a provocative and timely question in the debate over the energy policy: 'What would Jesus drive?' This is the centerpiece of a new energy conservation campaign, but some say the gospel has no place in the debate over gasoline. Here's NBC's Don Teague."*

Part of a television ad campaign: *"God saw that it was good."*

Reporter, Don Teague: *"As TV ad campaigns go, this is something different..."*

The ad campaign continues: *"Yet too many of the cars, trucks, and SUV's that are made, that we choose to drive, are polluting our air."*

Teague continues: *"...not because it carries an environmental message but because of the audience it targets."*

Commercial: *"So, if we love our neighbor and we cherish God's creation, maybe we should ask, 'What would Jesus drive?'"*

Switch to news anchor, Bill Hemmer, reacting to the commercial: *"What would Jesus drive, huh? Environmental evangelism: It is the new* *way to raise awareness about global warming. Our Fox religion correspondent, Lauren Green, joins us with more on that."*

Hemmer to Lauren Green: *"Good morning. Who's pushing green, Lauren?"*

Green: *"Hey, well, a lot of people and it really is across the board, theoretically speaking, or religiously speaking. Here are the top green religious people, according to Live Earth: We've got Reverend Joel Hunter. He is the senior pastor at Northland Church in Longwood, Florida. He actually was offered the head of the Christian Coalition but turned it down because he wanted to focus on issues like poverty and environmental protection. Norman Habel is a theology professor out of Australia. He edited something called the 'Earth Bible.'*

Then, of course, there's Pope Benedict the 16th and yesterday he issued a statement that said, 'The people of faith must listen to the voice of the Earth or risk destroying its very existence.' We also have the Archbishop of Canterbury, Rowan Williams, head of the Anglican Church; and, of course, the Buddhist leader, the Dalai Lama. The one thing you should add to this list is the National Evangelical Association, because two years ago it issued a letter to 50,000 members of its churches, which means its 30 million evangelicals, saying that, 'We affirm that God-given dominion is a sacred responsibility and that government has an obligation to protect its citizens from the effects of environmental degradation.' So, it is a big movement all across the board. "

Children singing an environmental pledge: *"I pledge allegiance to the earth, to care for land and sea and air, to cherish every living thing with peace and justice everywhere...I pledge allegiance to the earth, to care for land and sea and air, to cherish every living thing with peace and justice everywhere...I pledge allegiance to the earth, to care for land and sea and air, to cherish every living thing with peace and justice everywhere...with peace and justice everywhere."*

Instead of teaching our children to honor, love, and worship their Creator, (their true loving Father in Heaven Who put them here), these environmentalists are teaching our little kids to pledge their allegiance to rocks, dirt and trees (the earth). Also, did you notice that the so-called evangelical leaders representing tens of millions of evangelical Christians, are not pushing for a highfalutin campaign that promotes the Bible? Instead, they want to work toward control of God's climate that He can't seem to handle. Has God just lost control of the earth's weather? Those sorts of promotions by the environmental movement are just more earth worship.

What you read was a classic and dated message from James Coburn, who died in 2002 and hopefully knew Jesus Christ before he left this earth. But back when he said those things, he was promoting the same sort of Earth Day ideas that teach people to praise the Mother Goddess. The environmental movement is just another smokescreen to pull people into witchcraft with its Goddess worship. They turn God's created earth into some supposedly holy entity (Gaia) that they claim we all came from. But it is just the same pagan deity that occultists have been worshiping for thousands of years. And this time the Church is going along with it, just as Catholicism did when they jumped on board with paganism long, long ago.

Still, how could the Christian Church go along with all that? Well, many stopped teaching the Bible. Instead, they and their people crave things like the Inspirational Cube that will only give them pleasant thoughts. Hey, why not just cut out that annoying talk about sin and hell, right? And don't mention Bible prophecy or occult witchcraft because those are going to freak people out. Let's just discuss how we can all hold hands, working together to separate the recyclables into their appropriate bins. We can save the planet!

But no matter what we do, no one is going to save the earth. Wait until you see what God is going to do with our world during the soon-arriving Seven Year Tribulation. It will be trashed! What a waste of time while more and more people are dying each day without knowing Jesus.

Yet even Christians are signing onto this distraction and away from the true God. Even in our schools, the environmentalists have been able to slither in to lead our kids toward earth worship. That brings us to another area of our society that is promoting witchcraft. Hey, kids, "Go Green!"

The Green movement is just the same environmental movement that wants us to be one big earth-worshiping family. You already saw the video transcript about this kind of thing but now I want to share what is currently being taught in our "secular" schools. Notice that I emphasized secular. What is the solution to that major problem facing you and your child's entire life?! It rhymes with homeschool. Can you guess? Yes, it's homeschool. Get your kids away from the secular sewer pipe you are feeding them through secular education! The place that you send them is brainwashing your children daily. And unfortunately, 95% of the churches today aren't going to fix that with fluff preachers; not to mention that church only gets the kids for a fraction of the time those secular-indoctrination schools do.

And those in charge of that globalist system even let us know they are preparing the kids for a New World Order that the Bible warns us about. The Bible says dark forces will push for control of humanity through a One World Government and One World Religion. And the globalists are not even hiding from that term anymore. They think your kid belongs to them and that you have no right to build Christian morals into them. It is their job to teach them what kind of character to have and that will be based on the disastrous philosophy of moral relativism, which they are implanting in our children through secular public schools.

Why do you think the Democrats have fought so hard against school vouchers that would give parents more choice about who shapes their children's morals and character? We have homeschooled our children the whole way but still have had to pay taxes to support a secular education that we do not approve of for anyone's children. That is not right. Families are being punished for exercising their own constitutional right to raise their kids with a godly upbringing. And the globalists are so emboldened they even tell us they want our kids given to them each day so they can properly brainwash them into good communists and socialists that the fascist globalists can better control.

As part of that effort, secular schools are now even adding witchcraft to the lessons they are indoctrinating the kids into. You may not believe me, but they've really turned on that occult sewage pipe of instruction in recent years. While many parents are thinking their kids will be just fine because the parents also went through a secular school system and they came out okay, the schools today are not like what you and I went to. So, you cannot rely on that. Get them away from that endless push toward pagan beliefs! Every day in that school, anything goes, do what thou wilt, except for God, Jesus and the Bible. You thought you were sending your kids to get some math and English.

Instead, let me give you just a short (verified) list of those subjects currently being taught in our secular indoctrination centers, our public schools, including witchcraft: Daily, our children are learning Earth Worship (pantheism), Evolution, Socialized Medicine, the benefits of World Government, Animal Rights with animals seen as our brothers and sisters, and Redistribution of American Wealth to other nations, which is another indication that communists have taken over our educational system. They also get lessons on contraception and other aspects of reproductive health. Why would these globalists want to do that? It's so that our kids will begin thinking sexual thoughts, to start having fornication earlier in life, which is another way they can promote more abortion through their baby-murdering mills. We exposed that in great detail with our study, *Abortion: The Mass Murder of Children.*

Another idea the globalists put into our children's heads is debt forgiveness to third world nations. Hey, have we even mentioned Arithmetic or English yet? No! When do they have time for that? This is the sewer of ideas being taught to our kids in secular schools and we are not even done listing all of it yet. Globalists also considered it important for children to adopt the gay rights agenda, transgenderism, and how to become a good Muslim by learning to celebrate the Muslim holidays. That is all being fed to our kids in schools. The latter is something we exposed in our study, *Islam: Religion of War or Peace?*

Other indoctrination includes the elimination of the right to bear arms and setting aside massive amounts of the United States of America for human-free zones. Also taught to our kids are occult practices like how to get into an altered state of consciousness, Astrology, forms of Divination, Spiritism, Magic Spells, Sorcery, Occult Charms and Symbols, Solstice Rites, Sacred Sex and Serpent Worship. And on top of that, they are even teaching Human Sacrifice:

"Students are given lessons on death education and lessons to advocate the cultural endorsement of abortion and euthanasia [getting rid of those old folks that are costing the system too much money,] as a way to prepare the new generation to accept many forms of sacrifice, such as the notion of sacrificing oneself for the common good."

In our AI Invasion study, I'm going to expose that human-sacrifice issue that is basically what was seen on the popular 1976 movie, *Logan's Run*, about people voluntarily self-eliminating, even at a young age. That aspiration of the globalists is being ushered into our world through the programming of our children. And they are the ones who will make those decisions in the future. They are brainwashing kids to think people, including themselves, need to get with the common good and die when their controlling puppet masters tell them to. What does all that have to do with English, math, or spelling? One person said this:

"Is this what our children should be learning? Should schools turn children into earth and spirit worshipers? Should parents pay property taxes for public schools to promote pagan religions?"

Of course, the answer is "No!" And what happens behind those doors each day is why the schools often do not like the parents to see all they are teaching. But day after day they continue to get away with it because those in the church are keeping their mouths shut, blocking out "the negativity," and just passing the Inspiration Cube—press #27 to learn about being a better you and #28 is all about positive thinking. It is no wonder Wicca witchcraft is on the rise. And here is another promoter of it that we already talked a bit about:

Wicca and other witchcraft are also being promoted through our very influential music industry. We saw that with our exposure of superstar Beyonce, who admits being possessed with a demon (Sasha) that gives her special abilities. We also saw that witchcraft crossroads are popular in the blues industry. In fact, a movie called *Crossroads* came out in 1986, staring Ralph Macchio from *Karate Kid*. It was based on the idea of musicians selling their souls to the devil to get special musical abilities. That exchange is actually happening with musicians today because the music industry is flooded with occult witchcraft. The practice used to be kept behind the scenes so a person would have to attend a private party to learn the occult practices an artist was involved with. But that was in the past. Today, musicians are flat-out using their music as a platform to encourage other musicians and their social media fans to practice witchcraft. They are instructing people on how to get involved in witchcraft. A recent musician doing this is Azealia Banks. Folks, they are not hiding it anymore. The music industry has musicians flat-out saying they are witches and encouraging everyone to join them in the practice. Here is the video transcript with an interview of Azealia Banks:

Reporter: *"Hi, I'm Gabby Bess. I'm headed to Fox Grove studios to meet with musician, Azalea Banks. Recording artist, Azealia Banks, landed a recording deal at the age of 17. By the age of 20, she shot to fame with her breakout single: 212. Despite her obvious talent, Azalea is well known for controversy. The rapper separated from XL Recordings and then Interscope; all before her debut album, 'Broke with Expensive Taste,' was even released. Infamous for her unabashed opinions and Twitter feuds, which have even spread to our own 'Broadly' correspondents, Azalea Banks is truly an independent artist, whose work deserves a closer look."*

Bess interviews Banks: *"Thanks for inviting me to your studio."*

Banks: *"Thanks for coming. Thanks for coming to check me out."*

Bess: *"You've tweeted, sometimes, about witchcraft, like, very cryptically. Do you practice magic?"*

Banks nods.

Bess: *"What are your favorite spells?"*

Banks: *"The egg spell. You cleanse yourself with an egg, right; pass the egg all over yourself, praying for all of your negativity to go away into the egg, right. But usually you do it when somebody messes with you to get what the person is doing off of you; crack it in a crossroad, and you walk away and you don't look back. That (stuff) works."*

Bess: *"When did that start?"*

Banks: *"My mother practiced...white-table magic, prayers for the ancestors, and prayers to saints and cleansing and praying for protection and all types of (stuff) like that, you know. You know, my mother used to be doing, like, all kind of, like, candles and crazy (stuff) and then she'd be playing DMX (a rapper), like, while ironing my Catholic School uniform, you know, like, putting my little, like, Bible study book in my book bag and I'm, like, walking out the house, like, mimicking singing rap."*

Switch to Banks talking to her fans online: *"Hey guys, it's A.B. I'm in the witch cave right now. I just wanted to come here to you in the witch cave today, you know, because I've been talking a lot today and just wanted to give you guys a real peek at what it's about. The amount of (grime) that's about to come off my floor right now, guys—Oh my god!"*

Banks shows the floor where she does witchcraft and it is covered in black grime.

Banks showing the grime: *"Three years' worth of brujeria."*

As we saw with South American witchcraft, brujeria is just the Spanish word for it. Banks showed her fans the grimy walls and floor with the black and charred remains from three years of witchcraft rituals done on her floor. That is what goes on in today's music industry where people no longer have to get exposed to witchcraft by going to musician's parties or concerts because these artists are coming right out to say they are witches. And did you notice how Bank's Catholic upbringing, apparently, merged well with the occult?

But hey, if you think that's bad, while all this is going on to supercharge our society deeper and deeper into flourishing witchcraft, what is the church doing? They are passing around the inspiration cube: "We all must get the cube! Where is that cube? Can I borrow your cube?" Folks, this is nuts! And it is why witchcraft is on a massive rise. Of course, Azealia Banks is not the only witch in music. There is an entire occult movement going on in the music industry.

Depictions through their photos, art, and symbols give occult signals. All the occult symbols mean something. Common examples are their triangles and the all-seeing eye of providence that is even on the back of our dollar bill. And occult signaling through the music and movie industry is flooded with the stuff. Yet, parents who do not want to take responsibility will say, "Hey, it's just music. Maybe I don't like it, but my parents didn't like mine. If my child is into it that's fine. It's no big deal."

But more is going on there with your kids than them just liking some music. Let's say I encouraged you to do something like eat chicken. And what if I repeated it over and over in a sing-song way: "Go eat chicken, go eat chicken, go eat chicken..." Maybe I'd also throw in a chorus of something like, "Hey, go to KFC and Keep Feeling Cruddy because that's what it stands for...Hey, go to KFC and Keep Feeling Cruddy..." How would that be if I just kept saying that to you or your kid over and over? Or pick a sin and replace the chicken because you might not consider that one a sin, even though others do. But if I kept hitting you with the same encouragement to commit a certain sin, I'd be acting horribly, right? Let's say somebody encourages you or your child in that way to get involved with sexual immorality. And maybe that person is sitting next to you in the front seat of your car, constantly pushing sexual immorality. What would you do? We would ask them what they were thinking and tell them to shut their mouth, right?

But apparently, it is okay if they sing it to me or my child. Folks, those are the lyrics of that music. The musicians are including catchy suggestions that push anti-God, anti-Jesus, and murderous rotten behavior into our kid's brains. Much of it will stay in their heads for months or even years if they really like a song. But somehow that is okay and will not affect our children. That idea is wrong, and the lyrics are consistently getting worse and worse. It's full-blown demonic occult that doesn't just involve the music. These people, who have been made popular through their music are using that platform and their concerts to push idols and promote witchcraft. And that is just the music industry. Another area of our society promoting this stuff is the media:

By media I mean social media, television ("tell a vision"), cartoon, books, movies and all kinds of other media sources these days. We talked about one prominent media promoter of witchcraft: the *Harry Potter* books and movies.

The *Harry Potter* following is massive and certainly contributing in a big way to the rise of witchcraft. We also talked about Disney's cartoon movies that are said to be about magic but are really promoting witchcraft and other occult practices. As we saw, Disney just grabbed onto the coattails of the Brothers Grimm witchcraft books that presented witchcraft and other occult practices from around the world. Besides those Grimm stories, Disney also found other witchcraft traditions from all over our planet and then glamorize them through cartoons. Disney seems to find every country around the world that has some sort of pagan practice and then popularizes it with us and our kids. In fact, Disney just came out with another cartoon called, *The Owl House*, which is flat-out witchcraft and getting heavy promotion. As we saw before, owls are a prominent aspect of witchcraft. This show is one more of Disney's latest cartoons that promote occult practices to our children, training them to be good little witches like it is just a wonderful life. They are selling the idea that a child with a messed-up home, need only practice witchcraft to have a whole new home environment that is spectacular. Here's young Luz, a witch apprentice that is promoting her new cartoon:

Luz: *"Hi, there. I'm Luz Nosada. So, this one day, I found a portal and ended up someplace I could have never imagined. OK, well, I totally have imagined it."*

Luz is shown in front of a mirror with a witch magazine and she is wishing hard for such a place. The scene switches to the new land she found.

Luz: *"But this is even better. This is the Boiling Isles* (a very skully and boney land is shown) *It's amazing; the kind of place you just want to wake up to every day and say, 'Good morning, terrifying fantasy world.'"*

Seven-eyed sea monster: *"Good morning."*

Luz: *"Such friendly neighbors. And this is the Owl House, the best place on the Isles."* That's Hootie (an owl on the door that can project out like a snake,) *he is always hanging around. The Owl House is where I live with the King of Demons and Eda, the Owl Lady, the most powerful witch on the Boiling Isles! She is fierce. She is fearless. And someday I'm going to be just like her."*

Luz puts on a witch apprentice name tag and shows that she is Eda's #1 fan in the Eda Fan Club.

Luz: *"Want to see more of the Isles? Just a short staff ride away is the town of Bonesborough. Is there anything better than people-watching in a demon world? The marketplace has the best stuff in town."*

Luz talks to a Centaur (half man, half horse).

Luz: *"There's the library* (spell books shown) *and Hexide, the most amazing magic school ever! So, that is the Isles. I know sometimes it can seem a little different."*

King of Demons, her pet: *"It's very stinky."*

Eda, her witch mentor: *"And gross."*

Luz: *"But, if you look at it from a different perspective, it looks just like the home."*

Hey kids, is your home life messed up? Try witchcraft and create and new home environment for yourself. Of course, they fail to warn about the real demons that might materialize in your bedroom. If you don't think these sorts of media have an effect on kids, wait until you read the last video transcript at the end of this book. It is the true story of a girl who turned to witchcraft because of a television series about witches and a Disney witchcraft movie.

Besides Disney, an enormous number of Hollywood movies these days encourage people to get involved in witchcraft. From only the last few years, let me give you just a small fraction of the movies promoting the occult and witchcraft, including one with that Luz character we saw in the new Disney *Owl House* cartoon series:

Nocturne, The Third Day, Gretel & Hansel, The Grudge, Black Christmas, Doctor Sleep, Luz: The Flower of Evil, Scary Stories to Tell in the Dark, Fantastic Beasts (there are a couple now), *The Burial Of Kojo, Hellmington, Chilling Adventures of Sabrina, We Have Always Lived in the Castle, Hell House, The Winds: Demons of the Praire, Suspiria, The Devil's Doorway, Primal Rage, The Pledge, The Witch in the Window, Constantine: City of Demons, The Field Guide to Evil, don't Leave Home, Luz II, They Remain, Hereditary, Mandy, The Babysitter, Muse, Hagazussa, The Ritual, Tokyo Vampire Hotel, Mother, Veronica, Death Note, Jackals, Double Date, The Killing of a Sacred Deer, November, Get Out, Brackenmore, The Night of the Virgin, Miss Peregrines Home for Peculiar Children, The Void, Without Name, The Autopsy of Jane Doe, Rupture, A Dark Song, The Birch, The Neon, Demon, Raw, Darkness, The Wailing, The Girl Without Hands, The Alchemist Cookbook, The Love Witch, Hell House L.L.C., The Last Witch Hunter, Regression,*

*Southbound, Devil's Candy, The Childhood of a Leader, She Who Must
Burn, Embrace the Serpent, Tale of Tales, Ava's Possessions, The
Imitation Game, The Circle, The Hollow, Bridgend,* and *Partisan.*

That's just a tiny portion of those from one list online that had 466
total movies from recent years. And I am sure there are a ton more with all
the B movies not on that list. Also, that is just the movies, so it doesn't
even account for the huge number of sitcoms and cartoons out there that
are also promoting witchcraft and other occult topics. With all that, why
are we, as a society, not concerned about the impact on our country? And
if that is not bad enough, look at all the other ways witchcraft is getting
promoted on social media, streaming channels, and otherwise through the
Internet.

Witches know exactly what they're doing. In fact, another sneaky
tactic they use has to do with those that watch clips of *Harry Potter*
online. While watching, a person can click on links to be taken straight to
witchcraft sites. The witches are loving it! They will even admit *Harry
Potter* has done more for them than anything in the history of witchcraft.
Now, let me rip through some other online promoters of witchcraft,
including step-by-step instructions. A prominent one is YouTube:

We could literally spend years flipping through all the YouTube
channels that promote witchcraft. And it's growing every day. Let me just
give you a couple of them, starting with "Spells8":

That channel is video after video, minutely detailing the
instructions for every ritual or spell out there. It lists every tool with how-
to instructions for performing witchcraft. And it is all free for anyone of
any age to access anywhere in the world. Another very popular site is
"The Green Witch":

There's a lot of witch celebrities online who are encouraging
people to go down that route. Even older folks who have been in
witchcraft for a long time have learned to promote it on YouTube.

Here is the transcript of her welcoming video from her streaming site called, "House of Witchcraft":

"Hello, hello! Welcome to the House of Witchcraft. I'm Taren S, an old-school witch that's been in the community for almost forty years now. And this is my corner of the Web. On my website, I hope you find articles that are inspiring and empowering. And on our YouTube channel, it is all things witchy and I really hope you check us out. Thanks so much. Hope you have a bright, blessed day."

I don't think so, witch lady. If you watch her video online, it's just a bit creepy but that might just be me personally. We created Get A Life Media to give a godly counter to all this kind of promotion from occultists like these witches who are getting their message out in so many forms of media. As a ministry we look for any possible way to electronically share the gospel. However, we have to remember all these can also be used by witches. Witches and the occult are doing the same networking while the vast majority of the church is keeping their mouths shut. Witches are riding their free-pass wave and loving it. Where are the Christians?! Who will counter these occult practices if the Christians won't? Where are the Christians who will warn people out of love for them?

Well, praise God that at least we are! But where is everyone else? Maybe they are passing the inspiration cube, arguing over whether they should add more drums on stage and a new fog machine, or whether the overhead projector is working with the whole mood of the music. It's not a concern about whether they are missing a golden opportunity to use their media for electronically reaching people to warn them about these witches and other occultists that are sucking people into the dark arts. We need everyone to get busy on that while we still have the freedom to use God's Word in the media to counter those destructive and eternally consequential practices.

Besides YouTube and other video-streaming channels like Rumble.com, the Internet also has a ton of social media:

The reach of social media has gotten massive and new companies are popping up every month. First let's deal with the classic one, Facebook.

If you have a Facebook account, just do a general search for witchcraft or Wicca and you will be scrolling through profiles for days. Still, that is what is going on today on websites like Facebook. And it is the same with Twitter.

Just doing a quick search for Wicca or witchcraft on Twitter brings up "Wiccan Academy" where you can learn practices like ritual purifications. And I'm telling you, with just a quick search you or your children can scroll, and scroll, and scroll through witchcraft profiles for days. Social media provides a gargantuan sewage pipe for spreading Babylonia-conceived Wicca witchcraft here in the twenty-first century. Here is the latest more prominent social media site that a lot of young people are getting on today, and that is TikTok.

Hey, the witches didn't wait around to get on there so we Christians need to be doing the same. Our mentality needs to be that we should want to be right there with God's Word whenever something new comes along. TikTok has become very popular in a short time even though they were supposed to be banned in the U.S. at one point. And after you see what goes on there, you'll know why it probably should be banned. TikTok actually has a witch-talk channel that I'm going to give you a taste of. With this video transcript, pay attention to how these kids are instructing each other in witchcraft while parents don't even know what their own kids are putting out there on these smart phone apps and what they're watching. All these examples of witches are middle or high school children, who are putting their craft out there on TikTok for other children to learn from and do. School-age witches are giving each other explicit details on how to do witchcraft personally in school and out. Then at the end, notice what they are saying about the acts of Jesus. This is nuts:

Girl Witch One: *"Everyone's been asking me for some easy spells, and when I made TikToks doing the spells, they got removed. So, I'm just* *going to tell you guys how to do them instead of actually performing it myself. So, what you're going to need is a marker, sticky notes, moon water, and two cups. At 3 a.m., you're going to take the two cups and, on one of the cups, you're going to write on the sticky note, what you have. And on the other cup, you're going to put the sticky that is what you want. And in the cup that has what you have, you're going to fill it with moon water and then you're going to pour into the cup that is what you want. And then you drink it. And that's all."*

Girl Witch Two: *"Witchcraft to do's at School: 'Moon water/Crystal water in your water bottle. Sigils on your classwork. Bless your food. Wear crystals. Journal your day/write letters to your deity.'"*

Girl witch showing tarot cards: *"Movies that are witch-themed/Occult: 'VVitch. Hereditary. Bell, Book and Candle. The Craft. Eve's Bayou. The Love Witch. Rosemary's Baby. Haxan. Black Sunday. The Pagan Queen. The Wicker Man. Apostate.'"*

Boy witch with a small cauldron: *"Having a bad day? Watch this: Black salt to keep away evil. Dragon's blood to increase potency of the spell. Thyme to dispel negativity and grief. Rosemary to purify. Lavender to uplift mood, dispel negative energy, and bring calm. I cast it for you all (shows a heart.)"*

Girl witch four: *"When people say it's impossible for me to be a Christian and a witch, I just have a couple of things to say about that: immaculate conception—witchcraft!; rising from the dead—witchcraft!; stars leading to a baby—witchcraft!; gifts of frankincense, myrrh, and gold—witchcraft!; walking on water—witchcraft!; turning water into wine—witchcraft!; healing people instantaneously—witchcraft!"*

How could someone even think that?! Unfortunately, it is how our kids are being raised by secular society and away from Biblically sound churches that teach all of God's Word. I can't say for this young lady's upbringing, but she seems to have been taught in such a way that has caused her to denigrate the miracles of Jesus Christ, accusing him of being a sorcerer!

Contextually, that's called blasphemy of the Holy Spirit. However, in order for that to fully be the offense, Jesus has to be in front of the person physically. At the time of the book of **Matthew,** He was. Back when Jesus walked this earth and did miracles, to His face people accused Him of performing those under the power of satan. Jesus replied that all would be forgiven except that accusation, which is blaspheming the Holy Spirit. But it is one of the most abused passages of the Bible. Accusers want to claim things like, "Those who bowl are blaspheming the Holy Spirit," or "You talked bad about that preacher, so you committed blasphemy of the Holy Spirit." No, that is not true. Read your Bible. Again, it is accusing Jesus of doing his miracles by the power of satan. But technically you have physically got to be there in His face while claiming that.

Still, it is the sort of thing that young lady was saying, and how does she get away with it? How could that even come out of someone's mouth? Well, I have got a theory that goes like this: You see, in the church today, nobody wants to hear what is in the Bible anymore. In fact, it is so much so that congregations will only hire a pastor to speak in their pulpit who will give fluffy fun messages like those found on the Inspirational Cube. Hey, we'll put you in that pulpit but don't say anything negative or we'll either get you fired or leave the church. And when I go, just know I'm taking my money with me. That's the kind of baloney that's going on in "churches" today and that's why young girls can grow up in our society to accuse Jesus of doing his miracles through occult witchcraft. It is because the churches keep their mouths shut.

Now, you've noticed that every chapter of both books on witchcraft had unique Bible passages that warned against witchcraft. They were easy to find because they are all over the Bible throughout the Old and New Testaments. What is God's central message in all of it? He tells us to never get involved with witchcraft or other occult practices! Those who practice that are called on the carpet because God knows it will lead them down a dark, demonic path. And since we are the ones getting equipped, it's our job to let those on that tragic trajectory know what they are in for. Ask them in love, "How's that working for you?"

Social media and other media are not just helping this merge of Catholicism with the occult. Now they are even twisting Christianity and merging with Christianity like the "Christian" witches we saw earlier. The problem includes the facts that people are not being brought up to study the Bible and they never have anyone to warn them about witchcraft. At the same time, they have been taught that life is all about them so they should just do whatever feels good (moral relativism).

All that opens people wide to fall for a false path being promoted in a massive way by Wicca through all these different areas of today's media. I haven't nearly covered them all. And I just scraped the surface, as far as the Internet. In fact, I conducted a general online search for Witchcraft and Wicca, the former came back with over 55 million results. And here is what's crazy: Right after that "Wicca" actually came back with over 76 million hits. Why was Wicca almost 50% more? It is because the occult repackaged witchcraft with a new name that has made it more palatable. In fact, it's getting so bad that they're now allowing Wiccan ritual "prayers" in the government. Here is that from a news report:

"The Iowa House of Representatives started the day, Thursday, with a controversial prayer by a Wiccan priestess, prompting some Christian leaders in the state to call for a prayer protest, calling it an unprecedented challenge to Iowa's spiritual life. This is the first time a Wiccan prayer has been performed at the legislature. Some lawmakers decided to skip the prayer while others stayed and silently protested by turning their backs to the prayer."

Hey, that's going to make a difference, right? Whenever a witch has the audacity to come into a government building and publicly give us their ritual witchcraft, just turn your back to them. That will do it, right? Just be sure that witch understands you may pull out the turned back maneuver on him or her. That will stop it quick, right? Wrong! And what was the so-called church's response? They warned that they would be forced to have a prayer protest. So, between a couple turned backs and someone throwing out a prayer in protest, I'm sure that witch will think twice before getting up there again. Actually, the witch got a free pass, so she's probably encouraged and will most likely do it again as soon as possible.

Meanwhile, the church says nothing of substance. They don't even throw down some simple Bible passages, they certainly didn't take the time to teach what the Bible warns about that woman's witchcraft ways, they won't share how or why the Bible says it's wrong, they don't even attempt to have a rational discussion with the witch, and they won't warn the witch in love from the Bible. Instead, the approach is just to turn the back and say a prayer. I'm all for praying but what about some effort! Are you kidding me?! And you wonder why this stuff keeps growing and growing. How about speaking up when this kind of thing is being condoned in our society? How about letting people know their Creator calls those witch's prayers an abomination. Why not say something like, "Hey, right here in this government facility right now, I need to warn everyone sitting with her that **Deuteronomy 18** tells us not to imitate the detestable practices of the pagan nations and it's why God took those nations out. It was because of their abominable witchcraft practices like sorcery and mediumship?

Why can't we face that witch's prayer with information from God's Word? Would that maybe sting a bit more than a turned-back? The Word of God is not only for encouragement but also to correct and rebuke. God corrects us for our own good. He rebukes us because He loves us. He sees dangerous paths we could go down, and God corrects that scary route. But instead of calling upon the helpful Words from our Creator, the answer that seems more appropriate to these politicians is, "Hey, don't make me turn my back and pray! We will just get in the corner away from you and whisper. That will teach you!"

Another bothersome response to wicked behavior is this: "Hey, you are out of bounds now! You're leading us down the dark destructive path of witchcraft. So, do you know what we might do? We're thinking about protesting with a full thirty-seconds of silence. Don't make us do it!"

Are you kidding me?! People that need conviction of their sins certainly prefer thirty seconds of nothing, to a rebuke from the Word of God. That thirty seconds of silence has nothing negative for the offender so, of course, they prefer it. But what they call negative, God really provides for our good. Do you see how twisted it has become? Yet, we wonder why witchcraft is on the rise. It is because the Church is keeping their mouths shut and just passing the cube. And even when there is an easy opportunity to make a difference, good people also shut their mouths and turn their backs. God called it again with **Revelation 9** when He told us how bad it would get in these last days with the silent church that allows witchcraft to be promoted and thrive. And by now you know where it's all going. Our world's people will end up in the Seven Year Tribulation where they will be inundated with God's judgment but still won't repent or give up worshiping demons that have them commit murders on a massive scale.

Two thousand years ago God warned us about exactly what we are watching today, which means the Seven Year Tribulation is close and the Rapture of the Church is even closer. Folks, that **Revelation** society is us! When we stir all this media promotion together, the potion they have created is going to explode the amount of witchcraft and other occult practices all around us. It is already happening now, but it's going to grow exponentially as we live through these last days.

What do we need to be doing about it? We must finish strong. We certainly do not settle with shutting our mouths, turning our backs, or hitting them hard with thirty seconds of silence. We pray, but we don't just leave it at a prayer protest. I'm not against prayer, but we also must speak up. People need to know the dangers they face in the occult, so we need to preach the Word, being a faithful church in season and out of season, whether the people like it, or not. We continue presenting God's Word through threats and deplatforming of our social media channels. We go through those walls, find another channel, and keep doing so until Christ takes us home. That is what we need to be doing because some will respond. They may not be getting it from their church anymore because 95% of them are playing the pleasant cube game, but we too can be out there speaking up electronically, as well as in our churches when they come into our midst and also individually when we're physically out in society doing the work of ministry.

We can lead them to Christ, just like the story I want to give you of a young lady who had people love her enough to tell her the truth about Jesus. She not only got saved from them, but also notice how, early in childhood, she got involved in witchcraft because her home life was messed up and she was searching for answers. Here is the video transcript of Hunter's story and what influenced her to start going down the occult route:

Hunter Osborne: *"An eighteen-year-old, that was a friend of a family, sexually abused me. I was nine at the time and so that, more than anything, really messed with me."*

Narrator: *"In addition to being sexually abused as a young girl, Hunter Osborne suffered physical and emotional abuse as well."*

Hunter: *"It was from things like my mom looking at me as being physically unattractive and saying, 'I'm sorry that you were born with the ugly genes. I'm sorry your head is misshapen.' My nickname was 'ugly smugly,' by her. And she had a little song she would sing sometimes with it. When she would be angry, which was often, she would grab whatever was there and just hit us over the head. She got frustrated and would smack us. My self-image as a child was broken almost before life even got started."*

Narrator: *"Much of the abuse continued throughout her teen years."*

Hunter: *"I was struggling to find acceptance; someone just to love me; someone to prefer me."*

Narrator: *"She became curious about witchcraft because of the control it promised."*

Hunter: *"Growing up, we would watch shows on Disney Channel like 'The Worst Witch' or 'Hocus-Pocus.' And I always loved these witches. It seemed innocent. It seemed fun. It seemed intriguing. It seemed so cool to have that kind of power."*

Narrator: *"Hunter practiced witchcraft for over seven years."*

Hunter: *"I bought every book on witchcraft. I recognized I was a very spiritual person, who believed in a divine power. When you cast spells, it's just like saying a prayer and we believed that, as long as you don't harm anyone, do whatever you want."*

Narrator: *"She says her sexual activities began to take on a darker nature."*

Hunter: *"I was constantly with guys trying to search for that knight in shining armor, that rescuer, that guy who was going to be the one. I constantly cohabitated with anyone that I was with. I believed that, in order to truly understand who I am spiritually, I need to be sexually free. That began a very dark period."*

Narrator: *"That period culminated one unnerving weekend in Chicago."*

Hunter: *"The summer of 2005, we were at a hotel room and I was in bed by myself, but I suddenly became very aware of a very dark presence. I was paralyzed and I just knew, if I pulled down my covers, I would see a dark image above me. I was just so afraid. But eventually I broke free of that paralysis and I pulled down the covers and nothing was there. But it rocked me. It was so scary."*

Narrator: *"The encounter made Hunter question her lifestyle. Then she took a job at a local bookstore."*

Hunter: *"All the women at this bookstore were all believers; fierce, godly women and I was very loud and proud about my witchcraft. Because I was so vocal about it, this one particular older woman, she knew exactly how to meet me where I was at. She started speaking the love of God to me. We would have these little discussions, and she would keep pointing me to Scripture."*

Narrator: *"Over time, Hunter's heart began to change."*

Hunter: *"I mean, God was just prompting, prompting, prompting. They kept referring to Jesus. I had heard that this one church in our community was huge. And I knew if I went, nobody would notice me."*

Narrator: *"Hunter began attending this church and was later invited to a Bible study."*

Hunter: *"I did not know the Biblical God. I didn't know who He was. But the Bible talks about how, 'They bowed down and worshiped' and 'things were made—creature versus Creator.' That definitely penetrated my heart of witchcraft."*

Narrator: *"During a conversation with the pastor, Hunter realized her need for Christ."*

Hunter: *"I know that God pulled back the veil of who he was. I saw sin for what it was, and I saw it in my life and recognized the depravity and the depth of my sins and the bondage of my sin. But I did also hear the good news of Jesus. And the pastor explained to me that salvation comes through faith alone; through Christ alone and believing in Him. And that very moment I believed."*

Narrator: *"Hunter accepted Christ and began to mature in her faith."*

Hunter: *"I bought myself a Bible. I wanted to know God. I wanted to know Him more. Everything that I possibly could do, I wanted to be of Christ. I had lived such a dark life. I didn't want that life anymore. I was* *done with that life. It was not going anywhere. It was on a very fast track to a dark place. I knew I still wanted to be married, but it was different: I did not have a desire to pursue men anymore. I knew that, if God wanted me to be married, he would bring to me a godly man who loved Him. "*

Narrator: *"God did bless Hunter with a godly husband, Chad who is a pastor, and four beautiful children."*

Hunter: *"The only man I wanted to have my heart was Christ's heart. Jesus is that knight in shining armor that I was looking for. As soon as He revealed Himself to me, the truth of who He was, I knew that I was satisfied; my soul was justified. All the emptiness of my heart, the hole in my heart, He filled."*

How did she find that out and have her life completely transformed for the better? Someone loved her enough to speak up about her need for Christ. They didn't pass her the Inspirational Cube from Joel Osteen. They spoke up from God's Word and, to this day, she's been set free. That's what we need to do. That is how we need to finish. We need to be a part of the solution instead of contributing to the unfolding prophetic problem that is happening here in our day, in these last days. We will all stand before God to answer for what we chose to do at this time. Amen?

How to Receive Jesus Christ:

1. Admit your need (I am a sinner).

2. Be willing to turn from your sins (repent).

3. Believe that Jesus Christ died for you on the Cross and rose
    from the grave.

4. Through prayer, invite Jesus Christ to come in and control
    your life through the Holy Spirit. (Receive Him as Lord and
    Savior.)

What to pray:

Dear Lord Jesus,

I know that I am a sinner and need Your forgiveness. I believe
that You died for my sins. I want to turn from my sins. I now
invite You to come into my heart and life. I want to trust and
follow You as Lord and Savior.

In Jesus' name. Amen.

Notes

https://www.christianpost.com/news/jesus-was-a-sorcerer-bible-a-book-of magic-say-christian-witches-ahead-of-first-annual-convention.html
https://en/Wikipedia.org/wiki/European_witchcraft
https://www.forbes.com/sites/davidkroll/2017/10/31/the-origin-of-witches-riding-broomsticks-drugs-from-nature-plus-shakespeare/#344c060f61a9
https://en.wikipedia.org/wiki/Witches%27_Sabbath
www.SabbathTruth.com
https://en.wikipedia.org/wiki/Witchcraft
https://en.wikipedia.org/wiki/Sigil
https://en.wikipedia.org/wiki/List_of_sigils_of_demons
https://en.wikipedia.org/wiki/Crossroads_(mythology)
https://en.wikipedia.org/wiki/Crossroads_(1986_film)
https://en.wikipedia.org/wiki/Fairy
https://en.wikipedia.org/wiki/Leprechaun
https://en.wikipedia.org/wiki?Hobgoblin
https://en.wikipedia.org/wiki/Will-o%27-the-wisp
https://en.wikiedia.org/wiki/Witch_Trials_in_the_early_modern_period
https://en.wikipedia.org/wiki/witchcraft_Act_1735
https://en.wikipedia.org/wiki/Brothers_Grimm
https://en.wikipedia.org/wiki/Grims%27_Fairy_Tales#:-:text=Grims'Fairy Tales%2C originally known published on 20 December 1812
https://en.wikipedia.org/wiki/Harry_Potter
https//www.google.com/search?q=how+much+have+the+harry+potter+films+made&riz=1C1CHBF_enUS894&oq=how+much+have+the+hary+potter+made
https://www.cbsnews.com/news/English-occult/
https://christianpost.com/news/witches-outnumber-presbyterians-in-the-us-wicca-paganism-growing-astronomically.html
https://www.metalfloss.com/article/75472/11-hulking-facts-about-green-giant

https://en.wikipedia.org/wiki/Wicca#History
https://en.wikipedia.org/wiki/Margaret_Murray
https://ayrshirewica.wordpress.com/lessons/brief-history-of-wicca/
https://en.wikipedia,org/wiki/Aleister_Crowley#United_States:_1914-1919
https://en.wikipedia.org/wiki/File:Supposed_channeled_entity_by_occultis t_crowley.jpg
https://en.wikipedia.org/wiki/Book_of_Shadows
https://witchcraftandwitches.com/book-of-shadows-terms-book-of-shadows/
https://en.wikipedia.org/wiki/Wicca#History
https://en.wikipedia.org/wiki/
Gerald_Gardner_(Wiccan)
https://www.independent.co.uk.arts-entertainment/Doreen-valiente-mother-modern-witchcraft-whose-spells-are-still-used-today-wicca-brighton-gardner-a6973196.html
https://www.amazon.com/Bucklands-Coplete-Witchcraft-Llewellyns-Practical/dp/0875420508
https://www.washingtonexaminer.com/weekly-standard/representative-of-her-age-8586
http://godreports.com/2016/03/Hillary-clinton-has-her-methodism-been-influenced-by-seances-spiritism-and-new-age-spirituality/
https://www.orlandosentinel.com/news/os-xpm-1994-12-25-9412240789-story.html
https://www.rgi.com/story/news/2019/06/26/hagar-harry-reid-convinced-ufo-sightings-real-defends-funding-secret-research/1576640001/
https://www.politico.com/magazine/story/2017/12/16/pentagon-ufo-search-harry-reid-216111
https://www.newsweek.com/pentagon-ufo-program-disclosure-aliens-poltergeist-top-secret-bigelow-948051
https://www.usatoday.com/story/news/politics/201/06/15/trump-briefed-ufo-but-doesn't-particularly-believe-them/1465077001/
https://www.frontpagemag.com/point/21944/liberals-less=likely-knpw-earth-revolves-around-daniel-greenfield
http://big/asset.huggingtonpost.com/tabs_ufo_0906072013.pdf

https://www.pewforum.org/2018/04/25/whenamericans-say-they-believe-in-god-what-do-they-mean

https://fivethirtyeight.com/features/why-democrats-struggle-to-mobilize-a-religious-left

http://politicalhat.com/2020/08/21/fighting-racism-in-academia-with-witchcraft

https://en/Wikipedia.org/wiki/left-hand_path_and_right-hand_path#Left-hand_path

https://en/Wikipedia.org/wiki/The_book_of_Abramelin

https://en.widipedia.org/wiki/sex_magic

https://en.wikipedia.or/wiki/motion_picture_production_code

https://occult-world.com/sanders-alex/

https://en.wikipedia.org/wiki/dianic_wicca

https://en.wikipedia.org/wiki/zsuzanna_budapest

https://en.wikipedia.org/wiki/dianic_wica

https://occult-world.com/Budapest-z/

https://www.theguardian.com/world/2015/feb/24/witch-symbol-feminist-power-azealia-banks

https://www.apologeticsindex.org/4557-modern-witchcraft

https://www.apologeticsindex.org/w05.html

https://en.wikipedia.org/wiki/wiccan_rede

https://www.apologeticsindex.org/w05.html

https://www.gotqustions.net/printer/Asherah-pole-PF.html

https///www.prophecynewswatch.com/article.cfm?recent_news_id=2787

http://www.spiritoferror.org/2017/12/the-christia-tarot-card-controversy-at-bethel-church-in-redding-california/7409

https://pulpitandpen.org/2017/12/11/charismaics-now-using-christian-tarot-cards/

https://carm.org/what-is-wicca

https://carm.org/beliefs-wicca

https://en.wikipedia.org/wiki/Pan_(god)

https://www.revelist.com/arts/wiccan-tattoos/4819/the-spirit-goddess/5

https://www.learnreligions.com/pagan-and-wiccan-symbols-4123036?print

https://simple.wikipedia.org/wiki/Bonfire

https://www.britannica.com/print/article/371092

https://en.wikipedia.org/wiki/May_Day

http://users.belgacom.net/gc674645/grave/lastword.htm

https://en.wikipedia.org/wiki/Akashic_records
https://en.wikipedia.org/wiki/Star_of_David
https://en.wikipedia.org/wiki/Unicursal_hexagram#.-:text=The unicursal hexagram is a, with the points touching.
https://en.wikipedia.org/wiki/Hermetic-order-of-the-Golden-dawn
https://en.wikipedia.org/wiki/witch%27s_ladder#.-:text=A witch's ladder (also known, magical intention in the cords
https://en.wikipedia.org/wiki/Power_of_Three_(Charmed)#.-:text=in the original charmed series (1998-2006)%2Cthe, witchcraft%2C the Book of Shadows
https://www.britannica.comn/print/article/1086220
https://www.gty.org/library/print/sermons-library/53-8
https://wiccaliving.com/wheel-of-the-year-wiccan-sabbats/
https://cvltnation.com/a-thinning-of-the-veil-samhain-and-the-pagan-roots-of-halloween/
https://www.history.com/topics/halloween/history-of-halloween
https://www.countryliving.com/entertaining/a40250/heres-why-we-really-celebrate-halloween/
https://www.crosswalk.com/special-coverage/halloween/pagan-roots-of-halloween.html
https://www.jw.org/en/bible-teachings/questions/origin-of-halloween/
https://www1.cbn.com/the-pagan-roots-of-halloween
https://wiccaliving.com/wiccan-rituals/